Bible Brain Builders Book 2

Other Bible Brain Builders

Bible Brain Builders Book 1

Bible Brain Builders
Book 2

THOMAS NELSON
Since 1798

NASHVILLE   DALLAS   MEXICO CITY   RIO DE JANEIRO

© 2011 by Thomas Nelson Publishers, Inc.

Published in Nashville, Tennessee, by Thomas Nelson. Thomas Nelson is a registered trademark of Thomas Nelson, Inc.

Book design and composition by Graphic World, Inc.

Original puzzles and mazes created by W. B. Freeman.

Thomas Nelson, Inc., titles may be purchased in bulk for educational, business, fund-raising, or sales promotional use. For information, please e-mail SpecialMarkets@ThomasNelson.com.

The material in this book originally was published in other forms in *Nelson's Super Book of Bible Word Games, Book 1*, © 1992, *Nelson's Super Book of Bible Word Games, Book 2*, © 1993, *Nelson's Super Book of Bible Word Games, Book 3*, © 1993, *Incredible Mazes, Book 1*, © 1993, *Incredible Mazes, Book 2*, © 1994, *Nelson's Amazing Bible Trivia Book 2* © 2000, 2011 by Thomas Nelson Publishers, Inc., all rights reserved.

ISBN: 978-1-4041-8350-6

Printed in the United States of America

14 13 12 11 QG 1 2 3 4 5 6

Songs of Joy

*T*he angels were the first to sing at Christmastime as they announced the birth of the Savior praising God saying, "Glory to God in the highest, and on earth peace, goodwill toward men." The singing of carols has become a favorite custom worldwide, proclaiming the glad tidings of the Christmas message.

The word *carol* comes from a word that meant a dance performed in a circle. It is thought that originally the dance was accompanied by flute music and eventually by singing. Carols were sung between acts of the mystery plays that told the stories of the gospel before the Bible was widely available to the general public. Through the years, carols were sung and performed at different seasons and holidays but are now associated primarily with Christmas.

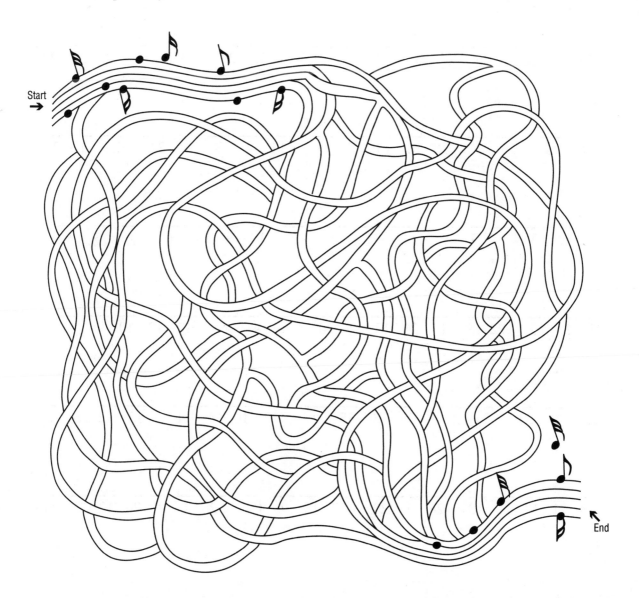

What is the Lord's due and why? Solve this cryptogram to discover a Bible answer.

Clue: MESSIAH *is* 2 18 11 11 10 26 12

‾‾ ‾ ‾‾ ‾‾ ‾ ‾‾ ‾‾ ‾ ‾ ‾‾ ‾‾ ‾‾' ‾ ‾ ‾ ‾ ‾‾'
23 3 15   26 9 18   19 3 9 13 12 23   3   4 3 9 20

‾‾ ‾ ‾ ‾‾ ‾‾ ‾‾ ‾‾ ‾‾ ‾‾ ‾‾ ‾ ‾ ‾ ‾‾ ‾‾ ‾ ‾‾
13 3   9 18 22 18 10 17 18   14 4 3 9 23   26 1 20

‾‾ ‾ ‾ ‾ ‾ ‾‾ ‾ ‾‾ ‾ ‾ ‾‾ ‾‾ ‾; ‾‾ ‾ ‾
12 3 1 3 9   26 1 20   5 3 19 18 9   16 3 9

‾‾ ‾ ‾‾ ‾‾ ‾ ‾‾ ‾‾ ‾‾ ‾‾ ‾‾ ‾‾ ‾ ‾‾ ‾‾ ‾‾ ‾ ‾‾ ‾‾
23 3 15 22 9 18 26 13 18 20   26 4 4   13 12 10 1 14 11

‾‾ ‾ ‾‾ ‾‾ ‾‾ ‾‾ ‾ ‾‾ ‾ ‾‾ ‾‾ ‾ ‾ ‾‾ ‾‾ ‾‾ ‾‾
26 1 20   24 23   23 3 15 9   19 10 4 4   13 12 18 23

‾‾ ‾‾ ‾‾ ‾‾ ‾‾ ‾‾ ‾ ‾‾ ‾‾ ‾‾ ‾ ‾‾ ‾‾ ‾ ‾‾ ‾‾ ‾‾ ‾‾ ‾‾.
18 21 10 11 13   26 1 20   19 18 9 18   22 9 18 26 13 18 20

Unscramble the letters in Column B to find the names of the brothers and sisters of the person(s) in Column A. When you finish with this acrostic you will discover a word that describes how Christians, as brothers and sisters in the Lord, are related to one another.

Column A

1. JAMES (Matthew 4:21)
2. TAMAR (2 Samuel 13:1)
3. JACOB (Genesis 25:26)
4. AARON, MIRIAM (1 Chronicles 6:3)
5. JOSEPH (Genesis 35:24)
6. ABEL, CAIN (Genesis 4:25)
7. MAHLON (Ruth 1:2)
8. MARY, MARTHA (John 11:1–3)
9. SIMEON, LEVI (Genesis 34:25)
10. PHINEHAS (1 Samuel 4:4)
11. ALEXANDER (Mark 15:21)
12. KOHATH, MERARI (Genesis 46:11)
13. ASAHEL, ABISHAI (2 Samuel 2:18)
14. ELIAB, DAVID, SHAMMAH (1 Samuel 17:13–14)

Column B

1. NOHJ
2. BALSAMO
3. USEA
4. SOMES
5. NINEJAMB
6. THES
7. HONILIC
8. AZURASL
9. HANDI
10. POHINH
11. FURSU
12. SHERGON
13. ABOJ
14. BANDAIBA

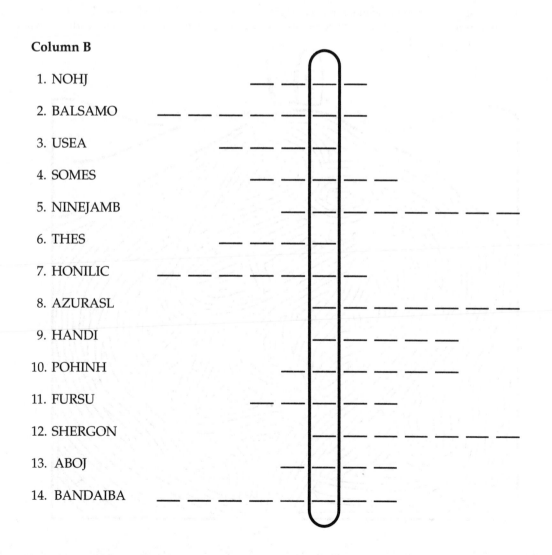

Moses The Mediator

Moses met with God on the mountaintop and received a code of law for the people of Israel and the great promises of God to be with His chosen people. But before he left the mountaintop, Moses was warned of trouble ahead.

While Moses was away, the shortsighted Israelites grew impatient and lost hope. And so they made for themselves another god — an idol, a calf of gold — and danced around it.

When Moses got down from the mountain and saw these rebellious people, his "anger became hot," and he smashed the stone tablets of God's Law into pieces. He announced he would go back to the Lord: "Perhaps I can make atonement for your sin."

Moses asked God to forgive their sins. But sin could not be overlooked, and God said those who sinned would be blotted out of His book. He also told Moses that He would send His angel before them to the promised land but that His presence would not go with them. The people mourned when they heard this bad news. So Moses met again with God on behalf of the people, "If Your Presence does not go with us, do not bring us up from here."

God listened to Moses, and Moses found grace in God's sight. And because he did, God renewed His covenant with the people saying, "Before all your people I will do marvels such as have not been done in all the earth. . . . It is an awesome thing that I will do with you."

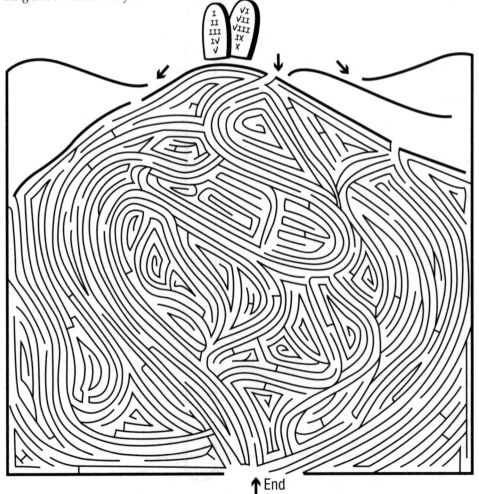

↑ End

Pursued!

When Saul heard the women sing, "Saul has slain his thousands, and David his ten thousands," it put him over the edge. For him it was the ultimate put-down; his very reputation as king had been based on his great success as a warrior and military commander. But the Scripture says, "Saul was very angry, and the saying displeased him. . . . So Saul eyed David from that day forward" (1 Samuel 18:8–9).

Saul's obsessive jealousy over David consumed his final years as Israel's king. One day when David was playing music to calm Saul's madness, Saul came to him with a javelin. Saul led his best men in pursuit of David as he hid in the wilderness from the enraged king. All this happened in spite of David's expressed and real loyalty to King Saul.

Saul's last days were tragic. The army of Israel fell against the enemy Philistines. And when the Philistines pursued Saul and his sons, they killed Jonathan, Abinadab, and Malchishua and wounded Saul. The fallen king then took his own life rather than risk abuse at the hands of his enemies.

Help David escape without being captured by Saul's army. Note: King Saul and his soldiers are looking for David in all four directions.

Nehemiah's Late-Night Ride

*A*fter Nehemiah returned to Jerusalem and had been in the city three days, he got up in the night and, taking only a few men with him, rode around the city of Jerusalem. He thoroughly surveyed the broken-down walls, the burned-out gates, and the rubble of the city. The Bible says that none of the officials of the city knew where Nehemiah had gone or what he had done. Nehemiah had not yet told the Jews, the priests, the nobles, the officials, or the workers about his plan to rebuild the city. (See Nehemiah 2:11-16.)

The project of reconstructing the city's walls took fifty-two days to complete under Nehemiah's skillful and courageous leadership (Nehemiah 6:15). When the Israelites' enemies heard of it, they were disheartened because they knew such a great task could only be accomplished with God's help on the Israelites' behalf.

Help Nehemiah find his way all around Jerusalem without being spotted by anyone who may be looking out the windows labeled *W*.

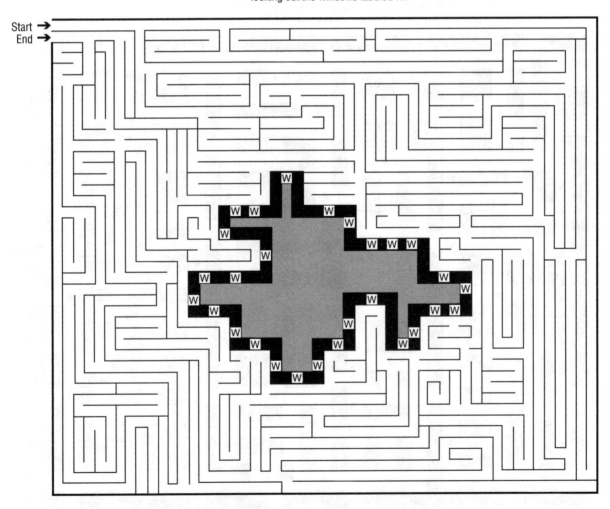

Find the names of the seven who were appointed to "serve tables".

E	S	N	S	P	H	I	L	P	A
M	S	A	A	R	P	E	T	S	P
A	P	N	L	N	P	H	E	A	R
C	S	T	E	O	N	E	R	N	O
I	T	E	L	I	C	M	T	I	C
N	E	O	C	O	E	I	S	C	H
S	P	A	S	N	S	P	N	A	O
O	H	H	A	R	N	A	T	P	R
N	E	S	I	T	O	C	E	R	U
P	N	M	I	L	M	I	P	O	S
R	O	N	A	C	I	N	N	M	E
E	T	S	M	I	T	P	S	A	N

Rulers – yet still subject to the Lord God, King of the universe!

Across

1 He ordered the priests to receive offerings to repair the temple

8 He is described as the king "who sinned and who made Israel sin"

9 His evil wife was Jezebel

10 The Lord was pleased with his request for an "understanding heart"

12 He burned the king's house down around himself and died in the fire

14 Jeroboam's son, he ruled Israel only two years

15 He was only 8 years old when he became king, and he did "what was right in the sight of the LORD"

17 Jeroboam's son, he reigned over Israel in Samaria only 6 months

18 He gave the king of Assyria 1,000 talents of silver to buy peace

20 King of Judah, he made peace with the king of Israel

21 Son of Ahab, he worshiped Baal and provoked the Lord God of Israel to anger

23 He reigned only a month in Samaria before he was killed

25 He became a leper and lived in an isolated house

28 He "did not leave to Jeroboam anyone that breathed until he had destroyed him"

30 The king of Egypt deposed him after he ruled only 3 months

31 He was killed in the citadel of the king's house

32 Ahab's son; he did evil in the Lord's sight

Down

1 He became king at age 18 and reigned 3 months before king Nebuchadnezzar took him to Babylon

2 Israel's first king

3 Son of Solomon, he reigned in Judah

4 He bought the hill of Samaria during his 12-year reign as king of Israel

5 He reigned in Hebron over Judah for 7-1/2 years and in Jerusalem over Israel and Judah for 33 years

6 Even though his heart was not loyal to God, the Lord "gave him a lamp in Jerusalem" for the sake of his father David

7 Best known for building the Upper Gate of the Lord's house

11 He sent the silver and gold from the Lord's house to enlist the military aid of the king of Assyria

13 He shed innocent blood "till he had filled Jerusalem from one end to another"

16 He "trusted in the Lord God of Israel, so that after him was none like him among all the kings of Judah"

19 He killed 10,000 Edomites in the Valley of Salt

22 King of Judah, he warred against Baasha, king of Israel, "all their days"

24 He built Elath and restored it to Judah

26 He "sacrificed to all the carved images which his father Manasseh had made, and served them"

27 Jehu conspired against him

29 He wrote a series of letters to Ahab's 70 sons in Samaria

Word Pool

ABIJAM AHAB AHAZ AHAZIAH AMAZIAH AMON ASA AZARIAH
BAASHA DAVID HEZEKIAH JEHOAHAZ JEHOASH JEHOIACHIN JEHORAM
JEHOSHAPHAT JEHU JEROBOAM JORAM JOSIAH JOTHAM MANASSEH
MENAHEM NADAB OMRI PEKAHIAH REHOBOAM SAUL SHALLUM SOLOMON
UZZIAH ZECHARIAH ZIMRI

RESURRECTED!

The butterfly is not mentioned in Scripture, but it has become a popular symbol of the new life in Christ and the resurrection. Metamorphosis, the life cycle of the butterfly from the egg to the larva, the pupa, and finally the beautiful adult butterfly, symbolizes the conversion of the Christian as he or she becomes increasingly Christlike, conformed to the image of Jesus. The butterfly emerges from its cocoon with a "glorified" body to soar to heights impossible to the insect in its life as a caterpillar.

*B*y adding and subtracting the numbers in this puzzle, you will find the difference in the number of books in the Old and New Testaments.

The number or books in the Old Testament   _____

Plus ...
The number of books in the Pentateuch   +   _____

Plus ...
The number of books of Old Testament history   +   _____

Minus ...
The number of epistles in the New Testament   −   _____

Minus ...
The number of books of Old Testament prophets   −   _____

Plus ...
The number of books in the Old Testament of poetry and wisdom   +   _____

Plus ...
The number of gospels about the life and ministry of Jesus   +   _____

Equals ...
The number of books in the New Testament   =   _____

*H*ere you'll find the tall and the short!

Across

2 Giants were thought to be the ____ of the sons of God and the daughters of men

4 Tall tower name ____ "because there the LORD confused the language of all the earth"

6 The spies "____ our hearts" by telling of a people greater and taller in the promised land

10 "There were giants on the ____ in those days.... Those were the mighty men who were of old"

12 The Israelites felt like this in comparison to Anak's descendants

15 Giant slain by David

16 Goliath was called a "____" of the Philistines

17 One of Goliath's brothers

22 Known as giants, they lived in a valley (see #20 Down)

23 Name given to the city formerly known as Kirjath Arba, the name of a giant

24 From his shoulders upward he was "taller than any of the people"

25 Greatest man among the Anakim

Down

1 Name for the region "at the top of the skies"—the place where the Tower of Babel reached

2 "I will cut down its tall ____ and its choice cypress trees"

3 Jacob dreamed of one so tall that its top reached into heaven

5 The Moabite name for the tall people in the land of Ar

7 King of Bashan, his bed was 9 cubits long

8 A giant who lived in this place had 24 fingers and toes

9 Son of a giant

11 With Argob, all of this region was called "the land of the giants"

13 The staff of Goliath's was like a weaver's beam

14 Bible people noted for their great height

15 The Anakim and Emim peoples

18 The giants were called the "____ men who were of old"

19 King was taller than any of his people "from the shoulders ____"

20 The ____ of Rephaim may be translated "Valley of the Giants"

21 The people of Babel built a ____ "whose top is in the heavens"

Word Pool

**ANAKIM ARBA BABEL BASHAN CEDARS CHAMPION CHILDREN DISCOURAGED
EARTH EMIM GATH GIANTS GOLIATH GRASSHOPPERS HEAVENS HEBRON
LADDER LAHMI MIGHTY OG REPHAIM SAUL SPEAR SIPPAI TOWER
UPWARD VALLEY**

String together the words to reveal a famous choice. What will YOUR choice be?

C	H	V	E	S	T	Y	W	W	U
S	O	L	S	H	I	A	H	I	O
O	E	E	R	S	D	O	M	Y	L
W	I	F	U	O	V	R	E	S	L
E	L	L	O	Y	B	E	A	S	O
W	S	T	H	R	U	T	M	R	F
E	E	E	E	L	H	Y	M	E	A
R	V	S	U	O	O	R	D	D	N

*I*t was more than just a dream; it was prophecy. Unscramble the words on the left and match them with their correct description on the right.

1. ASRMEOPG

— — — — — — — —

2. RSSDIA

— — — — — —

3. SEHSUPE

— — — — — — —

4. DAELIACO

— — — — — — — —

5. RATHITAY

— — — — — — — —

6. LAHIDPIHEPLA

— — — — — — — — — — — —

7. YASMNR

— — — — — —

A. And he who overcomes, . . . to him I will give power over the nations.

B. Be faithful until death.

C. Be watchful, and strengthen the things which remain.

D. I will make those of the synagogue of Satan, . . . come and worship before your feet.

E. You have there those who hold the doctrine of Balaam.

F. I counsel you to buy from Me gold refined in the fire.

G. Remember . . . from where you have fallen.

Match

1 - ___

2 - ___

3 - ___

4 - ___

5 - ___

6 - ___

7 - ___

14

There are many instances in the Bible of God's revealing His plans and speaking to people in their dreams. Fill in the answers below with answers that relate to dreams in the Bible.

Across

1 In matters of wisdom and understanding, Daniel and his three friends were ten times better than____(Daniel 1:20)

4 In his dream, eleven ____ bowed to Joseph (Genesis 37:9)

7 "____for you, O king, thoughts came to your mind while on your bed" (Daniel 2:29)

9 King Nebuchadnezzar was____ by his dreams (Daniel 2:1)

13 In Jacob's dream, this device stretched to the heaven (Genesis 28:12)

14 Solomon asked to be able to discern between good and____ when God asked him in a dream what he wanted (l Kings 3:9)

15 Joseph interpreted the baker's dream that he would hang from a ____ (Genesis 40:19)

16 Solomon explained to the Lord that he was a "little child; I do not know how to go____or come in" (l Kings 3:7)

17 This man was released from prison to interpret a dream for Pharaoh (Genesis 41:14)

20 Evening (old English)

21 Jacob lifted his____"and saw in a dream" (Genesis 31:10)

22 God____(past tense) Pharaoh in his dreams "what He is about to do" (Genesis 41:25)
24 This Babylonian king could not sleep because of his dreams (Daniel 2:1)
27 God revealed to Abimelech in a dream that____was Abraham's wife (Genesis 20:3)
29 When he told his brothers his dreams, Joseph ended up in this far country (Genesis 37:28)
30 This ruler had dreams about the years of plenty and famine that would come to his nation (Genesis 41:25)
32 To awaken;____up
34 When Jacob awoke, he said, "Surely the LORD is in this____" (Genesis 28:16)
35 Images or a message occurring during sleep: God sometimes communicates in this way
38 Joseph was told in a dream that Mary's son would save people from their____(Matthew 1:21)
40 In a dream, God told Jacob "the ____on which you lie I will give to you and your descendants" (Genesis 28:13)
41 Joseph asked, "Do not interpretations belong to ____?" (Genesis 40:8)
42 This man remembered Joseph's interpretation of his dream and introduced him to Pharaoh (Genesis 41:9–12)
44 The angel told Joseph in a dream, "Do not be____" (Matthew 1:20)
45 The butler dreamed that the vine brought forth this fruit (Genesis 40:10)
46 In Jacob's dream, the____of God were ascending and descending the ladder
49 Opposite of #16 Across
51 The top of #13 Across reached to ____(Genesis 28:12)
52 On the third____,which was Pharaoh's birthday, the baker and butler were released from prison (Genesis 40:20)
53 These animals, fat and gaunt, represented years of abundance and famine in Pharaoh's dream (Genesis 41:26–27)
54 The angel let Joseph know in a dream that Mary was the fulfillment of the prophecy "Behold, the virgin shall____ with child" (Matthew 1:23)
55 In Joseph's dream, eleven of these bowed to Joseph's____ (Genesis 37:7)
56 The number of good heads of grain in Pharaoh's dream (Genesis 41:5)
57 The feet and toes of clay and iron in Nebuchadnezzar's dream indicated the kingdom will be ____(Daniel 2:41)

Down

1 God spoke to this king of Gerar in a dream (Genesis 20:2–3)
2 The Angel of God told Jacob in a dream, to look at this animal (Genesis 31:12)
3 In a dream, God told #23 Down to speak neither____nor bad to Jacob (Genesis 31:24)
5 The butler and baker were ____ when Joseph came in to them (Genesis 40:6)
6 The sheaves and stars____to Joseph in his dreams (Genesis 37:7, 9)
8 In his dream, this man was reassured of God's covenant with him and his people (Genesis 28:13–15)
9 In the butler's dream, the ____ branches were ____ days (Genesis 40:12)
10 Joseph's____hated him when he told them his dreams (Genesis 37:8)
11 Joseph told the baker, "The birds will____your flesh from you," (Genesis 40:19)
12 The Lord appeared to Solomon in a dream at____(l Kings 3:5)
18 She, opposite
19 "He, who ____s secrets has made known to you what will be" (Daniel 2:29)
23 Jacob's father-in-law (Genesis 31:24)
25 Formerly Luz: where God spoke to Jacob in a dream (Genesis 28:19)
26 The butler dreamed that he pressed the grapes into Pharaoh's____(Genesis 40:11)
28 God told Solomon in a dream, "____! What shall I give you?" (1 Kings 3:5)
31 Solomon asked for an understanding____(1 Kings 3:9)
33 The king commanded that all the ____men of Babylon be killed (Daniel 2:12)
34 Jacob made a____out of the #47 Down he had slept on and poured oil on it (Genesis 28:18)
35 "God has shown Pharaoh what He is about to ____" (Genesis 41:25)
36 Joseph did as the angel____ and took to him Mary as his wife (Matthew 1:24)
37 "There is a God in heaven who reveals ____" (Daniel 2:28)
39 Daniel asked the king for time that he might be able to____ the king's dream (Daniel 2:16)
42 This man's dream foresaw his demise (Genesis 40:22)
43 Solomon asked God for the ability to____between good and evil (1 Kings 3:9)
47 The____that Jacob had used for a pillow, became #34 Down (Genesis 28:18)
48 Joseph told the Pharaoh, "It is not in____; God will give Pharaoh an answer" (Genesis 41:16)
50 God told #1 Down in a dream that he had taken another man's ____(Genesis 20:3–8)
51 In a dream Joseph was told to "take the young Child and____ mother, flee to Egypt" (Matthew 2:13)
55 God gave Solomon wisdom, riches, and honor "____that there shall not be anyone like you among the kings all your days" (1 Kings 3:12–13)

This cryptogram is part of a sermon.

Clue: MESSIAH *is* CHNNKUJ

R B H N N H S   U W H

Q J H   E Z Z W   K D

N E K W K Q'   Y Z W

Q J H K W N   K N   Q J H

.

I K D F S Z C   Z Y

J H U M H D.

*T*he earth provides food and shelter for God's creatures. Hidden in the letter box below are the names of some of God's creatures, and the food and the habitation that He provides for them. All the words are found in Psalm 104:10–26.

```
S  Y  E  K  N  O  D  P  O  N  S  S  T  O  R  K
X  F  O  P  O  R  S  M  A  N  T  P  L  X  N  Q
A  S  F  I  T  A  Q  W  G  N  X  R  U  O  L  U
Z  V  L  I  V  E  G  E  T  A  T  I  O  N  I  Q
L  Z  A  B  L  Q  B  A  N  D  O  N  R  S  O  B
E  A  T  T  I  C  E  O  Y  G  S  G  N  O  N  S
O  A  T  R  U  E  A  Q  T  R  U  S  T  A  S  M
B  A  D  G  E  R  S  T  A  O  G  X  H  P  O  T
C  O  A  W  E  R  T  S  E  E  R  T  P  O  X  N
I  C  E  O  I  S  P  O  X  N  A  L  I  E  P  O
S  S  R  A  D  E  C  Z  B  I  S  O  W  N  P  Q
A  B  B  O  D  A  O  N  V  A  S  L  L  I  H  Z
P  B  I  R  D  S  N  E  O  Z  L  G  P  W  J  N
P  O  N  Q  G  X  L  P  N  Q  U  T  R  I  F  N
```

Word Pool

BADGERS BEAST BIRDS BREAD CATTLE CEDARS CLIFFS DONKEYS
FIR GOATS GRASS HILLS LEVIATHAN LIONS MAN
OIL SEA SPRINGS STORK TREES VEGETATION WINE

*I*t was King David's desire to build a permanent temple for the Lord that would be the center of worship for the children of Israel. But because David was a man of war God did not allow him to build the temple. Instead God told David that his son, Solomon, would build it. The details of the temple "blueprints" are spelled out in 1 Kings 6. Fill in the correct numbers in this puzzle, perform the math functions and you will arrive at the number of years it took to build the temple. All of the measurements are in cubits.

The length of the temple   _____

Multiplied by …
The height of the side chambers $\times$ _____

Plus …
The length in front of the temple sanctuary $+$ _____

Divided by …
The number of cherubim in the inner sanctuary $\div$ _____

Plus …
The height of the temple $+$ _____

Divided by …
The width of the temple $\div$ _____

Plus …
The length of each wing of the cherub $+$ _____

Plus …
The length of the vestibule in front of the sanctuary $+$ _____

Divided by …
The width of the lowest chamber $\div$ _____

Equals …
The number of years it took to build the temple $=$ _____

LIGHT IN THE DARKNESS

In the Scripture the lamp symbolizes guidance and wisdom, giving divine light and understanding. The Bible describes the Word of God as a lamp unto our feet and a light to our path (Psalm 119:105). "For the commandment is a lamp, and the law a light" (Proverbs 6:23). Scripture also describes the Lord as our lamp, the One who lightens our way: "For You are my lamp, O Lord; the Lord shall enlighten my darkness" (2 Samuel 22:29).

Jesus used the metaphor of the lamp to teach believers about their responsibility to those in darkness. In the Sermon on the Mount, Christians are told to set their lamp on a lampstand so that it will give light to "all who are in the house" (Matthew 5:15). Christians are to allow the light of Christ in their lives and their good works to give light to those in darkness.

In the parable of the ten virgins, Jesus taught that Christians are also responsible to keep an adequate supply of oil in their "lamps" so they are not without light. It was the wise virgins who kept enough oil in their lamps to keep them burning until the bridegroom came.

In Genesis 46, we are told about Jacob's family members as they left for Egypt. Below is Jacob's family tree. Your challenge is to put the names in the grid provided on the opposite page. We've given you some letters as a starting point. Unscramble those letters to learn something about these people.

_ _ _ _ _ _ _   _ _ _ _

_ _ _   _ _ _ _ _ _ _ _

(4 words)

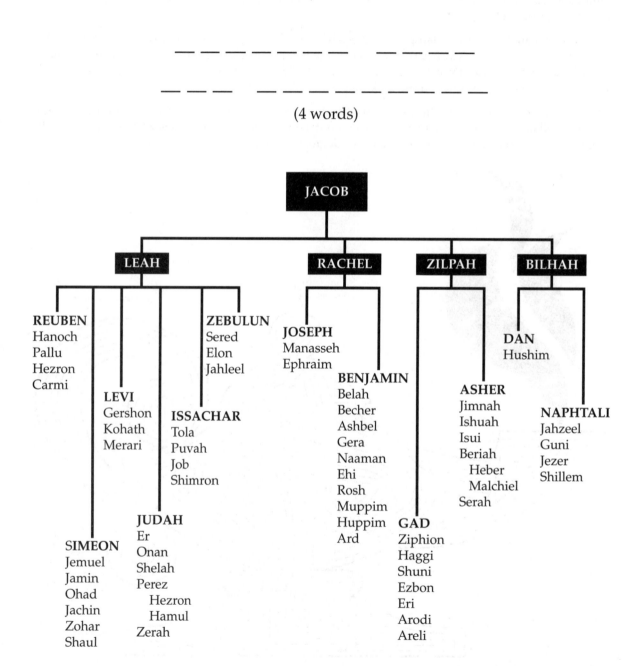

JACOB

LEAH   **RACHEL**   **ZILPAH**   **BILHAH**

REUBEN
Hanoch
Pallu
Hezron
Carmi

ZEBULUN
Sered
Elon
Jahleel

JOSEPH
Manasseh
Ephraim

DAN
Hushim

LEVI
Gershon
Kohath
Merari

ISSACHAR
Tola
Puvah
Job
Shimron

BENJAMIN
Belah
Becher
Ashbel
Gera
Naaman
Ehi
Rosh
Muppim
Huppim
Ard

ASHER
Jimnah
Ishuah
Isui
Beriah
Heber
Malchiel
Serah

NAPHTALI
Jahzeel
Guni
Jezer
Shillem

JUDAH
Er
Onan
Shelah
Perez
Hezron
Hamul
Zerah

GAD
Ziphion
Haggi
Shuni
Ezbon
Eri
Arodi
Areli

SIMEON
Jemuel
Jamin
Ohad
Jachin
Zohar
Shaul

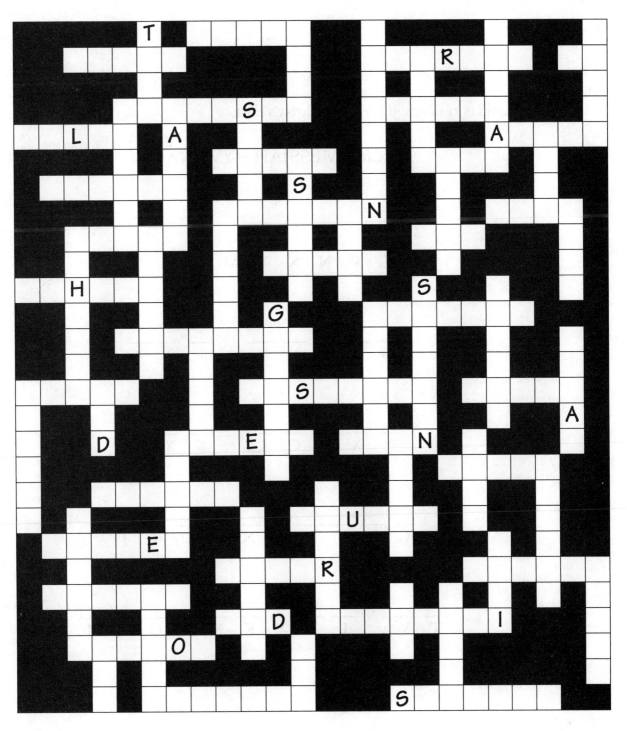

*E*ven grief is redeemed through Christ's love.

Clue: MESSIAH *is* YVNNAUZ

T J V N N V M   U C V

G Z X N V   F Z X

Y X Q C I'   K X C

G Z V E   N Z U J J

T V   L X Y K X C G V M.

*T*here's a right time for everything. Fit words from Ecclesiastes 3:1–8 into the grid below. We've given you some letters as a start.

Unscramble the circled letters to complete this verse:

To everything there is a ___ ___ ___ ___ ___ ___, a time

for every ___ ___ ___ ___ ___ ___ ___ under heaven.

(Ecclesiastes 3:1)

Word Pool

**BORN   BREAK   BUILD   CAST   DANCE   DIE   EMBRACE   GAIN   GATHER   HATE
HEAL   KEEP   KILL   LAUGH   LOSE   LOVE   MOURN   PEACE   PLANT   PLUCK
REFRAIN   SEW   SILENCE   SPEAK   TEAR   THROW   WAR   WEEP**

Link the letters below in an unending string to reveal one of Jesus' greatest promises to us.

```
A    N    U    O    Y    D    N

D    S    A    W    D    K    I

I    T    K    N    I    F    N

I    W    K    A    L    L    O

L    B    E    S    U    C    U

L    E    E    O    K    O    M

G    V    Y    N    A    Y    A

E    I    O    D    O    T    T

N    T    T    I    T    E    H

I    W    B    E    P    D    W

L    L    E    O    N    E    7:7
```

Hezekiah's Tunnel

King Hezekiah led his people in a revolt against Sennacherib. In preparation for war, he strengthened his forces and defenses internally and made alliances against Assyria. He also assured the supply of water to Jerusalem by closing off the outlet of the Gihon spring (outside the walls of Jerusalem). The spring water was diverted by means of a tunnel to the Pool of Siloam (inside the city walls). (See 2 Kings 20:20.)

The tunnel was an engineering feat in its day. Two groups began digging at opposite ends of the proposed tunnel route, and after a mid-course correction, they met with only a few inches of adjustment required.

Work this maze from both directions.

Start

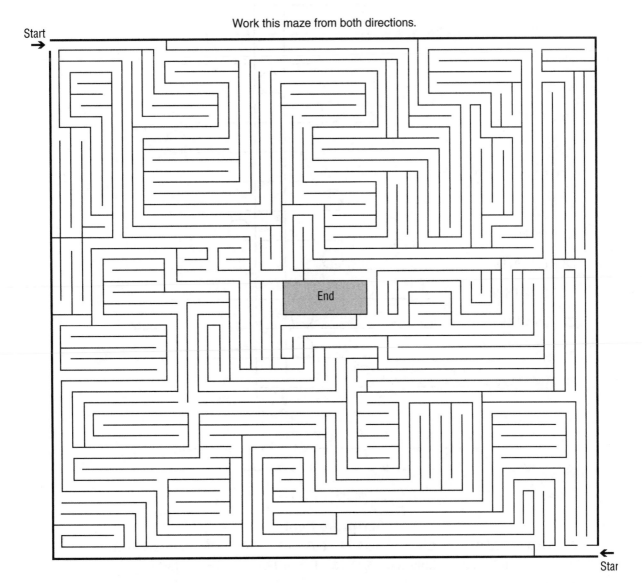

End

Star

24

Scripture uses the metaphor of marriage to illustrate the relationship between God and His people. Below is a list of scrambled words from the Bible that all pertain to marriage. Unscramble the words to reveal the relationship of all Christians to Christ. Then unscramble the circled letters to reveal Christ's invitation to each person.

VINEIT — — — — — ◯

DANBUSH — — — — — ◯ —

FEWI ◯ — — —

BOARNHOLE — ◯ — — — — — —

DERBI — — ◯ —

SIKS — ◯ — —

DEWGNID — ◯ — — — —

STAFE — — — ◯

VOLE — — — —

TGIF ◯ — — —

RUCHCH ◯ — — — ◯

DERTHBOTE — — — — ◯ — — —

GOMOREDIRB — — — ◯ — — — — —

CENTSAIDIF — — — — ◯ — — — —

STUGSE — — ◯ — —

SENTMARG — — — ◯ — — —

— — — —   — —   — — —
— — — — — — —

(Matthew 22:4)

Scripture Pool

Matthew 22:9–11   1 Corinthians 7:14   Luke 1:27   John 3:29   Genesis 29:11

John 2:2, 9   Ephesians 5:22, 25   Psalm 45:12   Hebrews 13:4

*F*ind all twelve tribes of Israel in the puzzle below. The names run in all directions.

```
P  N  I  M  A  J  N  E  B  W  I  R  J  K  L
O  A  S  D  F  G  H  J  K  H  L  R  M  O  S
J  P  E  M  I  A  R  H  P  E  A  X  J  I  O
Y  H  X  C  E  R  J  I  W  O  T  D  S  E  W
B  O  J  E  R  T  D  X  I  O  H  K  U  S  E
N  M  R  A  H  C  A  S  S  I  P  A  N  J  R
M  R  O  E  S  I  N  O  P  E  A  M  U  I  D
F  E  G  H  U  S  I  M  E  O  N  O  L  E  S
I  U  S  G  H  B  K  S  I  E  W  O  U  S  L
I  G  E  O  D  G  E  R  E  H  S  A  B  I  R
R  D  L  A  E  S  T  N  M  O  P  S  E  S  E
P  M  G  H  E  S  S  A  N  A  M  P  Z  P  I
```

Most of the clues and answers to this crossword are based on the person, work, and ministry of the Holy Spirit.

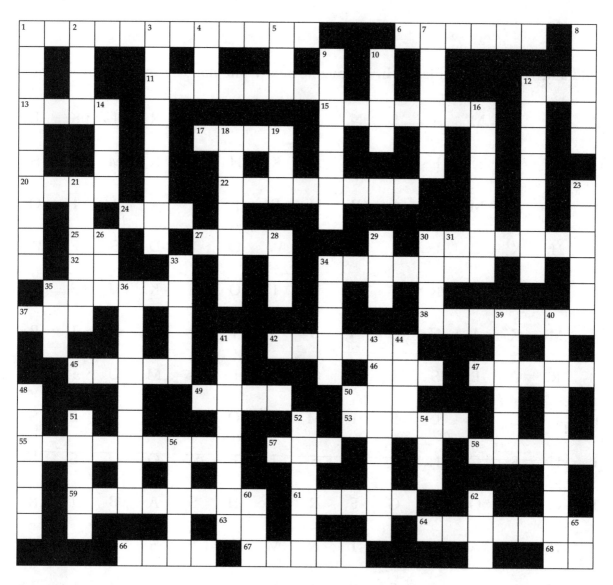

Across

1 Petition on behalf of another
6 He sent the Spirit
11 Make evident, reveal
12 Male person
13 The Spirit knows what to pray for according to God's ____
15 Guarantee
17 Daddy
20 The Spirit gives ____
22 The Spirit is Jesus' ____ in the believer
24 The Spirit ____ Jesus into the wilderness to be tempted
25 Los Angeles (abbr.)
27 Those who were "with one accord" in one place described the coming of the Spirit as a mighty ____

30 Testify

32 Lines (abbr.)

34 The Spirit was sent to show us Jesus and ____ Him

35 Counselor

37 By the Spirit we know that we belong to ____

38 Jesus' ministry inaugurated the ____ of God

42 Extinguish

45 Instruct; one of the functions of the Spirit

46 Not cold

47 Presents

49 Symbol of the Holy Spirit

50 Flank

53 Sinful nature

55 For Jews, a feast day of the firstfruits

57 The Holy Spirit told Simeon he would ____ the Christ before he died

58 Like Father, like Son

59 The Spirit moved upon the face of the waters at ____

61 The Holy Spirit gives us ____ to live the new life in Christ

63 Northeast (abbr.)

64 Gift of the Spirit to bring wholeness

66 He that searches the heart, knows the ____ of the Spirit

67 Time between the Resurrection and Pentecost: seven ____

68 The Spirit enables believers to fulfill the great commission to ____ into all the world

Down

1 Living within

2 Speak, declare

3 Jesus went away so He could send the ____

4 Transgression

5 Father, Son, Holy Spirit: ____ God

7 By the Holy Spirit we have ____ to the Father

8 We are renewed in the ____ #12 Across

9 The Bible says this man was full of the Holy Ghost

10 Appeared in the shape of cloven tongues

12 Evidence of God's reign

14 The Holy Spirit gives an abundance of this in our hearts

16 Three in one

18 Water, fire, and Spirit

19 Wonder, amazement

21 Elisabeth, Zacharias, and John were all ____ with the Holy Spirit

23 Sagacity

26 Everything

28 If you live after the flesh, you ____

29 Fruit of the Spirit

30 Fuse

31 Conditional

33 The Spirit guides into all ____

34 The Holy Spirit is the #20 Across -____

35 In what way

36 Name for the Holy Spirit

39 Sadden

40 Flowing out

41 We become God's #43 Down by ____

43 As ____, then heirs

44 A Christian's ____ is not disappointed

48 Change your mind

50 High frequency (abbr.)

51 Ask, seek, ____

52 Our bodies are the ____ of God

54 At His baptism, Jesus received anointing for ministry, and assurance as God's ____

56 Frequent

60 Those who were filled with the Holy Spirit were not drunk with ____ wine

62 Brings death

65 The "Men of Galilee" saw Jesus ____ into Heaven before He sent the Holy Spirit

Unscramble the related words below and then unscramble the circled letters to reveal God's special delivery agency.

BEALGRI ⊂⟩ _ _ _ _ _ _

HRBIUCME _ _ _ _ _ _ _ ⊂⟩

HSEETVLYNHOA _ _ _ _ _ ⊂⟩ _ _ _ _ ⊂⟩ _ (2 words)

CELAHIM _ _ _ _ _ ⊂⟩ _

ARNCAGHLE _ _ _ _ _ _ _ ⊂⟩ _

REFICUL _ _ _ _ ⊂⟩ _

RSHAMPIE ⊂⟩ _ ⊂⟩ _ _ _ _ _

_ _ _ _ _ _ _ _

Sackcloth and ashes are not exactly party fare, but the results could cause rejoicing.

Clue: MESSIAH *is* ZBMMTDE

A R L C B M M   N R I Q

P Q B M K D M M B M   P R   R L B

D L R P E B Q'   D L V   K Q D N

C R Q   R L B   D L R P E B Q.

P E D P   N R I   Z D N

W B   E B D Y B V   P E B

B C C B A P T O B'   C B Q O B L P

K Q D N B Q   R C   D

Q T X E P B R I M   Z D L

D O D T Y M   Z I A E.

*H*as there ever been a more faithful daughter-in-law than Ruth? When Naomi's husband and children passed on, leaving her all alone, it was Ruth who willingly left her home and said to Naomi, "Your people shall be my people, and your God, my God." God recognized Ruth's selflessness and gave her a new husband—and made her part of the genealogy of Jesus Christ. Refer to your New King James Bible to find any answers you don't know.

Across

1 Naomi's other daughter-in-law

3 At mealtime during the gathering of crops, Ruth dipped part of her loaf in this condiment

5 Naomi, her husband, and her sons moved here from #6 Down because of #8 Down

7 Following Naomi's instructions, Ruth went to the threshing floor and placed herself at her future husband's ____, and waited for him to tell her what she should do

9 Ruth deserved one of these for being so faithful to Naomi

12 Ruth's brother-in-law

13 Ruth used this garment to carry home food from the threshing floor

15 Oats are one

16 Ruth's great grandson

18 Ruth's husband

20 A dry measure equal to from three-eighths to two-thirds of a bushel

21 How many elders observed the transaction that resulted in Ruth's remarriage?

22 One of the two "cereals" that Ruth gathered by following the reapers

25 #2 Down told Ruth that when she felt this way, she should "go to the vessels" and partake of what the young men had drawn

26 Naomi's hometown was in the land of _____

27 #11 Down's nearest kinsman would have been forced to pass this up if he had exercised his option on #11 Down's property

29 This tragedy in the family was one reason that Naomi wanted to return to her homeland. (The other reason was that "the Lord had visited His people" in giving them food; #8 Down was over.)

30 Ruth sought refuge under these, belonging to the Lord God of Israel

32 According to Israel's law, the nearest relative was given the opportunity to do this with his late kinsman's property before any other relative could

33 Naomi lost two of them

34 The meaning of the name that Naomi took when she returned home (see #10 Down)

35 Naomi and Ruth arrived home at the beginning of this "time of gathering up crops"

36 Naomi sought this for Ruth, "that it may be well with you"; a good husband could provide it

Down

1 Ruth's son

2 Ruth's second husband

4 To go along behind the reapers and pick up the parts of the crop they drop or miss

6 Naomi's hometown, it was later the birthplace of one of Ruth's descendants

7 Where the seeds were planted

8 It drove Naomi and her family from their hometown

10 The name that Naomi took when she returned to her hometown

11 Naomi's husband

13 In Israel, taking this off signified that a deal had been made

14 The hour at which #2 Down awoke and found Ruth at the end of his pallet

17 The second of two "cereals" that Ruth gathered by following the reapers

19 Naomi's "condition" when she left her hometown; it expresses "having it all"

23 This is the foodstuff that God restored to His people when the land was fertile and productive once more

24 Being a Moabitess, Ruth was considered one of these in Naomi's hometown

26 Ruth's grandson

28 Ruth found this with her late father-in-laws kinsman; it meant food on Naomi's table

31 Naomi originally left her hometown as #19 Down, but returned this way

Unscramble the original given letters to find a descriptive word for Naomi:

__ __ __ __ __ __ - __ __ - __ __ __

*T*ry to solve the equation below without consulting the Scriptures!

The number of days after birth a male child was to be circumcised

_____

The number of days journey from Horeb by way of Mount Seir unto Kadesh-Barnea

× _____

The number of days the children of Israel wept for Moses in the plains of Moab

+ _____

The number of days Jesus stayed with the Samaritans at Sychar

+ _____

The number of days Lazarus was in the tomb before Jesus called him back to life

÷ _____

The number of days Moses was on the mountain with the Lord God

+ _____

The number of days between the time Nabal's heart "died within him" and the time he actually died

− _____

The number of days the "prince of the kingdom of Persia" withstood the heavenly messenger who came to interpret Daniel's vision

+ _____

The number of days required to build Nehemiah's wall

− _____

The number of days set aside for celebrating Purim

+ _____

The number of days the Lord God took to complete His creation

− _____

The number of Joseph's brothers who went to buy grain in Egypt

+ _____

The number of days it took Paul and his disciples to sail from Philippi to Troas

+ _____

The number of days it rained on the earth at the time of the Great Flood

= _____

Unscramble the related words below to reveal the identity of an Old Testament judge.

TALETB __ __ __ __ __ O

DANESMIITI __ __ O __ __ O __ __ __ __

PGA O __ __

HUOST __ __ O __ __

PAMSL __ __ __ __ __

ICHETRPS __ O __ __ __ __ __ __

FECELES __ __ __ __ __ __ __

__ __ __ __ __ __

SIGNIFICANT SEVENS

Although Bible scholars do not all agree on the significance of the number *seven* in the Scripture, there is little doubt that it has played a frequent role in God's dealing with man. From the seven days of creation in Genesis to the seven seals in Revelation, the number occurs in nearly every book of the Bible. Some of the most memorable occurrences include the seven loaves, which at Jesus' hand fed the multitude and then filled seven baskets; the year of Jubilee which followed seven cycles of seven years; the seven times the Israelites marched around the walls of Jericho; and the seven statements of Christ from the cross.

Travel any direction to an adjacent block with the number seven from beginning to end.

↓ Start

7	6	5	3	2	5	1	6	7	7	7	9	4	9	5	0	2	7	1	4	7	7	5	9	4	0
0	7	7	7	9	7	8	7	4	2	1	7	7	7	0	7	8	7	7	5	6	1	7	7	7	6
7	9	5	0	7	0	7	0	3	3	4	8	0	1	7	7	3	2	7	0	4	3	2	0	3	7
7	6	3	1	8	2	6	7	0	4	9	6	5	2	8	6	7	5	7	7	2	7	1	9	1	7
4	7	7	4	4	7	5	7	7	0	8	6	5	7	4	6	7	9	2	8	7	7	8	0	7	3
2	1	5	7	6	7	7	0	9	7	5	7	7	9	7	0	2	7	5	4	7	9	2	7	4	2
1	5	7	3	9	8	7	4	3	2	7	1	6	8	5	7	3	7	6	7	5	2	7	3	1	6
6	7	0	4	5	8	3	8	6	2	1	7	0	2	3	7	9	1	7	7	8	5	0	7	7	7
2	8	1	7	7	7	9	7	7	5	0	1	7	9	8	7	4	9	7	3	2	0	4	7	5	0
2	1	4	7	6	0	7	8	9	7	5	8	0	8	7	4	1	7	3	7	9	5	4	7	1	4
3	7	9	3	7	5	3	1	3	7	6	3	1	9	7	5	6	5	0	8	7	2	7	9	5	0
7	7	2	2	7	4	7	5	7	6	8	4	7	7	6	7	3	1	7	7	3	4	1	7	2	0
7	4	2	7	2	4	6	7	3	5	4	7	3	8	0	7	4	7	0	4	9	5	8	7	5	2
3	3	4	7	0	0	2	7	1	5	0	7	4	9	1	7	1	7	2	8	3	6	7	7	7	7
4	0	2	5	7	6	9	7	2	4	7	8	5	8	7	0	2	4	0	7	0	7	9	2	3	9
7	7	7	7	7	3	8	5	7	7	8	4	7	7	9	2	3	1	8	0	7	3	5	7	7	4
1	2	5	0	7	4	1	3	9	5	6	2	4	9	5	7	4	2	9	7	3	8	3	0	7	9
5	7	7	4	7	7	7	7	7	8	0	1	7	8	9	7	7	4	7	0	7	7	7	2	7	0
7	6	9	0	5	8	2	8	7	5	3	7	5	7	8	2	4	7	5	3	8	5	7	9	7	3
7	5	6	7	7	7	1	7	4	7	7	2	3	9	7	7	7	3	7	2	5	1	7	7	4	0
7	7	7	7	5	9	7	5	9	0	4	6	7	7	1	2	0	5	0	7	2	7	3	9	7	7

↑ End

MORE THAN CONQUERORS

God knows the attacks, temptations, and the enemies that come against Christians. He knows what it takes to defeat the enemy, so He has equipped the believers with the "armor of God." To quench the fiery darts of the wicked one, Christians are given, above all, the shield of faith. (See Ephesians 6:14-17.)

How is it that the shield of faith defends against the enemy? Just what is it that Christians receive by their faith for the defense of soul and spirits? The Bible says that by faith we have salvation, justifications, pure hearts, peace, joy, everlasting life, access to God, healing, and victory that overcomes the world. By faith, Christians have all they need to be more than conquerors.

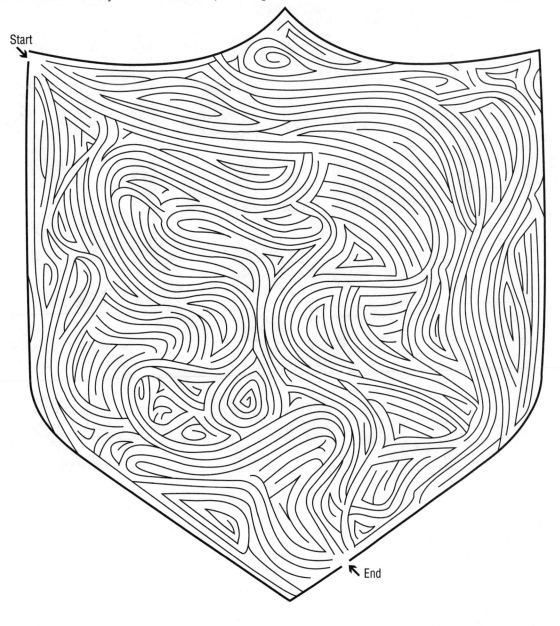

The Kingdom of Heaven is like . . . fill in the answers with clues pertaining to the Kingdom of Heaven and Jesus' parables on the Kingdom.

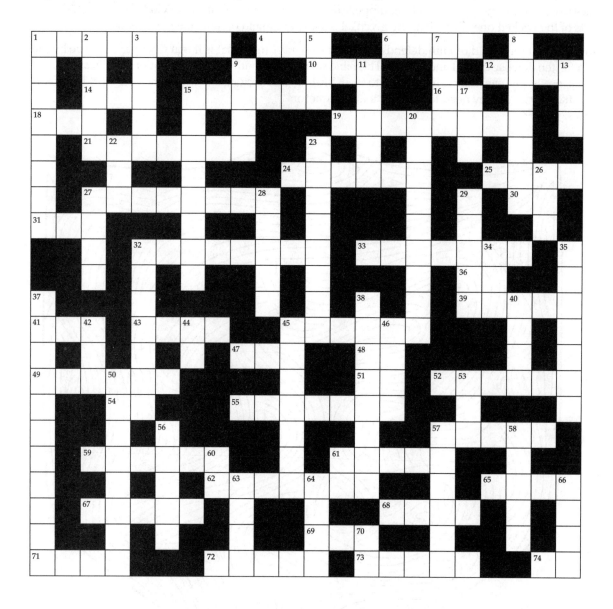

Across

1 Stories with more than one level of meaning
4 When the wood, hay, and stubble are burned up, this will be left
6 Planted
10 The cost of the pearl of great price
12 Desire, search out
14 Atmosphere
15 Those who accept the invitation
16 Southeast (abbr.)

18 Friend

19 God's provision of righteousness for wedding #15 Across

21 This seed makes the point that inauspicious beginnings don't determine success or failure

24 What we'd call the men in Matthew 22:6

25 Those who think they are first may be in for this surprise

27 This person knew real value when he saw it

30 Land- ____

31 Affirmative (bibl.)

32 A day's wages

33 Day of Judgment

36 Leading edge (abbr.)

39 Sows bad seeds

41 Time

43 This was stored in vessels; the rest was tossed out

45 In the Kingdom of Heaven, God rules in our ____

47 If this functions properly, you are blessed

48 Associate Arts degree (abbr.)

49 Yeast

51 Near (abbr.)

52 Message of Jesus' forerunner

54 Pronoun without gender

55 Hell

57 Fruit of the #67 Across

59 Jesus revealed what had been ____

61 Wringing of hands, tearing one's hair, #15 Down of ____

62 Maidens

65 Hearts and taskmasters

67 Ground

68 A bird's home

69 Not new

71 Exchanged for something else of value

72 Rule

73 Discovered

74 Ancient name for God

Down

1 Jesus spoke in #1 Across', fulfilling __

2 Domain

3 God's winged creatures

5 Everyone who __ will be given more

7 These women heeded the motto: "Be prepared"

8 The expected One

9 Sons of the Kingdom or of the wicked one

11 Smallest

13 Peter was given the __ (sing.) of the Kingdom

15 What the tormented do

17 In the ____, the weeds and the wicked will meet their ____

20 Only God can shed some light on these

22 Good stewards put their #35 Down to good ____

23 The heart and this are in the same place

26 ____ of Man sows good seed

27 A large number are called

28 9:00 AM; ____ hour

29 Where treasure was hidden

32 This was full of good and bad

34 Not everyone who has #47 Across can ____

35 Gifts, abilities

37 Those who are involved in this have no place in the Kingdom

38 The far reaches of the Kingdom

40 Wicked

42 Estimated time of arrival (abbr.)

44 Wedding feast fare

45 This activity should result in understanding

46 Offspring of the wicked one

50 Where there is work to be done

53 If you have this, you can pay attention

56 If the #47 Across and #53 Down don't function, and the #45 Across (sing.) is #65 Across it will be difficult to know this

57 Select few

58 Gem

60 Television (abbr.)

61 Tennessee (abbr.)

63 Unprofitable

64 Image

66 Not sharp

70 Damage free (abbr.)

In the box of letters below find seven things at which the Queen of Sheba marveled when she came to see King Solomon.

```
L   O   M   B   I   C   S   T   E   I   P   O

S   E   R   V   D   O   M   E   T   O   R   S

W   Y   R   O   H   E   S   E   O   H   I   R

I   S   A   A   E   W   I   S   D   O   M   E

S   O   N   T   P   T   N   A   V   U   W   R

V   I   S   C   U   P   B   E   A   S   P   A

A   C   O   S   T   N   A   V   R   E   S   E

E   H   U   A   E   B   M   S   P   A   P   B

N   C   E   D   S   I   W   A   C   P   V   P

T   M   H   E   M   O   D   E   O   E   R   U

S   O   C   R   T   G   N   R   S   E   N   C

H   M   O   P   R   A   E   B   R   E   S   T
```

*T*his Bible verse, found in the New Testament, is a familiar one. It's one of God's promises that ultimately means the end of the old life and the beginning of the new. (Hint: There's no code number for the letter "Z"—you won't need it. And to make this a little more difficult, the words are scrambled; they form two sentences.)

Clue: MESSIAH *is* 3 5 4 4 4 1 3

Unscramble the letters:

___ ___ ___ ___ ___   ___ ___ ___ ___ ___ ___   ___ ___ ___   ___ ___ ___ ___
4   5   1   4   4   1   4   5   5   4   5   1   4   4   3   5   3   5

   ___ ___ ___ ___ ___   ___ ___ ___   ___ ___   ___ ___ ___ ___
   5   1   5   4   4   3   4   3   3   5   4   5   5   3

___ ___   ___ ___ ___ ___ ___ ___   ___ ___ ___ ___   ___ ___ ___ ___ ___
3   5   2   5   3   5   2   4   3   4   2   2   2   5   4   3   5

  ___ ___   ___ ___ ___   ___ ___ ___ ___   ___   ___ ___ ___ ___
  1   5   1   4   4   4   5   5   3   4   3   4   5   3

___ ___ ___ ___ ___   ___ ___ ___   ___ ___   ___ ___   ___ ___ ___ ___
1   4   5   3   1   5   3   5   3   5   4   1   3   4   5   3

   ___ ___ ___ ___   ___ ___ ___   ___ ___   ___ ___ ___
   4   4   4   5   5   3   5   5   5   1   4   4

___ ___ ___   ___   ___ ___ ___ ___ ___   ___ ___   ___ ___ ___
1   4   4   4   3   5   1   3   4   4   4   3   4   3

Unscramble the words:

_____

_____

_____

_____

_____

*T*here was no retirement for Sarah, the wife of Abraham. At an age when most women were bouncing great grandchildren on their knees, Sarah was still waiting to have her first child. Her doubts were many, but as we read her story in Genesis, her underlying faith in God comes through. God kept His promise, and Sarah and Abraham took their place in the bloodline that led to the birth of Jesus Christ.

Across

2 God's agreement with Abraham

5 The "surrogate heir"

6 As God was known to the patriarchs in Old Testament times: ____ Shaddai

8 The land where Sarah and Abraham resided; it was God's gift to them

10 She really was this to her husband, by half

14 The women of the house of #30 Across found theirs closed because of Sarah

16 Sarah's father-in-law

18 Of God's agreement with Abraham, there would be no ____

19 Sarah was pleasing to it

20 Abraham's original name, meaning "exalted father"

22 Sarah was buried in this

23 Sarah gave this woman to her husband to be his wife when she herself could not conceive

26 In the wilderness on the way to Shur, he is the

one who comforted the mother of Abraham's first child after she fled from Sarah's presence

28 Because of his fondness for Sarah, Pharaoh didn't make Abraham wait for some of these

30 God talked in his sleep and kept him from touching Sarah, then this ruler gave Abraham some valuable property and money and returned Sarah to him

31 Abraham had to pay for Sarah's final resting place. How many hundred shekels of silver did he give to Ephron?

32 The town that #30 Across ruled

36 Long may he reign

37 Abraham couldn't count them, can you?

38 Location of the field where Sarah, Abraham, Isaac, Rebekah, Jacob, and Leah were buried; it was the only property the patriarchs owned (that is, purchased) in the Promised Land

39 The son of Abraham's brother Haran

40 This document, confirming Abraham's ownership of Sarah's burial place, was a good one

Down

1 The city where Sarah died

2 Sarah's was so beautiful, Abraham passed her off as a sibling

3 Sarah was over ____ years old when her son was born

4 How long had Abraham and Sarah lived in the Promised Land when Abraham's first son was born?

7 "Morsels" of money

8 Taxi of the desert; Abraham received this type of animal from Pharaoh

9 A unit of measure for Abraham's inheritance from God

11 Sarah's original name also meant "princess"

12 You could accuse her of wool-gathering; she figured in the oath that Abraham made with #30 Across

13 God's promise fulfilled

15 Is there one in the house? (abbr.)

17 What Sarah might have exclaimed at the thought of conceiving a child at her age

21 It turned out to be a temporary (albeit long-lived) condition for Sarah

24 #30 Across had one that saved his life

25 Sarah didn't cook this animal for their heavenly visitors; she was busy making cakes

27 Sarah giggles

28 These were a standard unit of weight in Old Testament times

29 Refreshing water was available at this spot in the wilderness; Sarah's servant found solace there

33 A mate for #12 Down. He was part of the proof that Abraham would inherit the Promised Land

34 #22 Across probably had walls made of this

35 She waited on Sarah while Sarah waited on God

Unscramble the given letters to reveal the means by which Sarah received strength to conceive seed:

—— —— —— —— —— —— ——   —— —— —— —— ——

(Hebrews 11:11)

Old orders stand until new orders arrive.

Clue: MESSIAH *is* DVJJZRY

X F   K Y V I V W F I V   R E U

D R B V   U Z J T Z G C V J   F W

R C C   E R K Z F E J'   S R G K Z Q Z E X

K Y V D   Z E   K Y V   E R D V   F W

K Y V   W R K Y V I   R E U   F W

K Y V   J F E   R E U   F W   K Y V

Y F C P   J G Z I Z K'   K V R T Y Z E X

K Y V D   K F   F S J V I M V   R C C

K Y Z E X J   K Y R K   Z   Y R M V

T F D D R E U V U   P F L;   R E U   C F

Z   R D   N Z K Y   P F L   R C N R P J

V M V E   K F   K Y V   V E U

F W   K Y V   R X V.

Chosen Bride

*T*o find just the right bride for his beloved son Isaac, the aging Abraham sent his trusted servant off to his homeland of Mesopotamia. The servant loaded up ten camels with some of Abraham's best things and began the journey. When he arrived, he felt the full weight of his task, and he prayed, "O Lord God of my master Abraham, please give me success this day, and show kindness to my master Abraham. . . . Now let it be that the young woman to whom I say, 'Please let down your pitcher that I may drink,' and she says, 'Drink, and I will also give your camels a drink' — let her be the one You have appointed for Your servant Isaac" (Genesis 24:12, 14).

Before he was even through praying, beautiful Rebekah came out with her water pitcher. He asked for a drink of water and she agreed. Then she offered to draw water for the camels. It didn't take this servant long to realize his prayers for his master had been answered. After Abraham's servant made arrangements with Rebekah's family, she made the journey back to the land of Canaan to become Isaac's wife and the mother of his children, continuing the lineage of Abraham.

*H*e's best known for "dry bones," but Ezekiel was a prophet whose words we would be wise to heed, even in this day. When God chooses a people, makes a covenant, and pours out His blessings upon them, what should their response be? What is *our* response to the God who loves and blesses and keeps and saves us? This puzzle deals with the entire book of Ezekiel; use the New King James Version to find the answers.

Across

1 The priests couldn't drink this in the inner court of the temple

8 The foolish prophets of Ezekiel's day gave this type of vision; it was useless

9 One of the six men in one of Ezekiel's visions carried this writer's implement at his side

10 Ezekiel found the scroll of this surprisingly tasty

11 God sought a man to make a wall and stand in the _____ before Him on behalf of Israel; there was no one

14 God promised to leave this after destroying most of the people of Israel

15 As men gather bronze, iron, _____, and other metals, and place them in a furnace, God will put Israel there to burn

16 God said He would bring Tyre down with those who descend into the ____

21 To sustain Ezekiel when he was symbolizing the years of Israel's and Judah's iniquity, God allowed him this amount of water: one-sixth of a ____

22 People who came to Ezekiel heard his words but ignored them. With their mouths they showed ____, but their hearts pursued their own gain

24 The prophets' visions were like building a boundary wall and plastering it with untempered ____; it will fall

26 Contraction for I am

28 God told Ezekiel to do this to his head and beard

29 In viewing the temple abominations, Ezekiel saw____ men of the elders with censers in their hands

30 When Ezekiel fell on his face before God, God commanded him to "____"!

33 Editor (abbr.)

35 This bird was used to symbolize Nebuchadnezzar, who carried away Israel's princes

36 God pressed Ezekiel to take this type of plate and set it as a wall between him and the city

37 God will spread His net over the prince in Jerusalem and catch him in His ____, like an animal

38 The king of Babylon used divination: shook arrows, consulted images, and looked at the ____ (without X-rays!)

40 Ezekiel's father

44 Five of the six men from #9 Across slew old and young men, little children, and ____

46 Article

47 The man from #9 Across scattered coals of ____ over the city

48 Ezekiel was to bake his cakes by using human waste for fuel; it was a sign of eating this type of bread among the Gentiles, where God would drive His people

49 In the valley of dry bones, God put ____ and flesh on the bones

51 Shepherds who fed themselves should have been feeding their ____

54 After his initial vision, Ezekiel went to the captives at this place and sat, astonished

55 The land of God's people was ruled with crimes and ____; none bothered to wipe it up

57 One of the four faces of the living creatures

58 Either . . . ____.

59 When God executes judgment, one-third of the people will die by this

60 The elders had these in their hearts, not the true God

62 The scroll contained writings of lamentations, mourning, and ____

63 One of three well-known men of God who could have saved only himself in the unfaithful land of Ezekiel's day

65 Moab, ____, and Phillstia would see the vengeance of God

66 This tribe received two portions of the land—for Ephraim and Manasseh

68 God said He'd put these in Gog's jaws and lead him out

69 When the land was divided by lots into inheritance, a ____ was set apart for God—a holy portion

71 God will make Rabbah, the Ammonites' city, a stable for this animal

72 Priests had to change these before leaving the temple's holy chamber (sing.)

73 Israel would become one ____ with one king

74 Men took one of these in exchange for killing

Down

1 The living creatures had four of these

2 A standard unit of measure, it equaled 17½ to 20 inches

3 Priests' clothes had to be made of this fabric

4 God said He'd purge these "unmanageables" from among His people; they wouldn't enter Israel

5 Another name for Samaria, meaning "She of the Tent"

6 One of the people that would judge Jerusalem, along with Babylonia and other Chaldeans

7 On His holy mountain, God will accept His people as a sweet ____ to His nose

12 Egyptians are originally from the land of ____

13 God's people were held ____ by numerous nations

17 Israel played harlot with the Egyptians and Assyrians and erected a ____ at the head of every road

18 God will knock the ____ out of Gog's left hand and arrows from his right

19 In an early vision, Ezekiel saw the walls of the temple, with creeping things, abominable ____ (sing.), and idols portrayed there

20 The six men of #9 Across each had a deadly weapon: A ____-ax.

23 How many months it would take Israel to bury Gog and his multitude

25 Another name for Jerusalem, meaning "My tent is in her."

27 The trees on the river bank near the restored temple had fruit for food and leaves for ____, for healing

31 At the end of the book: The name of the city shall be "The Lord is ____"

32 Another of the men from #63 Across

34 The people of God who survive destruction will escape to the mountains, like this bird of the valleys

39 Ezekiel was sent to the children of Israel because they were ____; they wouldn't obey God

41 The sons of ____ of the tribe of Levi could approach God

42 A priest could marry another priest's widow, or a ____

43 God said He would leave His people in the furnace to "become liquid"

45 The gateway of the temple's inner court (facing east) was only open on the Sabbath and the day of the ____ (two words)

50 When God gathers His scattered children, He will replace their hearts of stone with hearts of ____

52 Gog will come like a ____ to cover the Israelites' land

53 This city that burned was less corrupt than older sister Israel

55 When Gog comes, every man's weapon will be against this close relative

56 The house of Israel had become ____ from silver; it was impure

61 Those who survive God's punishment will have ____ hands and knees as weak as water

64 The taste of the scroll was like this sweet substance

66 God lifted His hand in oath to descendants of the house of ____ on the day He chose Israel

67 When His people seek____, they'll find none—only anxiety

70 An offering for the prince of Israel would be one lamb from a flock of how many hundred?

THE MOLINE CROSS

*E*ach arm of the Moline Cross ends in two graceful, outward-curving petals. The resemblance to the crossed iron, or moline, of the upper millstone is what gives this cross design its name.

The arms of the cross seem to evoke an all-embracing, far-reaching feeling, and thus the cross is frequently associated with the Great Commission: "Go therefore and make disciples of all the nations, baptizing them in the name of the Father and of the Son and of the Holy Spirit, teaching them to observe all things that I have commanded you; and lo, I am with you always, even to the end of the age" (Matthew 28:19–20).

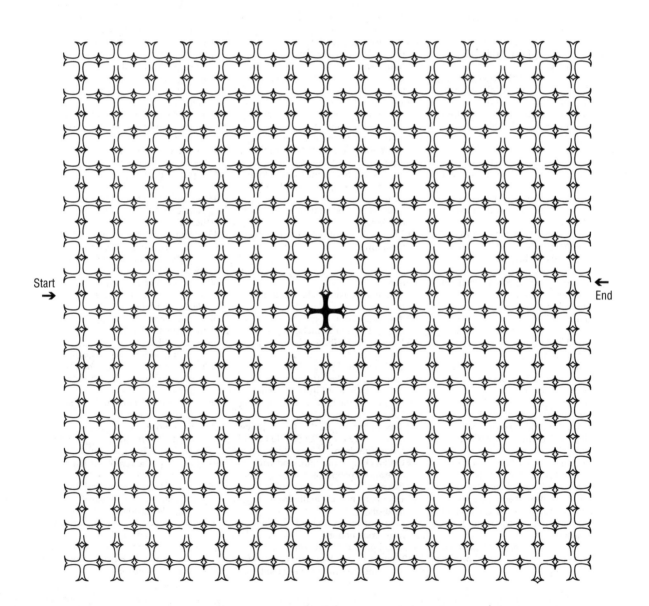

Start
→

←
End

*J*esus was asked the question, "Who do You think You are?" In the letter grid find 16 "I AMs" of Jesus.

```
R  R  O  O  T  O  F  D  A  V  I  D  Y
E  A  S  O  F  F  S  P  R  I  N  G  E
M  P  H  W  E  R  F  H  A  C  E  W  F
B  R  E  A  D  O  F  L  I  F  E  B  I
I  L  P  T  R  E  S  V  E  R  Y  R  L
O  L  H  Y  T  H  G  I  M  L  A  A  H
O  N  E  Z  E  I  N  E  S  G  H  T  T
D  I  R  N  T  I  A  M  E  P  A  S  U
R  O  D  H  I  O  N  M  L  S  E  G  R
U  G  G  W  E  V  O  A  T  R  A  N  T
F  I  G  R  S  A  E  W  O  R  K  I  Y
L  N  O  M  D  S  E  U  B  O  R  N  A
S  O  A  T  E  V  W  E  R  O  O  R  W
D  R  E  S  U  R  R  E  C  T  I  O  N
R  U  I  T  A  T  R  E  Y  A  R  M  D
```

Scripture Pool

John 6:35; 8:12, 58; 10:9, 11; 11:25; 14:6; 15:1; Revelation 1:8; 22:16

The books of the Old Testament provide the answers to this crossword.

Across

3 The temple rebuilt
4 The book of the weeping prophet
5 Prophesied the birthplace of the Messiah
6 Jerusalem plundered and Edom's demise
8 The prophet during the Babylonian exile
10 The crossing, the conquest, and the land
11 The people spared and the Feast of Purim begun
12 Return to the land
16 Book of praises
17 The wall is rebuilt
18 Loyalty rewarded
19 Nineveh's downfall
20 First book of the Pentateuch
24 In Hebrew, "The words, events, of the days"
26 Details laws on sacrifices
31 Wilderness wanderings
32 The shepherd prophet from Tekoa
33 This prophet's name means "My messenger"
34 Love story

Down

1 Eight visions
2 The prophet voices complaints about evil and God's justice
4 The problem of suffering
7 The farewell address, the law reviewed and the eve of the entrance to Canaan
9 Odes of woe
10 Prophesied the outpouring of the Spirit on all people
13 Central theme is the coming "Day of the Lord" that will bring destruction
14 End of the judges and the kingdom established
15 The one that (almost) got away
21 The great escape
22 The preacher
23 Practical wisdom
25 The kingdom divided
27 True love spurned
28 Prophesied the suffering servant
29 From Joshua to Samuel
30 Dreams, visions, and uncompromising loyalty

Jesus said He came to fulfill the Law and the Prophets, not destroy them. Indeed, heaven and earth will disappear before the least of the commandments. Unscramble the circled letters to reveal what Jesus said those are:

— — — — — — — — — — — —

Wood was a popular material in Bible times. It was used to make a variety of items, such as . . . well, we aren't going to tell you what it was used for. It's up to you to figure that out in this puzzle. Unscramble the letters and spell out items made of wood, things built with wood, types of wood, and the forms wood takes. Then, unscramble the circled letters and spell out a New Testament verse that tells you what is "king of the hill," so to speak.

DANHANWEOP

◯_◯_ _◯_ _ _ _
(2 words)

FATFS _◯_ _ _

SLESEVS ◯_ _ _◯_ _

KAR ◯_ _

SOSRC _ _◯_ _

SOLID _ _ _ _◯

ROODS ◯_ _ _ _ _

ARCT _◯_◯

EIRF ◯_ _ _

RLOOSF _ _ _◯_ _

COBKL _◯_ _ _

KEYSO _◯_ _◯

LOPES _ _ _◯_

BATSO _ _ _◯_

SARB _◯_ _

POCANY _◯_ _ _ _

WOBS _◯_ _

BURCHIME _◯_ _ _◯_ _

GAMERN _ _ _ _◯_

RACEVDGAMEI

_ _ _◯_ _ _ _ _ _◯
(2 words)

PETMEL _◯_ _ _◯

DOGS _ _ _◯

WARSRO _ _◯_ _◯

TARMLOFP _ _ _◯◯_ _ _

BEATL ◯_ _ _ _

SWEIKSORGE _ _ _ _◯_ _ _ _ _

SLACIUMMIRTSETNUNS

_ _ _ _◯_ _ _ _ _
_ _ _ _◯_ _◯_ _ _ _
(2 words)

LAWLS ◯_ _ _ _

TALRA _ _◯_ _

FIRNGEOF ◯_ _ _ _◯_ _ _

BACELEARNT _ _◯_ _ _ _ _ _◯_

OLDEMDMAIEG _ _ _ _◯_ _ _ _◯_
(2 words)

PHISS _◯_ _ _

DAROSB _ _ _ _◯_

GIESTRHHNPELESTIMMN

_◯_ _ _◯_ _ _
◯_◯_ _◯_◯_ _
(2 words)

PEOHRG _ _ _◯◯_

QAPUALNNI _ _ _ _◯_◯_ _

RAILPLS _ _◯_ _◯_

Verse:

_ _ _   _ _ _ _   _ _ _ _   _ _ _ _   _ _ _ _
_ _ _ _   _ _ _ _   _ _ _   _ _ _ _   _ _ _ _
_ _   _ _ _ _ _   _ _   _ _ _ _

*S*olve the following puzzle by connecting adjacent letters (in all directions) to reveal how to experience God's leading.

T	L	T	I	W	O	E	S	T	A
H	L	H	D	R	H	L	R	D	N
E	I	A	T	T	D	E	I	I	N
N	H	I	N	R	N	N	G	H	A
R	A	E	T	U	U	N	Y	T	L
T	A	N	S	T	O	W	A	W	L
L	D	O	H	T	O	E	N	Y	S
E	N	T	N	I	N	W	O	K	A
A	N	U	D	E	L	S	H	A	C
H	E	G	N	H	E	E	R	D	L
I	M	A	D	S	T	T	C	I	L
			H	H				
			Y	T				
			P	A				

Jesus taught that the Sabbath is created for our benefit and should not interfere with our decision to help others. After all, the greatest commandment is to love God with all your heart and soul, and then to love your neighbor as yourself—no matter what day of the week it is.

Across

2 After sacrificing their "hope for the future" to their idols, the people of Israel profaned the Sabbath by entering the sanctuary on the same day

8 A woman, who had a spirit of infirmity for ____ years was healed on the Sabbath, raising the indignation of the synagogue's ruler

9 In the wilderness, the Israelites were supposed to bake and ____ whatever foods were needed for the Sabbath, on the day before the Sabbath

10 When the Shunammite woman's son died, her husband, unaware of the death, asked why she was going to see this man of God, since it wasn't the Sabbath

12 This unit of measure is how much manna the Israelites gathered on the sixth day: two ____ instead of one, to prepare for the Sabbath

15 When Jesus stood and read the Book of ____ in the synagogue on the Sabbath, He told the people that the Scriptures had been fulfilled in their hearing

16 At the Feast of Firstfruits, the priest waved one of these before the Lord on the Israelites' behalf, on the day after Sabbath, to signify the first harvest

19 Not out

20 The day before the Sabbath, ____ Day, Joseph of Arimathea asked for the body of Jesus

22 When Jesus taught in the synagogue on the Sabbath, the people were astonished, asking, "What ____ is this which is given to Him, this Son of Mary?"

25 At Philippi, Paul, Silas, and Timothy went on the Sabbath to the riverside where "conversation with God" was customarily made (pl.)

27 If the Israelites didn't break the Sabbath the way their fathers did, and if they heeded God, then kings and princes sitting on the throne of David and riding in these would enter the gates of their city, a city which would remain forever

30 At the end of seven Sabbatical cycles (49 years) came the year of ____: That entire year, the people could not sow crops or reap

31 For the Feast of Weeks, the grain offering was two wave loaves of fine flour, baked with this fermenting agent

33 Preaching on the Sabbath at #1 Down, Paul said those in Jerusalem and the rulers didn't know Jesus or the voice of these "men of God" that were ready every Sabbath (sing.)

34 How many years did the Promised Land lay fallow to make up for the years when the people refused to observe the Sabbath?

35 One of three divisions of the psyche

37 Although the Israelites gathered twice as much manna on the sixth day, the extra portion didn't stink or have any of these when they ate it on the Sabbath

38 Visiting the house of a Pharisee ruler to eat bread on the Sabbath, Jesus healed a man of this disease

39 During the land's Sabbath rest, the people could not reap what grew of its own accord, nor gather these from untended vines (sing.)

40 In the wilderness, a man who was caught gathering sticks on the Sabbath was taken out and ____ as a final punishment

Down

1 Paul and his party stopped in this city and, on the Sabbath, Paul stood and preached Jesus; after the Jews left the synagogue, the Gentiles wanted Paul to preach the same to them on the next Sabbath

3 On the same day as #22 Across, many were offended by Jesus, resulting in fewer healings. Jesus was indeed a #33 Across without ____ in His own country

4 God said the land would enjoy its Sabbaths while it lay ____ (lonely) without the Israelites

5 Blessed is the man who keeps from defiling the Sabbath and keeps his hand from doing any ____

6 The men of Tyre who lived in the area were guilty of bringing this to sell on the Sabbath in Jerusalem

7 The king of Assyria, Tiglath-____ contributed to #14 Down's disregard for God's temple

11 At the Pool of Bethesda by the ____ Gate, this man wasn't fuzzy about the healing he received at Jesus' hand on the Sabbath; his 38 years of sickness were over

13 "My Sabbaths you shall keep,"(NKJ) God said. It was "a ____ between Me and you," an indication that God sanctified them

14 This king removed the Sabbath pavilion that had been built in the temple, possibly due to the influence of the king of Assyria

17 The Israelites couldn't kindle any of these in their habitations on the Sabbath (sing.)

18 From the day after the seventh Sabbath after the Feast of Firstfruits, the Israelites counted ____ days and celebrated the Feast of Weeks with a new grain offering

19 The gateway of this court (facing east) would be closed on the six working days, but open on the Sabbath and the day of the New Moon

20 In Corinth, Paul stayed with Aquila and ____, and reasoned in the synagogue every Sabbath, persuading many Jews and Greeks

21 This was made for man, not man for it

23 Anyone who profaned the Sabbath would suffer a premature one

24 In a song for the Sabbath day (found In Psalms), God's lovingkindness and faithfulness should be declared on an instrument of ten strings, and on the ____ and the harp

26 If one of these animals fell into a pit on the Sabbath, Jesus asked, wouldn't the Pharisees lift it out? So is healing on the Sabbath a sin?

28 From Mount ____ to Jerusalem is a Sabbath day's journey. The disciples made the trip after Jesus ascended to Heaven

29 God told Moses to tell the Israelites to "keep My Sabbath and reverence My ____,"or "holy place where the Lord was present"

30 This priest brought together Queen Athaliah's officers and bodyguards to provide protection for the rightful heir, Joash, at his coronation

32 The man in #11 Down was told to take this up and walk, but the Jews told him it wasn't lawful to carry it on the Sabbath (pl.)

33 For six years, the Israelites were to sow the fields, and ____ the vineyard and gather its fruit; the seventh year was a Sabbath for the land

34 At the Sabbath sunset, the whole city gathered at the door of this disciple's house, and Jesus healed many and cast out demons

36 In Ezekiel, the priests had profaned holy things, and had hidden their ____ from God's Sabbaths

THE ANCHOR CROSS

*T*he writer to the Hebrews speaks of hope as "an anchor of the soul" (Hebrews 6:19). Thus, this cross design is also called the Cross of Hope.

The cross design was popular among early Christians. It has been associated especially with St. Clement, Bishop of Rome, who according to tradition was martyred under the Trajan persecutions by being bound to an anchor and cast into the sea.

Start

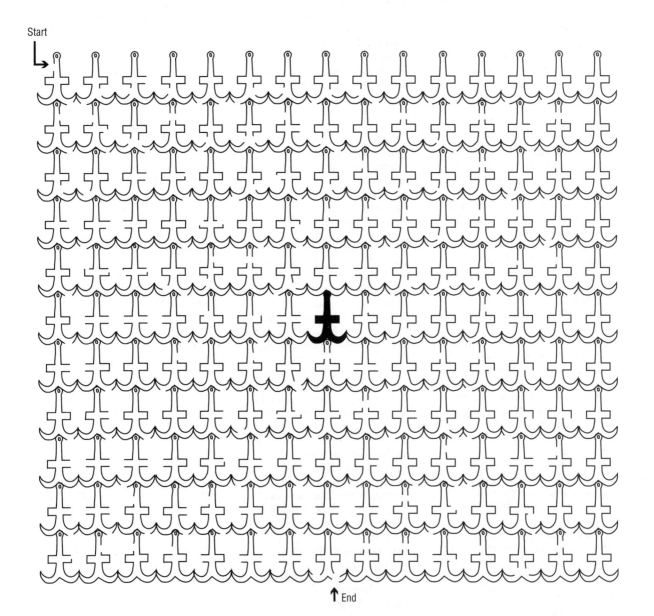

↑ End

*T*here are many hidden treasures of great and precious value to be searched out in the Word of God. In the letter box below "dig out" the buried treasures of the shiny and glittering kind that are found in the Bible.

G H O W P Z B T R E V X L M W

E T A G A X R O O D L O G Q W

X O W A R E A H I L Y R E B Z

Z P W S B V S O S N N P P R R

S A R D I U S T A M B E R O R

O Z R E W C K I P T R A L N E

E D N O M A I D P T O R X Z L

A N Y N O O L K H S I L V E R

B R A Y C A L E I T N O P T L

T O X X R A R M R H E T S I K

S A R E W P A M E T H Y S T B

A E M J E L E W N B B T R O N

S E E S I O U Q R U T T S U R

M H T N I C A J R G T E A C G

Word Pool

AGATE   AMBER   AMETHYST   BERYL   BRASS   BRONZE
DIAMOND   EMERALD   GOLD   JACINTH   ONYX   PEARL
RUBY   SAPPHIRE   SARDIUS   SILVER   TOPAZ   TURQUOISE

*T*ry to solve the equation below without looking up the references! All of the figures are from the book of Leviticus.

The number of days and nights Aaron and his sons were commanded to abide at the door of the tabernacle for their consecration _____

The number of the month in which the Day of Atonement falls on the Jewish calendar $+$ _____

The number of the day in the month on which the Day of Atonement falls $\times$ _____

The number of the day on which the unconsumed portion of a peace offering was to be burned $\times$ _____

The number of days each week in which work is to be done $\div$ _____

The day of the month in which Passover begins at evening $+$ _____

The number of loaves to be "waved" as an offering of firstfruits $\div$ _____

The number of the month that begins with a blowing of trumpets $+$ _____

The number of the day in the month on which the feast of tabernacles begins $+$ _____

The number of the month on the Jewish calendar in which Passover falls $-$ _____

The number of days the children of Israel were commanded to "dwell in booths" $\div$ _____

The number of birds to be brought for sacrifice by a leper at the time of his cleansing $-$ _____

The number of the day that is "the Sabbath of the Lord" $=$ _____

HUGS AND KISSES

*E*mbracing (or hugging) and kissing are customs that are noted thoughout the Bible. Among other things, biblical kisses were given as a blessing (Genesis 48:10–16), an anointing (1 Samuel 10:1), a sign of reconciliation (Genesis 33:4), and even a sign of false religion (1 Kings 19:18; Hosea 13:2). In Jesus' parable of the prodigal son, the kiss of the father to his son symbolized not only the great joy of reunion, but also forgiveness and acceptance. But perhaps the most well-known kiss in the Bible is the one by which Jesus was betrayed (Luke 22:47–48).

Travel any direction to an adjacent block with an X to get from one kiss to the other.

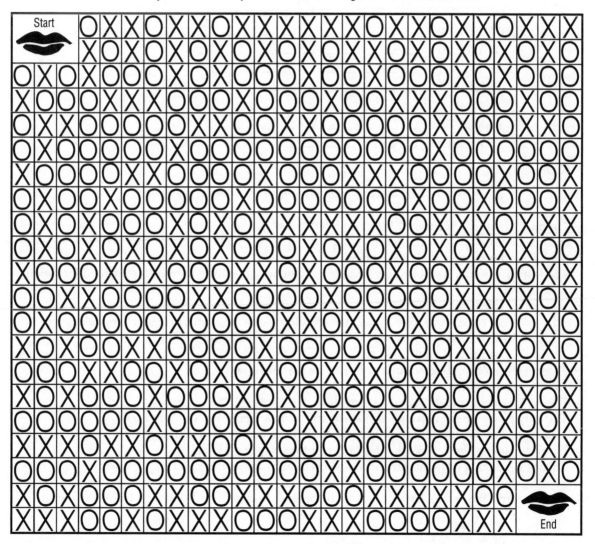

*U*nscramble the names below to reveal some of the more notorious Bible "villains"—some who waged war against God's people, others who refused to step in when the innocent were suffering. Use the clues only if you must!

RAIBMA DAN TADHNA _ _ _ _ _ _ _ _ _ _ _ Ⓞ _ _ _ (3 words)

HACNA _ _ _ _Ⓞ

ROHED RAGPIPA _ _ _Ⓞ_ _ _ _ _ _ _ _I (2 words)

HAAZ _ _ _ _

BEMRAJOO _ _ _ _ _ _ _ _I

BUAIH DAN DBANA _ _ _ _Ⓞ_ _ _ _ _ _ _ _Ⓞ(2 words)

MOANN _ _ _ _ _

HIHTALAA _ _ _ _ _Ⓞ_ _

GEOD HET MEETIOD _ _ _ _ _ _ _ _ _ _ _ _Ⓞ_ (3 words)

HAPRUSH _ _ _ _ _ _ _

BATLALANS _ _ _ _Ⓞ_ _ _ _

ORMHEAOB _ _ _ _ _ _ _ _

TUSLURTEL _ _Ⓞ_ _ _ _ _ _

EAKDEZHI _ _ _ _ _Ⓞ_ _

YALSEM _ Ⓞ_ _ _ _

(Note: The clues are not in the same order as the words above.)

1. Jeremiah renamed this priest "Terror on Every Side"
2. A sorcerer also known as Bar-Jesus
3. Saul's henchman, he killed God's priests
4. The last king of Judah rebelled against the Babylonians, resulting in his recapture and Jerusalem's destruction
5. He raped his half-sister, Tamar
6. This governor of Samaria tried to stop the rebuilding of Jerusalem during Nehemiah's time
7. The first king of Israel who established a nonlevitical priesthood
8. This prosecutor called Paul "a plague"
9. These sons of Aaron offered unholy fire and were consumed
10. He imprisoned Peter
11. The earth opened and swallowed them alive
12. The only ruling queen of Judah, she killed all the male heirs she could find
13. He caused Israel's defeat at Ai because be took items forbidden for him to have
14. He added to the heavy yoke that his father, Solomon, put on Israel
15. This eleventh king of Judah sacrificed his son in worship to other gods

Now unscramble the circled letters to reveal the fate of those who inflict evil on God's people:

__ __ __ __ __ __ __ __ __

*T*his conversation put new light on the matter.

Clue: MESSIAH *is* TRUUCKN

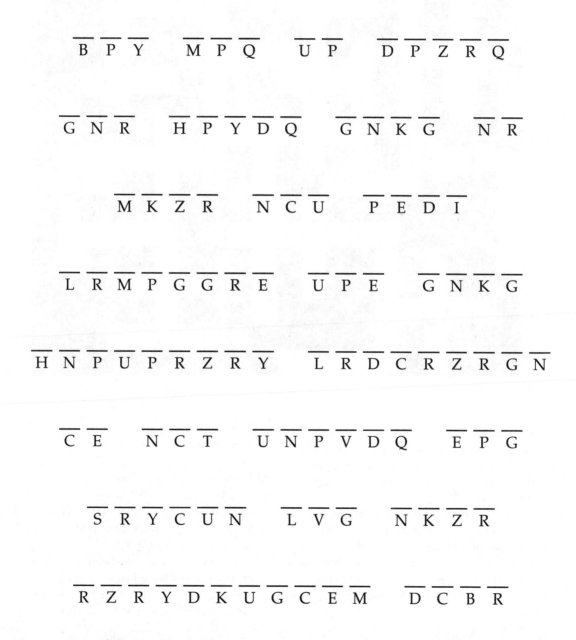

B P Y   M P Q   U P   D P Z R Q

G N R   H P Y D Q   G N K G   N R

M K Z R   N C U   P E D I

L R M P G G R E   U P E   G N K G

H N P U P R Z R Y   L R D C R Z R G N

C E   N C T   U N P V D Q   E P G

S R Y C U N   L V G   N K Z R

R Z R Y D K U G C E M   D C B R

It's easy to love the Apostle Peter. He wasn't perfect, but he tried hard. And he loved Jesus, although fear drove him to make three sorely regretted denials. The four gospels give slightly different accounts of what happened the night of Jesus' arrest.

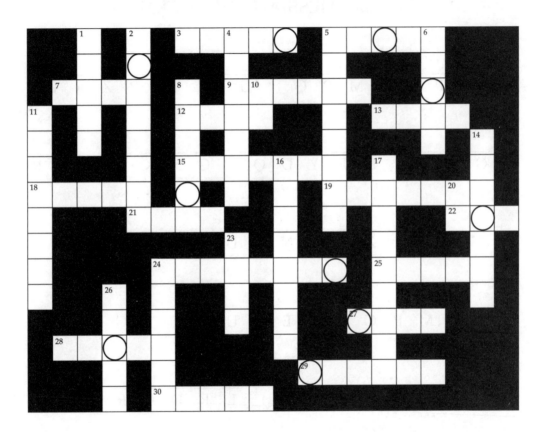

Across

3 To restore Peter after his denial, Jesus met with him and several other apostles at the Sea of Tiberias after the resurrection and first asked Peter to "Feed My ____"

5 Later in #3 Across, Jesus asked Peter to tend and feed His ____; Peter proclaimed his love for the Lord three times, effectively "canceling" his three previous denials of Jesus

7 When Peter realized that Jesus' prediction about his denials had come true, he ____ bitterly

9 Luke says that when #19 Across crowed, Jesus turned and ____ at Peter, no doubt with sadness

12 Peter's name means this

13 Another word for #19 Across

15 In Matthew, Jesus said all His apostles would be made to ____ because of Him, leading Peter to say that he would not

18 Peter was heard to "offer epithets" when accused of knowing Jesus

19 This bird's crow came after Peter's third denial in the book of Matthew (NKJ)

21 Jesus said Peter would "refuse to admit" that he knew Him

22 Peter was willing to be incarcerated or to _____ with Jesus.

24 This high priest had once counseled the Jews that it was expedient that one man should lose his life for the people; Jesus was taken to him the night of Peter's denial

25 How many times the bird crowed in the book of Mark

27 Jesus told Peter that although the devil would attempt to sway him, He had prayed that his faith would not _____.

28 Peter was the son of John, although some translations say his name was _____.

29 It was in the _____ of Gethsemane that Peter tried to prove his devotion to Jesus, but Jesus called him off

30 This fallen angel asked for Peter, but Peter had Jesus' prayers to buoy his faith

Down

1 #30 Across wanted to sift Peter as this grain

2 One person who accused Peter of knowing Jesus said that his speech, or accent, had _____ him; he was obviously from Galilee as Jesus was

4 This servant of the high priest lost his ear to Peter's sword in Gethsemane

5 Jesus said that when they struck the _____, the sheep of the flock—His apostles—would be scattered

6 Mark says Peter went out onto the _____ of the high priest's residence after his first denial, and heard #19 Across crow

8 It was ironic that Peter said he would follow Jesus into _____or to death itself, since he was indeed locked up in one in the book of Acts

10 All right (slang)

11 John says Peter and another "apostle" followed Jesus when He was taken from Gethsemane

14 At the high priest's residence, some of the people who were with him included elders and these teachers

16 Jesus' prayer for Peter, after the denials, was that he would return to Him and strengthen his _____—followers of Jesus who would be looking to him for leadership

17 It was in this area (NKJ) adjacent to the high priest's residence that servants and officers had gathered, and that Peter was approached by people who said he had been one of Jesus' followers

20 Editor (abbr.)

23 In Matthew, Peter denied with one of these strong words that he knew Jesus

24 The Aramaic name for Peter, used in Acts

26 John says that Jesus was taken to see this man first; he was the father-in-law of the high priest

Unscramble the circled letters to find out what Peter needed—and received—after be denied Jesus.

__ __ __ __ __ V __ __ __ __ __

MIRACLE OF LIGHT

*T*he menorah candelabrum is a central part of the Jewish Hanukkah celebration commemorating one of the great victories in Jewish history, the victory of Judah the Maccabee over the Syrian-Greeks under King Antiochus IV. In the second century B.C., the Jews of Palestine were under Greek domination and prohibited from practicing their Jewish rituals. The temple was defiled with the worship of Greek gods and the sacrifice of pigs.

A revolt against the Greeks broke out, led by the priest Mattathias and carried on by his son Judah and his four brothers. They successfully freed Jerusalem from the Greek control, and they set about to purify the temple. All except one cruse of oil had been desecrated by the Greeks, but when the menorah was lit in the temple, the one cruse of oil miraculously burned for eight days — the time it took to make more oil.

During Hanukkah the eight candles of the menorah are lit — one each day of the holiday. A ninth candle, the *shamash*, is a "servant" candle which is used to light the others but is not regarded as one of the lights. Because of the tradition of lighting the candles, Hanukkah is also called the Festival of Lights.

*U*nscramble the words to the left to reveal what belongs ultimately to God.

RSTUT ___ ___ ___ ___ ___

HOPWRSI ___ ___ ___ ___ ___ ___

GSETNRTH ___ ___ ___ ___ ___ ___ ___

RLYGO ___ ___ ___ ___ ___

NODIMION ___ ___ ___ ___ ___ ___ ___

ILEF ___ ___ ___ ___

REGNEY ___ ___ ___ ___ ___ ___

DWONKLEGE ___ ___ ___ ___ ___ ___ ___ ___ ___

IKONGMD ___ ___ ___ ___ ___ ___ ___

NSAEWRS ___ ___ ___ ___ ___ ___ ___

EWRRAD ___ ___ ___ ___ ___ ___

GLAEALICNE ___ ___ ___ ___ ___ ___ ___ ___ ___ ___

ROONH ___ ___ ___ ___ ___

EBOIECDNE ___ ___ ___ ___ ___ ___ ___ ___ ___

TNOVIEOD ___ ___ ___ ___ ___ ___ ___ ___

TUFRUE ___ ___ ___ ___ ___ ___

EASRPI ___ ___ ___ ___ ___ ___

ESRROUCSE ___ ___ ___ ___ ___ ___ ___ ___ ___

TSJEAMY ___ ___ ___ ___ ___ ___ ___

OVLE ___ ___ ___ ___

OHCCIE ___ ___ ___ ___ ___ ___

ORWEP ___ ___ ___ ___ ___

RCWON ___ ___ ___ ___ ___

*L*ove. . . the greatest gift, the more excellent way.

Across

1 Forbearing
5 Juvenile (n.)
8 Anointing substance
9 Male offspring
10 Unfold
11 Very small child
12 Goes with cymbal
15 Wicked
19 . . . Now remain
   these ____ . . .
21 Considered,
   deduced
24 Profound

26 Harvest
27 Not black or white
   (alternate spelling)
29 Jealousy
30 Color
31 Obnoxious
32 Suspend
33 Vapor
34 Distant
36 Goes with gong
38 Rascal
40 Sick
42 Idea, consideration
43 A biblical language

44 Used to be

Down

1 Portion
2 Fact. verity
3 Simple
4 Languages
5 Group, family
6 The greatest of these
7 Relocate
13 Looking glass
14 Prediction
16 Referendum
17 Not out

18 Conducted
20 One of the three
22 Fury
23 Take joy
25 Enigmas
28 Twelve months
32 Corridor
33 Male people
34 One of the three
35 Despise
36 Bumpkin
37 Face or cup
39 Comprehend
41 Research room

Unscramble the names of the twelve people(s) below to reveal a place they all had in common.

IPILTHNSISE __ __ __ __ __ __ __ __ __ __

DNIEGO __ __ __ O __ __

INAHMOA __ __ __ __ __ __ __

SHSHTHOBIE __ __ __ - __ __ __ __ O __ __

BAHA __ __ __ __

EKALSMIATE __ __ __ O __ __ __ __ __ __

IJLHEA O __ __ __ __ __

BONTHA __ __ __ __ __ __

EEZEBJL __ __ O __ __ __ __

AJORM __ __ O __ __

EHJU O __ __ __

IMNIADTIES __ __ __ __ __ __ __ __ __ __

Unscramble the circled letters to reveal the name of one of the Bible's most famous valleys.

__ __ __ __ __ __ __

BITTER AND SWEET

*A*fter three days walking in dusty, dry, hot sand with nothing to drink, the children of Israel weren't sure whether to believe their eyes. It looked like an oasis up ahead — or were they imagining it?

They had just narrowly escaped from the Egyptian army, but now they were beginning to wonder if it was really going to be worth it. After all, when they were slaves in Egypt they at least had the security of knowing there would be enough to eat and drink. Now there was a lot of uncertainty. Even though they knew God had promised them a nation of their own, this seemed like an unlikely way for God to treat His chosen people.

Was it too good to be true? Well, it was an oasis all right — the name was Marah — but the water was bitter and not fit to drink. That was almost too much to bear. But Moses said the Lord told him to throw a tree into the water. It seemed like a strange thing to do, but at this point it was worth a try. And do you know what? The water turned sweet, and the Israelites drank all the water they wanted. This was a story they definitely would tell their grandchildren.

Start ↓

↑ End

No doubt, this was not what anyone had in mind.

Clue: **MESSIAH** *is* TXLLDVU

V E B   M U X I   H X Z X   V Q Q

C D Q Q X B   H D M U   M U X

U P Q I   L O D Z D M   V E B

A X Y V E   M P   L O X V R

H D M U   P M U X Z   M P E Y G X L

V L   M U X   L O D Z D M

Y V K X   M U X T

G M M X Z V E W X

*D*oes being a Christian really make any difference? Paul spells it all out in Romans, in straightforward language so there's no misunderstanding. Unscramble the letters and fill in the grid and you'll see the difference—like night and day.

REEF   — — — —

TRIPSI   — — — — — —

ROLGY   — — — — —

SHIRE   — — — — —

TRIBELY   — — — — — — —

FILE   — — — —

CONEDEBIE   — — — — — — — — —

MINTREEQUER (NKJ)   — — — — — — — — — —

NOSSNADSTAREDHUG   — — — — — — — — — — — — — — — —
(3 words)

TODOPINA   — — — — — — — —

APECE   — — — — —

SEJUSSHIRTC   — — — — — — — — — — (2 words)

ISITFUDJE   — — — — — — — — —

CAUDSEC   — — — — — — —

LANDMO   — — — — — — (2 words)

RACLAN   — — — — — —

DEGOBAN   — — — — — — —

SHELF   — — — — —

NITEMY   — — — — — —

INS   — — —

AWL   — — —

HATED   — — — — —

LUTIG   — — — — —

PINTOCUROR   — — — — — — — — — —

KESFEELINGS   — — — — — — — — — — — (2 words)

*I*n the days of satellite communications it's almost hard to imagine what the first Christians were up against to take the Gospel to all people. The fact that by the end of the first century the Word had been spread to three continents is a tribute to (among other things) the zeal and commitment of our ancestors in the faith. Find hidden in the letter box below the names of roads in Bible times and the available means of transportation.

```
U  I  O  S  B  N  V  V  I  O  L  H  H  D  Y
O  W  N  J  E  R  I  C  H  O  R  O  A  D  A
S  B  I  P  S  E  A  Z  E  L  W  R  B  U  W
R  O  A  D  T  O  E  M  M  A  U  S  T  R  H
B  A  L  T  I  R  G  W  R  M  N  E  Q  T  G
S  T  O  O  F  M  N  E  R  A  O  P  H  X  I
O  P  E  B  Y  C  A  R  P  O  D  G  T  I  H
S  Y  O  N  R  R  T  P  O  E  I  U  I  T  S
M  E  R  O  S  T  I  F  L  A  A  O  P  W  G
S  K  O  G  R  A  A  O  R  T  S  V  O  Y  N
O  N  D  A  N  O  Y  T  W  L  Z  H  H  O  I
B  O  R  W  N  I  S  U  T  E  R  X  I  V  K
O  D  A  M  A  S  C  U  S  R  O  A  D  P  L
T  Y  S  J  K  W  P  T  I  X  Y  W  A  L  N
```

Word Pool

APPIAN WAY   BOAT   DAMASCUS ROAD   DONKEY   FOOT
HORSE   JERICHO ROAD   KINGS HIGHWAY   ROAD TO
EMMAUS   SHIP   STRAIGHT   VIA EGNATIA   WAGON

*I*t wasn't easy being the children of Israel. They had to contend with the Pharaoh who refused to let them go. Then, when they finally got out of his clutches, they had to deal with a holy God who expected them to toe the line. To help them do that, God made laws for every situation, in addition to the basis for all laws: the Ten Commandments. In this puzzle, you examine "commands": God's, Pharaoh's, and a few others'.

Across

3 For the tabernacle, God said to make fifty of these of gold, and couple the curtains together with them (NKJ)

5 God said to celebrate the Passover, and to kill a sheep or a _____ at twilight

8 God said to tell Pharaoh to let His people go, or He would send swarms of flies all over Egypt—except in this land, where His people lived

10 God told Moses to take sweet spices —_____ and onycha and galbanum—to make incense

12 If a man stole an ox and slaughtered or sold it, he had to restore this many oxen for the stolen one

15 God told Moses to say, in the hearing of Joshua, that He would utterly blot out the remembrance of these people from under Heaven (use their ancestor's name)

16 The people were told to keep the Feast of Ingathering at this time of year

17 If a man delivered an animal to his neighbor and it died, was hurt, or ran away, and no one saw it happen, an _____ (affirmation) of the Lord was put between them that indicated noninterference

19 Before coming upon Mt. Sinai, God told Moses to have the people wash these as part of the sanctification rite

20 Every man had to give a ransom for himself to the Lord when Moses took this head count (NKJ)

22 If you take a neighbor's garment as a pledge, God said, return it to him before this goes down

23 The priest of _____ told his daughters to call Moses, "that he may eat bread," after Moses helped water their flocks

26 Take no ____, God said. It blinds the discerning (no doubt with dollar signs) (NKJ)

28 The first time God told Moses to put his hand in his bosom, he drew it out and found it was ____ like snow

30 If a maidservant didn't please her master and was betrothed to him, he had no right to sell her to this type of people, because he had dealt deceitfully with her (NKJ)

31 That is (abbr.)

32 To hallow Aaron and his sons as priests, Moses had to feed them unleavened ____ anointed with oil, made of wheat flour

33 If a servant refused to leave his master in the seventh year, the year of freedom, his master was to pierce his ear with this, and the servant would then serve him forever (NKJ)

36 White ____ snow

38 Aaron and his sons had to wash their hands and feet in a ____ made of bronze (NKJ)

39 To amplify #6 Down, God said He would cut off the Amorites, Hittites, Perizzites, Canaanites, ____, and Jebusites

41 Don't let her live, God said of a woman who practiced magic (NKJ)

45 I. . . you. . . he. . . she. . . ____

46 A "man of no means" could not be shown partiality in his dispute

47 Pharaoh told Moses to "plead his case" with God after the flies came

48 God said to tell the people not to touch this part of Mt. Sinai

49 God told Moses he could return to Egypt, because the men who had sought his life were ____.

51 God told Moses to leave Mt. Sinai and warn the people, lest they break through the bounds to gaze at the Lord and meet this fate

52 God said to celebrate the Feast of Unleavened Bread, to remember when God brought the Israelite "troops" out of Egypt

53 If a man acted with premeditation against his neighbor, and killed him with "craftiness," death was his sentence

Down

1 God said to carve six of these on each of the two onyx stones, for the twelve tribes

2 Meat that had been torn by beasts in the field had to be thrown to these animals, and not eaten by the people

4 After obeying God's command, Moses saw the waters of Egypt turn to blood; the fish died and the river "smelled bad"

5 If a thief was struck and killed when caught breaking in, there was to be no "remorse" for his bloodshed

6 If they did all that God spoke to them, the people could count on God's being one of these to their enemies

7 If a fire broke out and caught in "a rose's chief drawback," so that grain or a field was consumed, the kindler had to make restitution

9 After setting the altar of gold for the incense before the #27 Down, Moses had to put up the "partition" for the door of the tabernacle (NKJ)

10 God told Moses to tell the people to ask their Egyptian neighbors for articles made of this shiny material

11 Obey My voice and keep My covenant, God said, and you (the Israelites) will be "a special ____" to Me, something of value (NKJ)

13 If an ox tended to thrust with this in times past, and the owner knew it, and the ox killed someone, the ox and his owner had to be put to death

14 God said He would rescue the Israelites from ____, redeem them with an outstretched arm (NKJ)

18 On a plate of pure gold, the artisans were told to engrave "____ TO THE LORD"

19 God told Moses to say that He would send severe pestilence on all Egyptian livestock: cattle, horses, donkeys, ____, oxen, and sheep

21 A man who stole a sheep had to restore this many sheep for the stolen one

24 Don't "trouble" the widow or the fatherless child, God said

25 After setting up the tabernacle of the tent of meeting, Moses had to put the #27 Down in it and partition that that off with a __ (NKJ)

26 The boils in #37 Down broke out on man and___

27 God said to make this "container" for His Testimony of acacia wood

29 The people were to overthrow their enemies and completely break down their sacred "obelisks"

32 When eating the Passover meal, God said, wear a belt on this (NKJ)

33 On the lampstand's branches, God said to make three bowls like this "nut" blossom on each branch

34 If you make an altar of stone, God said, don't use hewn stone; that would ____ it (NKJ)

35 God told Moses to lift his rod over the Red Sea, causing it to ____

37 God told Moses and Aaron to take handfuls of these from a furnace and scatter them toward Heaven; they'd cause boils

40 God said to make altars of this "dirt"

42 God told Moses to stretch out his hand over the waters of Egypt: streams, ____, ponds, and pools

43 God said to tell all gifted artisans to make Aaron's garments: breastplate, ephod, robe, tunic, turban, and ____ (NKJ)

44 According to orders, the artisans left an opening for this in the middle of Aaron's robe (NKJ)

48 When preparing the Passover lamb, God said, don't do this to its bones

50 God told Moses to strike this with his rod so it would become lice

The Bible is full of good advice on how to conduct our lives. It tells us what to think about, what to do, how to treat others—and most important of all, how to relate to God our Father. This puzzle, a verse from the Old Testament book that's known for dispensing sage counsel, addresses the whole issue of how to use our heads.

(Note: The words of the verse have been scrambled.)

Clue: MESSIAH *is* 3 17 24 24 19 1 23

$$\frac{}{19} \ \frac{}{4} \quad\quad \frac{}{21} \ \frac{}{17} \ \frac{}{1} \ \frac{}{20} \quad\quad \frac{}{13} \ \frac{}{8}$$

$$\frac{}{7} \ \frac{}{8} \ \frac{}{20} \ \frac{}{13} \quad\quad \frac{}{5} \ \frac{}{17} \quad\quad \frac{}{8} \ \frac{}{14} \ \frac{}{4}$$

$$\frac{}{4} \ \frac{}{8} \ \frac{}{26} \quad\quad \frac{}{6} \ \frac{}{8} \ \frac{}{22} \ \frac{}{20} \quad\quad \frac{}{26} \ \frac{}{23} \ \frac{}{17}$$

$$\frac{}{13} \ \frac{}{17} \ \frac{}{12} \ \frac{}{1} \ \frac{}{20} \ \frac{}{26} \quad\quad \frac{}{14} \ \frac{}{19} \ \frac{}{24} \ \frac{}{17}$$

$$\frac{}{17} \ \frac{}{18} \ \frac{}{19} \ \frac{}{7} \quad\quad \frac{}{17} \ \frac{}{6} \ \frac{}{17} \ \frac{}{24}$$

$$\frac{}{1} \ \frac{}{4} \ \frac{}{13} \quad\quad \frac{}{21} \ \frac{}{20} \ \frac{}{8} \ \frac{}{3}$$

Unscramble the words:

_____

_____

_____

_____

Connect adjacent letters (in all directions) to discover how to experience enduring power. (Note: the first and last letters of the message are the same.)

A	K	L	A	W	L	L	A	H	S	Y	E	H
N	H	E	L	L	A	T	H	E	I	S	T	T
D	N	T	O	L	H	W	E	T	R	E	R	D
N	O	R	D	S	R	E	N	H	G	N	E	N
O	P	U	T	Y	E	H	T	L	G	A	S	A
T	A	T	W	I	S	S	E	H	A	L	A	Y
F	H	Y	A	A	H	T	S	U	R	L	S	R
A	T	H	E	L	L	H	Y	N	A	G	O	A
I	T	U	O	M	W	E	H	N	N	N	T	E
N	N	T	U	P	I	T	W	I	D	B	E	W

*T*his puzzle should be "E-sy." It's all about people, places, and things in the Bible that start with the letter "E." (We've also thrown in some adjectives and verbs that have special meaning.)

Across

3 He wanted a double portion of his mentor's spirit

4 Younger people, submit to the ____ person, Peter said

6 But deliver us from ____

7 This king of Moab defeated Israel

8 The priest who led the exiled back to Jerusalem

9 An animal commonly used in sacrifices

11 The Israelites battled King Og of Bashan at this place

13 A time to ____, and a time to refrain from this (third-person sing.)

14 A town in southern Judah that probably belonged to both Judah and Simeon (NKJ)

15 Great-grandfather of Samuel

17 It was perfect, except for the snake

18 "Strongly tell" servants to be obedient to their masters, Paul told Titus

19 On the road to this village, Jesus met two followers after His resurrection

20 The Israelites finally got out of here

21 Rachel to Jacob: "Give me children, or 'otherwise' I die!"

23 A priestly garment

24 Saul and his men encamped in this valley—and met Goliath

25 This left-handed Benjaminite stabbed and killed the king of Moab

29 Wrath kills a foolish man, and this slays a simple one

31 In Heaven, John said, the rainbow around the throne appeared like this gem

32 He put his stomach before his birthright

33 The father-in-law of #32 Across

34 Told that the ark had been captured, this high priest fell, broke his neck, and died

36 She replaced Queen Vashti

37 "God is with us"

38 A fellow worker with Paul

39 A son of Cain

40 In Psalms, God renews your youth like the bird's

42 Pharaoh Neco changed this king's name to Jeholakim

43 This Philistine city met God's wrath in Amos

44 The men of Dedan brought Tyre ivory tusks and this durable wood as payment

45 It took forty days to properly do this to the body of someone who had died

46 Samuel's father

47 Nehemiah prayed ". . . let Your ____ be attentive and Your eyes open"

3 She was first

5 Christ must reign until He puts all these under His feet

6 Son of Seth (Greek spelling)

7 The seventh angel in Revelation poured out his bowl, and this is what happened

10 His son, Gaal, fought against Abimelech

12 An encampment during the Exodus

16 A city in Judah (also a common anesthetic, in our century)

17 Is there taste in the white of this? Job asked

19 Jesus' tomb was ____ on the first day of the week

20 One of the seven churches in Revelation

22 The land south of #20 Across

26 Weeping may "last" for a night, but joy comes in the morning

27 Naomi's husband

28 Forever

30 A letter

31 Another name for #32 Across

34 "I will ____ You, I will praise Your name," said Isaiah (NKJ)

35 Like an ____ of gold is a wise reprover to one who listens and obeys

36 God made him a watchman for the house of Israel

37 A descendant of King Saul, and brother of Azel

41 A dry measure that's a little over a U.S. bushel

43 ____ for an ____

Down

1 A son of Aaron

2 Joshua built an altar to the Lord in Mount ____, to renew the covenant

If you found the crossword puzzle "e-sy," you'll want to find out what the Bible says is easy. The letter "e"—and all the other vowels, including "y"—have been taken out of this verse. Add the vowels where they are needed to complete the words in this Scripture.

FRMKSSNDMBRDNSLGHT.

_____

_____

_____

*T*ry to solve the equation below, based on the ages of people in the Bible, without consulting the references!

The age of Enoch when he "walked with God" (Gen 5:23-24) _____

The age of Lamech when his son Noah was born (Gen 5:28) $+$ _____

The maximum age of the children Herod ordered to be killed in Bethlehem (Matt 2:16) $\times$ _____

The age of Noah when the rains began to fall (Gen 7:11) $-$ _____

The age of Methusaleh when he died (Gen 5:27) $+$ _____

The age of Abram when he departed out of Haran with Sarai and Lot (Gen 12:4) $-$ _____

The age of Adam when his son Seth was born (Gen 5:3) $+$ _____

The minimum age of males counted in the giving of portions by Hezekiah (2 Chron 31:16) $\div$ _____

The age of Jared when his son Enoch was born (Gen 5:18) $+$ _____

The age of Seth when his son Enos was born (Gen 5:6) $+$ _____

The age of Cainan when his son Mahalaleel was born (Gen 5:12) $+$ _____

The age at which Levites began to have a course of service under Hezekiah (2 Chron 31:17) $-$ _____

The age of King Jehoiada when he died (2 Chron 24:15) $+$ _____

The age of Joseph when he became second in command to Pharaoh (Gen 41:46) $-$ _____

The age of Enoch when his son Methuselah was born (Gen 5:21) $+$ _____

The age of Jesus when he went to Jerusalem for Passover and "tarried behind" in the Temple (Luke 2:42) $+$ _____

The number of years that are as a day in the Lord's sight (Ps 90:4) $=$ _____

Unscramble the twelve words below, which are all associated with one of the most evil people in Israel's history.

TAEHBLA __ __ __ O __ __ __

OPREPTHS __ __ __ __ __ __ __ __

EUQNE __ __ __ O __

ISADINON (NKJ) __ __ __ __ __ __ __ __

NOTBAH __ __ __ __ __ __

CUNHUES O __ __ __ __ __ __

IEJHLA O __ __ __ __ __

SGDO __ __ __ __

EERLJEZ __ __ O __ __ __ O

YVNAEIDR __ __ __ __ __ __ __ __

UJEH O __ __ __

BAAH __ __ __ __

Unscramble the circled letters to reveal the name that has become so closely associated with the word "wicked":

__ __ __ __ __ __ __

The names of the New Testament books will complete this crossword.

Across

1 The Lord's return
5 Letter to seven churches
6 Christ is supreme
8 The King's Gospel
10 I am the Son of God
12 True religion
13 The Church is born
15 Glory of the Church
16 Paul's thank-you letter
17 Fullness in Christ

Down

1 Paul's last word
2 Written to Theophilus, a Gentile Christian
3 The Servant of the Lord
4 Church problems
7 The Gospel manifesto
9 Letter to church leader in Crete
10 Contend for the faith
11 Do Gentiles have to become Jews to become
   Christian?
14 Slaves and brothers
16 Hope in suffering

In the Old Testament and the New, God was there for the people in their present; but He wanted them to know that He would be in their future as well. He used prophets to tell the people some of what they could expect in the years—and centuries—and eternity—to come. As we read the prophets, we see some precious promises, and we see them fulfilled before the Bible's last page was written. The verse below is just one of those promises—good news for everyone. (Note: The words are scrambled.)

Clue: MESSIAH *is* 15 2 20 20 3 1 11

16 1 15 2   7 4 5 16 20 2 14 4 19

2 22 2 19 14 1 20 21 3 16 10   23 3 14 14

3 20   1 16 8   9 4 19   5 20   4 9

7 11 3 14 8   10 4 22 2 19 16 15 2 16 21

5 16 21 4   1   17 19 3 16 7 2

20 11 4 5 14 8 2 19   20 4 16   10 4 8   5 20

11 3 20   3 20   17 2 1 7 2   1   10 3 22 2 16

5 17 4 16   1 16 8   5 16 21 4   6 4 19 16

7 1 14 14 2 8   15 3 10 11 21 25   6 2   11 3 20

23 4 16 8 2 19 9 5 14   21 11 2

23 3 14 14   6 2   9 1 21 11 2 19.

Unscramble the words: _____

_____

_____

_____

Find the names of the eight men who linked Adam to Noah in the box of letters below.

```
E   M   B   W   S   L   T   N   L   A   M   E
N   A   E   N   I   A   J   U   H   T   E   M
S   J   H   T   A   C   A   S   H   A   M   J
O   A   M   E   H   D   R   E   O   A   H   A
C   J   A   I   N   U   E   L   I   N   E   L
L   A   M   E   C   H   S   A   H   C   E   R
E   R   N   A   L   C   R   E   A   E   P   U
T   E   S   H   M   A   E   H   L   S   N   E
H   D   P   C   N   I   D   A   I   A   O   S
E   A   R   A   E   N   L   E   H   U   H   E
D   I   D   M   J   A   M   N   E   T   T   L
A   N   A   S   H   N   H   C   O   N   E   A
C   E   L   A   H   A   M   O   D   E   S   H
A   N   M   I   A   C   U   I   R   A   J   I
```

*U*nscramble the names of these ten Bible figures, who shared a common experience.

OSSME   __ __ Ⓞ __ __

ALNAB   __ __ __ __ __

ASMHE   __ Ⓞ __ Ⓞ __

AVDDI   __ __ __ __ Ⓞ

AJZZI   __ __ __ __ __

EBLA   __ __ Ⓞ __

JBOCA   __ __ __ __ __

ORLD   __ __ Ⓞ __

EOHJSP   __ __ __ __ Ⓞ Ⓞ

BAHAMRA   __ __ __ __ __ __ __

Unscramble the circled letters to reveal the profession associated with them all:

__ __ __ __ __ __ __ __

*P*aul's high-sea adventure on his way to Italy for trial is one of the most dramatic stories in the New Testament. Most of the clues and answers relate to that famous journey.

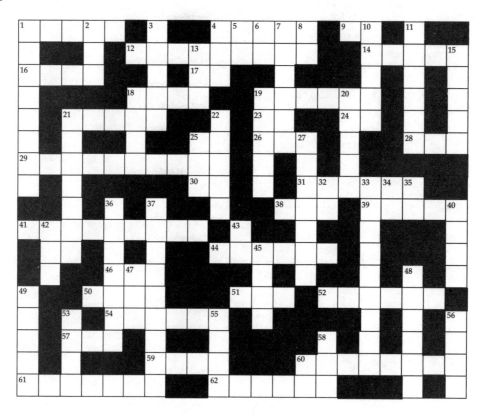

Across

1 A welcome sight to the crew and passengers on board the ill-fated Alexandrian sailing vessel

4 To act for another's benefit

9 You and me

12 Cornelius was a _____ of the Italian army

14 When Paul prayed and put these on the sick, they got well

16 Destination

17 Not off

18 Bow of a ship

19 Roman emperor

21 Grain

23 Agriculture (abbr.)

24 Northeast (abbr.)

25 Enlisted army man (abbr.)

26 Representative (abbr.)

28 _____ aground

29 "Northeaster"

30 Doctor of Divinity (abbr.)

31 Related to

38 Not healthy

39 Venomous creature

41 Perilous

44 Mediterranean island

46 Penitentiary (abbr.)

50 Lifeless

51 Inlet of the sea
52 Wrecked
54 Used for kindling
57 Inclined
59 Larger inlet
60 Hospitality
61 Unit of measurement; one is the length of arms outstretched
62 Get away

Down

1 Killer
2 Fasten
3 Be encouraged; take ____
4 While the storm raged, this was not seen
5 Emergency room (abbr.)
6 Rhode Island (abbr.)
7 Nautical journey
8 Half an em-space
10 Beach
11 Mainstay
13 Pull
15 Rear end of a boat
18 He had been through it all—shipwrecked, beaten, imprisoned, stoned
19 Freight
20 God's messenger
21 Paul's was ignored

22 These were contrary, causing threatening sailing conditions
25 The island natives thought Paul was one of these because he seemed immune to poison
27 Chief official of #1 Across
32 Elevated (abbr.)
33 To lighten the ship so it could sail faster and farther, its contents were thrown here
34 Nickel (abbr.)
35 General practitioner (abbr.)
36 Violent storm
37 To measure depth, take ____
40 This fell on the already soaked crew and passengers
42 How many people would be saved from drowning in the shipwreck
43 Near
45 Implore deity
47 Paul encouraged the people on board to do this to survive
48 Made well
49 Light rowboat
53 What one does on the Day of Atonement
55 Not threatened
56 Paul predicted this if they sailed
58 Those aboard the ship had given up hope and expected to ____
60 Kitchen patrol (abbr.)

The Apostle Paul went through great hardships for the Gospel, and, according to tradition, he made the ultimate sacrifice—martyrdom—for his faith. How did Paul regard his suffering? The well-known verse below tells us. To find out, put the words in their proper sequence.

TO BE WORTHY THIS BE WHICH ARE IN TIME I THE NOT REVEALED SUFFERINGS THAT WITH GLORY FOR PRESENT OF CONSIDER THE COMPARED SHALL

_____

_____

_____

PETER'S PRISON RELEASE

*A*fter Herod killed James, the brother of John, and saw that it pleased the Jewish leaders, he arrested Peter and put him under the guard of four squads of soldiers. While Peter was sleeping, chained between two soldiers, an angel smote him on the side and ordered him to get up and put on his sandals in preparation for leaving the prison. As Peter arose, the chains fell off his wrists.

The angel then proceeded to lead Peter out of the prison past the first and second guard posts and out the iron gate (which swung open of its own accord) that led to the city. (See Acts 12:10.) After the angel had led Peter down a street, the angel disappeared from Peter's sight. Until that moment, Peter had thought that he was experiencing a vision. After the angel departed, the Bible tells that Peter "came to himself" and realized he had been delivered by the Lord. He immediately made his way to a house where Christians were in prayer for his release.

Find the route the angel took to free Peter. Note: The prison guards can guard a pathway in all four directions.

*T*ake a word of advice from our old friend Solomon: Read Proverbs and rediscover wisdom! Fill in the missing words, match up the two halves of each proverb, and unscramble the circled letters to describe "the right word at the right time."

1. Do not enter the path of the

__ __ __ __ __ Ⓞ.

A. But a foolish son is the

Ⓞ __ __ __ __ of his mother.

2. Honor the Lord with your

Ⓞ __ __ __ __ __ __ __ __ __ __

B. But love __ Ⓞ __ __ __ __ all

sins.

3. Evil Ⓞ __ __ __ __ __ __ __

sinners,

C. And do not walk in the way of

Ⓞ __ __ Ⓞ.

4. A wise son makes a __ Ⓞ __ __

father,

D. But to the righteous __ __ Ⓞ __

shall be repaid.

5. __ Ⓞ __ __ __ __ stirs up strife,

E. And with the

__ __ __ Ⓞ __ Ⓞ __ __ __ __

of all your increase.

Unscramble letters:

__ __ __ __ __ __ __   __ __   __ __ __ __

THE CELTIC CROSS

*T*his cross design is also called the Ionic Cross or Irish Cross. It is one of the most familiar forms of the cross, as well as one of the most ancient. It is widely used on church roofs and towers.

The primitive Celtic Christians trace their origin to a very early era. A number of these crosses are found in Great Britain and Ireland where they were first erected as cemetery and wayside crosses. Some of them are elaborately carved.

The circle that appears on the cross is a symbol of both eternity and wholeness. This cross design is therefore also called the Cross of Redemption.

Start ↘

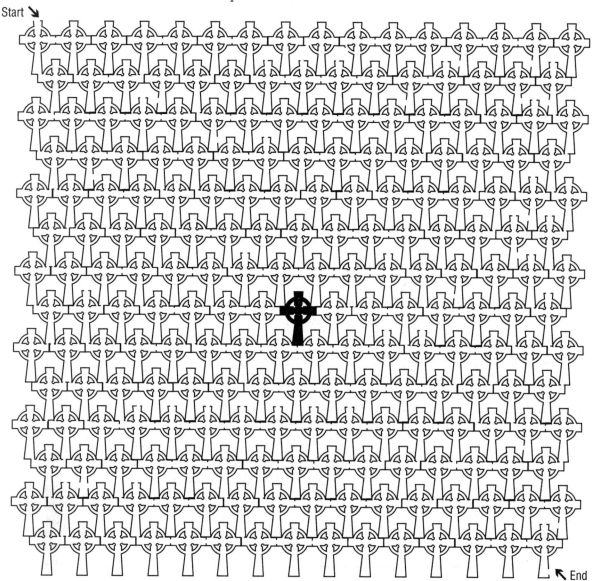

↖ End

Fill in the blanks to create a profile of the One we love.

Who hath believed our report? And to whom is the ____ (9) of the LORD revealed? For he shall grow up before him as a ____ ____ (13). And as a ____ (11) out of dry ground . . . there is ____ ____ (5) that we should desire him. . . . He is ____ (6) and ____ (14) of men: a man of ____ (1). And acquainted with ____ (16): . . . We did esteem him ____ (8), ____ (4) of God, and ____ (17) . . . he was ____ (12) for our transgressions, he was ____ (7) for our iniquities, the ____ (10) of our peace was upon him; and with his ____ (3) we are healed . . . The Lord hath laid on him the ____ (19) of us all. . . . He was ____ (18), and he was afflicted . . . as a ____ (15) before her shearers is dumb, so he openeth not his mouth. . . . For he was ____ ____ (2) out of the land of the living: for the transgression of my people was he stricken. (Isaiah 53:1-8)

1   — — — — — — —

2   — — — — — —

3   — — — — — — —

4   — — — — — —

5   — — — — — — — (2 words)

6   — — — — — — —

7   — — — — — — —

8   — — — — —

9   — — —

10 — — — — — — — — — — —

11 — — — —

12 — — — — —

13 — — — — — — — — — — (2 words)

14 — — — — — —

15 — — — — —

16 — — — —

17 — — — — — — —

18 — — — — — — —

19 — — — — — — —

When it comes to animals mentioned in the Bible, our best friend doesn't fare too well.

Across

1 Second Peter says this type of teacher fulfilled the proverb: A dog returns to its own vomit

4 This future king of Syria thought Elisha's prophecy made him sound like a dog

5 David's enemies, like a dog, would search for food and "wail" if they weren't satisfied (NKJ)

8 Gideon's 300 were chosen to fight these people because they (the 300) lapped from the water like a dog

10 Preposition

11 "Look out for" dogs and evil workers, says Philippians

15 Israel's leaders were like "money-grubbing" dogs, never having enough, says Isaiah

17 When this king's blood was washed out of his chariot, the dogs licked it up

19 Don't give what is "sacred" to dogs

20 This beggar sat by a rich man's gate while dogs licked his sores

21 These "killers" will be kept outside the New Jerusalem, along with dogs, sorcerers, the sexually immoral, idolators, and liars (sing.)

Down

1 As a dog returns to his vomit, this type of person returns to his folly

2 God brought David's enemies back from the depths of this "water" so his dogs could have their portion

3 Not a dog moved this "lapper" against the Israelites when God took the Egyptians' firstborn

4 When Shimei cursed David, Abishai called him a dead dog and asked to remove this from his body

6 David asked whom Saul was pursuing—a dead dog? This insect found on dogs?

7 A living dog is better than this dead animal, because he has hope

8 Holy men had to throw this beast-torn "flesh" to the dogs (NKJ)

9 Was Goliath a dog, that David came to him with ____?

11 Jehu said the dogs would eat whoever belonged to this king of Israel

12 Meddling in another's quarrel is like taking a dog by these "muff holders"

13 The dogs ate this queen by the wall of Jezreel

14 The dogs also ate whoever belonged to this king of Israel; his son Nadab succeeded him

16 A woman from this region wanted the crumbs from the Lord's table, because even dogs got those

18 Bringing the price of a dog to the "abode" of the Lord for any vowed offering was an abomination

*T*his puzzle is taken from the Gospels and Acts. The phrase that you are looking for is a "command" that all Christians should follow, with great joy. To make this a little more difficult, we have added 3 letters to each scrambled word. Once you've eliminated the unnecessary letters and unscrambled each word, you can then unscramble the circled letters and find the phrase. And when you're done, it should be obvious what the 13 words have in common. (Hint: The phrase has three words.)

APIEPIHTL Ⓞ __ __ __ Ⓞ __

NATEOMSI Ⓞ __ __ __ __

SIMTEJAO __ Ⓞ __ __ __

DEATHIDHGUSA __ __ __ __ __ __ Ⓞ __ __

SAIJNUDG __ __ __ __ Ⓞ

CMOSTHAIR __ __ __ Ⓞ __ __

JOINHER __ __ __ __

EASTJUME __ Ⓞ __ __ __

TREEPOST __ __ __ __ Ⓞ

DRAWERNET __ Ⓞ __ __ __ __

WARMTHIENT __ __ __ __ Ⓞ __ __

BALTIMOREHDOWN __ __ __ __ __ __ __ __ Ⓞ __

MIANEATDHTS __ __ __ __ __ Ⓞ __ __

Unscramble letters:

__ __ __ __ __ __   __ __ __   __ __ __ __

*T*hroughout the Bible, significant events happened at all hours.

Across

3 Daytime, He taught in the Temple; at night He stayed on this mountain, says Luke (NKJ)

6 The bird that fed Elijah day and night

8 He received an olive leaf from a dove one night

10 Jesus was delivered to him in the morning by elders and chief priests

11 These animals pursue their prey at night, says the psalmist

13 Mister (abbr.)

14 He visited Jesus one night and identified Him as "a teacher come from God"

17 Some of the disciples couldn't catch one of these on the morning Peter swam to shore to meet the risen Lord

18 This animal was part of the burnt offering prepared every morning, per God's orders in Ezekiel

20 This member of royalty had to appoint a portion of his possessions for morning and evening burnt offerings

21 A man who rules in the fear of God is like a morning without these

24 The psalmist declared God's loving kindness morning and night with this stringed instrument

25 The torment will go on day and night for this kind of prophet

26 Jesus could return at the early A.M. crowing of this bird

Down

1 David left his woolly charges with a keeper on the morning of the day he met Goliath

2 After Joshua's 5,000 men ambushed this city, Joshua hanged its king on a tree until evening

4 A landowner hired laborers to work in this early one morning

5 The Levites stood, morning and evening, to "offer appreciation to" the Lord

7 He had a vision one night that led him to go to Macedonia

9 Second Peter says to heed the prophetic word, as a light does this in a dark place, until the day dawns

12 The day and night are God's, said Asaph; He prepared this "sky light"

13 The princes of this country stayed with Balaam one night

15 "Prayerfully ponder" God's Word, as the psalmist does during night watches

16 David would "melodiously vocalize" God's mercy in the morning .

19 When Moses did this day and night—without a jury—Jethro suggested he get help

22 Jesus is the Bright and Morning ____

23 Put on this "coat" of light, said Paul; the day is at hand

PASS THE PLATE

One of the instructions Moses received from God when he was on Mt. Sinai was to take up an offering to build a tabernacle as a dwelling place for the Lord. The tabernacle would be a portable sanctuary that would go with the people through the wilderness, a place where the Lord could be among the people of Israel on their journey to the promised land. God gave Moses exact specifications for the construction of the tabernacle and its furnishings and for making the sacred garments for the priests.

Moses told the people the Lord commanded an offering for the tabernacle from "whoever is of a willing heart." The Israelites brought earrings, nose rings, rings and necklaces, jewelry, thread, fine linen, goats' hair, red rams' skins, badger skins, acacia wood, yarn, onyx stones, spices, and oil. They brought so many offerings that the Bible says, "the people were restrained from bringing, for the material they had was sufficient for all the work to be done — indeed too much" (Exodus 36:6–7).

Pass through each item of offering before bringing it to Moses. Do not cross back over a path that you have already used.   ◆ = Offering

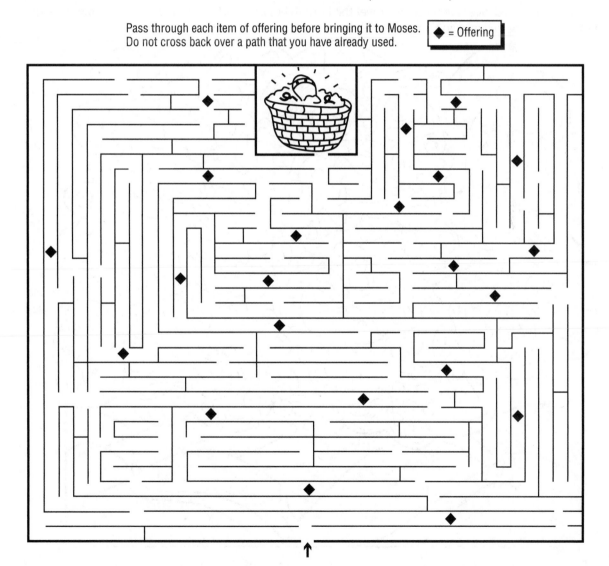

MOSES' MOUNTAINTOP EXPERIENCE

*T*he phrase "mountaintop experience" could have been coined by Moses, for indeed it was there that he saw the glory of the Lord. God told Moses to meet Him on top of Mt. Sinai. The invitation was extended to Moses, his brother Aaron, his nephews Abihu and Nadab, and seventy elders. Everyone else would worship from a distance, but only Moses was allowed to come near to God.

For six days a cloud covered the mountaintop. On the seventh day Moses saw the glory of the Lord which "was like a consuming fire." For the next forty days and nights, Moses was on the mountaintop while God gave him detailed instructions for offerings, tabernacle, furnishings, sacred garments for the priests, altars, sacrifices, and incense. And then before Moses left, God handed him two tablets of stone with the Law for the people to observe.

Mountaintop experiences are where we meet the Lord to be equipped for the business of living daily on the plain or in the valley. And that is what Moses was about to find out.

$\mathcal{U}$nscramble the words on the left that are among God's provisions for us. The circled phrase reveals our appropriate response to Him!

TAEWR   — — — — —

ICHLTONG   — — — — — — — —

HAIFT   — — — — —

AEDILVENREC   — — — — — — — — — —

EKDNLOWGE   — — — — — — — — —

HESETLR   — — — — — — —

SIGERVOFNES   — — — — — — — — — —

TNHISGI   — — — — — — —

IYVRCOT   — — — — — — —

DSWIMO   — — — — — —

RIFNEDIHSP   — — — — — — — — —

AIUNGDCE   — — — — — — — —

AENHGLI   — — — — — — —

ETSRGNHT   — — — — — — — —

OFOD   — — — —

PLUPSY   — — — — — —

DERRWAS   — — — — — —

IALSAVTNO   — — — — — — — — —

TAIRIPOSNIN   — — — — — — — — — — —

ECENSRPE   — — — — — — — —

TCPTREOOIN   — — — — — — — — — —

*H*ow do you keep those spiritual muscles from going soft?

Across

1 If we hang on and do the will of God, we'll receive this

3 Paul pressed on for the reward of the ____ ____ of God (2 words)

5 Once you've put your hand to this, don't look back to see who's gaining

7 Paul didn't just beat the air

8 An objective

11 We all run in this

13 If they're feeble, strengthen them

14 When Jesus comes, we'll receive headpieces of ____

15 Paul disciplined this

16 We don't have to run, if we do this in the light

18 Hanging on

19 If your calling is sure, you won't "trip"

21 They need straight paths

22 The race isn't to the "fast"

Down

1 Part of the race: "proclaim" the kingdom of God

2 If the Philippians were blameless, Paul hadn't run or ____ in vain

4 The reward

6 Don't become "tired" or discouraged in your souls

9 The end of our faith—the ____ of our souls

10 At the end, there will be an "opening" into the kingdom for us

12 Is yours imperishable?

17 Pursue this with all, and holiness, too

20 Our path is Jesus: The Way, the ____, and the Life

*I*n the letter box below circle the names of occupations of Bible times.

O W R O T C E L L O C X A T

A U O X B N W P D J N L F N

M W S D R E H P E H S R I A

B A K E R N E J O U R A S H

A O W N E O N R U E X O H C

S O M E L R G L N D O W E R

S B U T L E R N O U G A R E

A X S O U R A P L M N E M M

D O I R F T V S E T L O A Z

O R C S E N E O I L O Q N E

R O I E M B R O I D E R E R

S C A R P E N T E R O W J Z

O U N R R O T A R O P Z L A

Word Pool
AMBASSADOR   BAKER   BUTLER   CARPENTER   EMBROIDERER
ENGRAVER FISHERMAN   FULLER   JUDGE   MERCHANT   MUSICIAN
ORATOR   SHEPHERD   TANNER   TAX COLLECTOR   TILLER

85

G od asked the Israelites to make a place for Him where He could be in their midst. They followed His instructions to the letter, and when He was there, it was obvious.

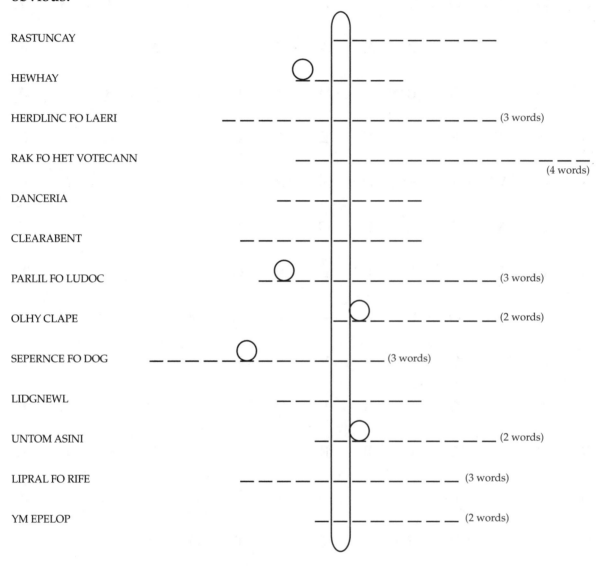

RASTUNCAY

HEWHAY

HERDLINC FO LAERI — (3 words)

RAK FO HET VOTECANN — (4 words)

DANCERIA

CLEARABENT

PARLIL FO LUDOC — (3 words)

OLHY CLAPE — (2 words)

SEPERNCE FO DOG — (3 words)

LIDGNEWL

UNTOM ASINI — (2 words)

LIPRAL FO RIFE — (3 words)

YM EPELOP — (2 words)

Unscramble the circled letters to reveal where God dwells now:

— —   — — —

(See 1 Corinthians 3:16.)

*T*he longest prayer of Jesus recorded in Scripture is one He prayed for Himself, His disciples, and for all those who would come to believe in Him. He prayed this prayer on the night He was betrayed. Some of His last concerns and requests on our behalf are found in this prayer in John 17. Most of the clues below are from that chapter.

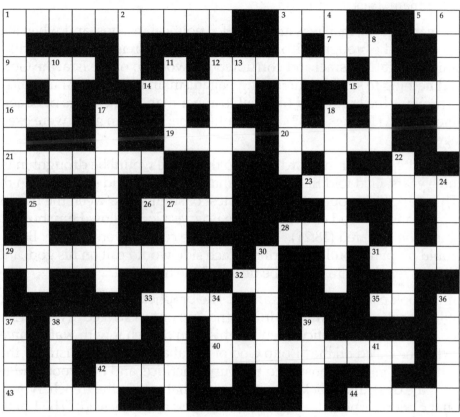

Across

1 Creation
3 Deity
5 In the world, but not ____ it
7 Is (pl.)
9 Designation
12 See
14 Granted
15 Actual fact
16 Male offspring
19 Sinister
20 Humanity
21 Never ending
23 Flawless
25 History
26 World's attitude toward Christians
28 God's attitude toward people
29 Made known
31 Remove
32 Not you
33 Task
35 You and I; in this instance, Father and Son
38 Sacred
40 Destruction
42 Go forth
43 Global perspective, ____-view

44 Savior

Down

1 Completed
2 Everyone
3 Bring honor
4 In Greek, "Abba"
6 Male parent
8 Inhabited plane
10 Jesus' 12 disciples were these
11 #21 Across ____, is to know God and His Son
12 To accept in faith
13 Half an em-space
17 Set apart

18 Accepted
22 Proclaim
24 Not false
25 When you speak to God
27 Power
30 Want
34 To be faithful to
36 God spoke these
37 Understand
38 Time
39 Jesus prayed that those God gave Him could be ____Him
41 United
42 Special delivery (abbr.)

Run for Your Life

Jezebel should have left well enough alone. When she came up against the prophet Elijah she had more than met her match. She didn't realize that her 450 priests of Baal and 400 prophets of Asherah were no contest for Elijah's God, the God of Abraham, Isaac, and Jacob.

Jezebel's marriage to Ahab was arranged for political reasons, and when she moved to Israel she brought with her the worship of foreign gods. The influence of paganism spread in Israel and corrupted the worship of the Israelite God. Ahab did nothing to stop the increasing paganism. In fact, King Ahab "did more to provoke the LORD God of Israel to anger than all the kings of Israel who were before him" (1 Kings 16:33). Critics of Jezebel's foreign gods were executed or avenged.

Elijah spoke the word of the Lord to Ahab that there would be drought in Israel. After three years, God told Elijah to tell Ahab that He would send rain on the earth. This was Elijah's opportunity for a test of strength between the pagan fertility gods and the God of Israel. "If the LORD is God, follow Him; but if Baal, follow him," he declared (18:21). The rules of the contest were simple: Both sides would prepare a bull for sacrifice. Each side would call on his god, and the god who answered by fire would be declared the true God.

The contest took place on Mount Carmel. The prophets of Baal invoked their god until evening to send fire, but in the end "no one answered" (v. 26). Elijah prepared his altar and sacrifice, then had his men drench it with water three times. When he called on the "LORD God of Abraham, Isaac, and Israel," the "fire of the LORD fell and consumed the burnt sacrifice, and the wood and the stones and the dust, and it licked up the water that was in the trench. Now when all the people saw it, they fell on their faces; and they said, 'The LORD, He is God! The LORD, He is God!'" (18:36–39).

In short time, a cloudburst came and ended the drought. A clear and decisive victory was won by Elijah's God. To bring an end to the pagan worship, Elijah put to death the prophets of Baal. When word reached Jezebel of the execution, she threatened the prophet with his life. "When he saw that, he arose and ran for his life, and went to Beersheba" (19:3).

Elijah's life has been threatened, and he needs to get out of sight in a big hurry. Help him escape to Beersheba through this maze without being seen by Jezebel's cohorts.

ELIJAH
(Start)

*Y*our destiny is awesome.

Clue: MESSIAH *is* QIGGMET

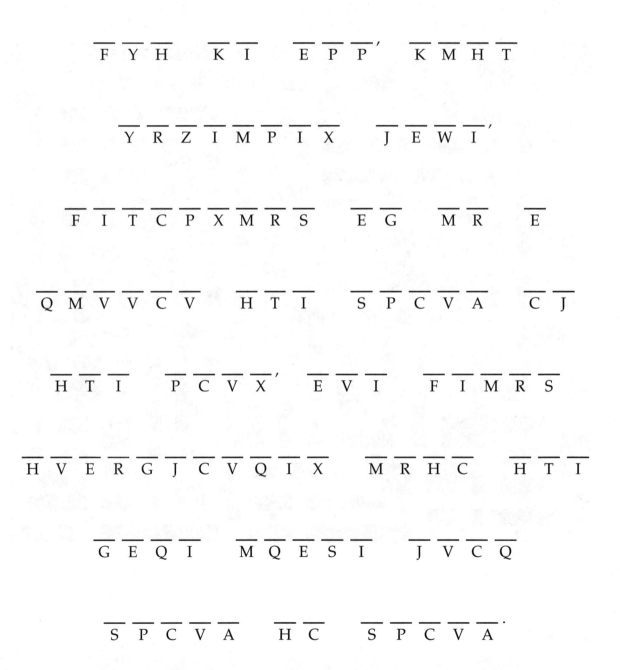

F Y H   K I   E P P '   K M H T

Y R Z I M P I X   J E W I '

F I T C P X M R S   E G   M R E   E

Q M V V C V   H T I   S P C V A   C J

H T I   P C V X '   E V I   F I M R S

H V E R G J C V Q I X   M R H C   H T I

G E Q I   M Q E S I   J V C Q

S P C V A   H C   S P C V A .

*T*he words of the song most commonly called "The Doxology" are used to complete this crossword grid. We've given you a word as a starting point. Fit in the rest of the words as quickly as you can. (Can you complete the puzzle in under five minutes?)

Praise God, from whom all blessings flow;
Praise Him, all creatures here below;
Praise Him above, ye heav'nly host;
Praise Father, Son and Holy Ghost.

STAYING LIT

*M*atthew 5:16 says, "Let your light so shine before men, that they may see your good works and glorify your Father in heaven." This candle has a breeze shield that allows the user to protect the flame from wind drafts.

The Holy Spirit both lights the flame of our light and provides us with protection against the winds of the enemy who tries to extinguish our light for the Lord.

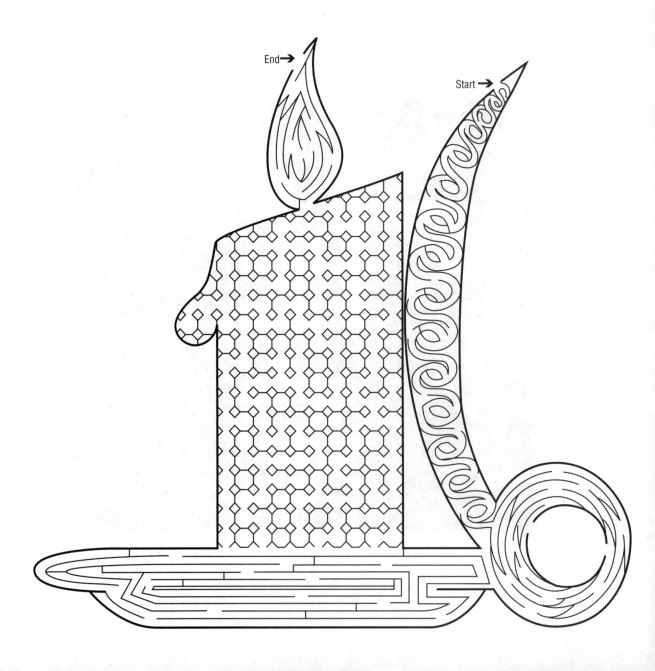

A number of life-changing events for Bible personalities took place "in the field" or out in the countryside. Find the names of twelve of these Bible people in the letter grid below. (One of the "names" is a title, two words.)

```
L B A N O S O J U R V D C A A I A N P
E U T E G Y A I T N I S N A A I T I T
G J O W I L F C I D O S A L V I D I S
Y A H M A N D S H E S A E G Y M P T A
P S E S M A A C A D A B A L A A M I U
J F P J T H R U R A S E B N H N A A C
O I H O O B A E N B G L A A I O A N B
N W E S U N H H A Y H E P D L A L S A
A H C E R P A T P D E H C A A H C B A
D O A P E H C T A I R S C B T S P A L
A A I H R T I N H V D L I U I W E A J
V M S U L A S O D A S A R D D I S C O
M A A D N U A J C D N B A A M F O I N
A N B A E L A H P E S V N O J E J S A
N O E V I A C S A J I O N A T H A R W
O A S A A C B A A C I W N A M H T U I
H R U T D A V I J O S E A E B A F G C
R L A B S I C A A C E B L G Y P N I A
```

Scripture Pool
GENESIS 4:8; 24:63; 37:13–15   NUMBERS 22:23   JUDGES 13:9   RUTH 2:2–3
1 SAMUEL 11:5; 16:11–13 19:2–3; 30:11   LUKE 2:8

*T*o keep … to follow … to obey. As Christians, we are admonished to keep the commandments, follow the leading of the Spirit, and "obey God rather than men" (Acts 5:29). Put together the two halves of these "obedience" verses and match each verse with its Scripture citation.

Column A

1. But God be thanked that though you were slaves of sin,

2. Since you have purified your souls in obeying the truth through the Spirit in sincere love of the brethren,

3. For as by one man's disobedience many were made sinners,

4. You shall walk after the LORD your God and fear Him,

5. Has the LORD as great delight in burnt offerings and sacrifices,

6. If anyone loves Me, he will keep My word;

7. Obey My voice, and I will be your God, and you shall be My people.

Column B

A. and My Father will love him, and We will come to him and make Our home with him.

B. and keep His commandments and obey His voice; you shall serve Him and hold fast to Him.

C. yet you obeyed from the heart that form of doctrine to which you were delivered.

D. And walk in all the ways that I have commanded you, that it may be well with you.

E. so also by one Man's obedience many will be made righteous.

F. as in obeying the voice of the LORD?

G. love one another fervently with a pure heart.

Column C

Deuteronomy 13:4

Romans 5:19

1 Peter 1:22

Jeremiah 7:23

John 14:23

1 Samuel 15:22

Romans 6:17

Column A	Column B	Column C
1	___	_____
2	___	_____
3	___	_____
4	___	_____
5	___	_____
6	___	_____
7	___	_____

As you complete the words of Isaiah 55 below, you'll have all the clues you need to finish the crossword!

93

"_____! Everyone who _____, come to the
70 Across   10 Across

_____ ; and you who have no _____, come,
4 Down   51 Down

_____ and _____ . _____, come, buy _____
72 Across   5 Down 48 Across   4 Across

and _____ without money and without _____ .
12 Down   3 Down

Why do you _____ money for what is not
20 Across

bread, and your wages for what does not

satisfy? _____ carefully to _____, and eat
78 Across   77 Down

what is good, and let your soul _____ itself in
34 Down

_____ . _____ your _____ , and come to _____ .
9 Across 44 Across 60 Down   15 Across

Hear, and your _____ shall live; and I will
41 Across

make an _____ _____ with you—the sure
13 Across 58 Across

_____ of David. Indeed I have given him as a
33 Down

_____ to the people, a _____ and _____ for the
75 Across   8 Down   27 Down

people. Surely you shall call a nation you do

not know, and _____ who do _____ know you
45 Down   61 Across

shall run to you, because of the LORD your

_____ , and the _____ One of Israel; for He
56 Down   65 Across

has glorified _____ ."
76 Down

_____ the LORD _____ He may be _____ ,
17 Across   49 Down   1 Down

_____ _____ Him while He is near. Let the
74 Down 55 Down

wicked _____ his _____ , and the _____ _____
46 Down   36 Across   79 Across 63 Across

his thoughts; let him _____ to the LORD, and
2 Down

He will have mercy _____ him; _____ to our
16 Across   6 Down

God, for He will abundantly _____ .
73 Across

"_____ My thoughts _____ not your _____ ,
1 Across   38 Across   43 Down

nor are your ways My _____ ," says the _____ .
11 Down   32 Down

"For as the heavens are _____ than the earth,
53 Across

_____ are My ways higher _____ your ways,
54 Across   26 Down

and My thoughts than your _____ ."
62 Down

"For as the _____ comes down, and the snow
7 Down

from _____ , and do not return there, but
40 Down

_____ the _____ , and make it bring forth and
71 Down   69 Down

_____ , _____ _____ may give _____ to the
39 Down 52 Down 42 Across   35 Across

_____ and bread to the _____ , so shall _____
68 Across   21 Down   63 Down

word be that goes _____ from My _____ ; it
23 Across   47 Across

shall not return to Me _____ , but it shall
14 Down

_____ what I _____ , and it shall _____ in the
59 Down   57 Across   67 Down

_____ for which I _____ it.
64 Down   22 Down

"For _____ shall go out with _____ , and be led
19 Down   18 Across

out with peace; the _____ and the _____ shall
51 Across   24 Down

break forth into singing before you, and all the

trees of the _____ shall _____ their hands.
23 Down   30 Across

Instead of the _____ shall come up the _____
28 Across   25 Down

tree, and instead of the _____ shall come
37 Across

_____ the _____ _____ ; and it shall be _____
66 Across 31 Across 29 Across   50 Across

the LORD for a name, for an everlasting sign

that shall not be _____ off."
25 Across

St. Andrew's Cross

*T*his cross shape has a number of other names, such as Cross Saltire, St. Patrick's Cross, the Scottish Cross, St. Alban's Cross, and Crux Decussata.

According to church tradition, the apostle Andrew died on this form of cross. Feeling himself unworthy to be crucified on the same type of cross as that on which his Lord, Jesus Christ, had died, he requested that the form of his cross be different. Tradition states that he died in prayer, just as Jesus did.

This emblem is frequently used as part of liturgical garments that are worn on St. Andrew's Day, November thirtieth.

As a silver cross on a blue background, this cross shape is the national cross of Scotland. When used as a symbol for St. Patrick, the cross is colored red.

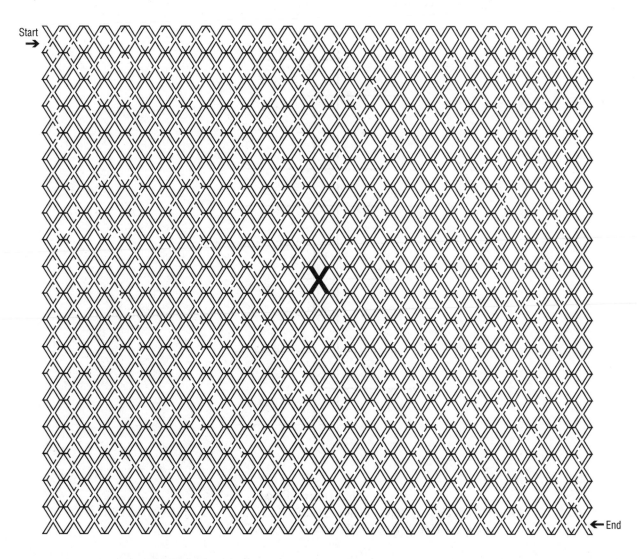

Start →

← End

*T*he words below are related in the Scriptures to one of the most frequently used analogies for material and spiritual prosperity. As you unscramble the words—and then fit them onto the grid below—you will discover the name of the one who watches over and takes care of this blessing.

OEWNR   UNRPE

ETDN   ARPGES

UFRIT   INVE

MSOSLOBS   SLCUETSR

NBARCHSE   SERKEPE

SICDPEWNIE (2 words)

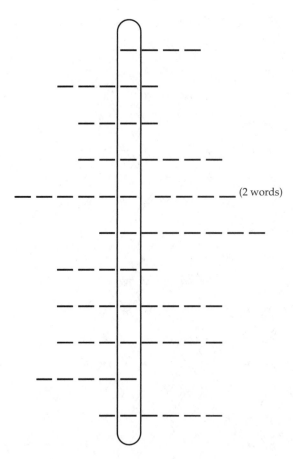

(2 words)

Scripture Pool

LEVITICUS 25:3   SONG OF SOLOMON 7:12; 8:2, 11–12   JEREMIAH 8:13
MATTHEW 20:8   JOHN 15:1, 4–5   REVELATION 14:18

*A*ll of the clues to this crossword begin with the letter *N*. See how many you can answer before looking up the Scripture references.

Across

2 The time of day Nicodemus came to Jesus (John 3:1–2)

3 Jesus raised a widow's only son from death in this city (Luke 7:11–15)

6 He was called a "mighty hunter before the LORD" (Genesis 10:9)

7 Commander of the Syrian king's army, he became a leper and was cured by dipping seven times in the Jordan River (2 Kings 5:1–14)

8 The Lord told Jonah to "cry out against" this wicked city (Jonah 1:1–2)

10 Hannah prayed, "No one is holy like the LORD, for there is _____ besides You" (1 Samuel 2:2)

11 King of Babylon, he built a golden image of himself and insisted that the people bow down and worship it or be thrown in a fiery furnace (Daniel 3:1–6)

12 In John's revelation, those who serve the beast have _____ rest (Revelation 14:11)

14 Deborah was the name of Rebekah's _____ (Genesis 35:8)

15 Servant of King Artaxerxes, he rebuilt the walls of Jerusalem (Nehemiah 1)

16 John had a vision of an angel having the everlasting gospel to preach to those of "every _____ , tribe, tongue, and people" (Revelation 14:6)

18 John wrote, "Let him who has understanding calculate the _____ of the beast, for it is the _____ of a man: His _____ is 666" (Revelation 13:18)

20 Jesus told the disciples to "cast the _____ on the right side of the boat" to catch fish (John 21:6)

21 "Let us therefore come boldly to the throne of grace, that we may obtain mercy and find grace to help in time of _____" (Hebrews 4:16)

22 Joshua's father (Joshua 1:1)

24 The psalmist described the rebuke of the LORD as "the blast of the breath of Your _____" (Psalm 18:15)

26 Abram had two brothers: _____ and Haran (Genesis 11:26)

27 The disciple whom Jesus saw "under the fig tree" (John 1:45–51)

Down

1 Thomas said he would not believe Jesus was resurrected unless he saw and touched "in His hands the print of the _____" (John 20:25)

2 Ruth's mother-in-law (Ruth 1:3–4)

3 Obadiah wrote, "The day of the LORD upon all the nations is _____" (Obadiah 15)

4 One of the first seven men chosen to take care of the "ministry business" of the early church (Acts 6:5)

5 The prophet who advised King David (2 Samuel 7:1–17)

8 The Lord showed Moses the land of promise from the top of this mountain (Deuteronomy 34:1–4)

9 Called "a ruler of the Jews," it was to him that Jesus said, "Unless one is born again, he cannot see the kingdom of God" (John 3:1–3)

10 Jesus' hometown (John 1:45)

11 Called "the city of the priests," it was attacked by Doeg the Edomite (1 Samuel 22:18–19)

13 Paul wrote that Jesus Christ is above "every name that is _____" (Ephesians 1:21)

15 Jesus healed the son of "a certain _____man" in Capernaum (John 4:46–53)

17 Jesus said that it is "easier for a camel to go through the eye of a _____ than for a rich man to enter the kingdom of God" (Matthew 19:24)

19 The name of the first month of the year on the Jewish calendar (Esther 3:7)

21 Abigail's first husband (1 Samuel 25:3)

23 Builder of the ark (Genesis 6:13–14)

24 The name of the thirty-fourth book of the Bible

25 Either, or; neither, _____

Some of the answers to this petal puzzle are people or things God uses to prophesy; some of the other answers are the fulfillment of prophecies. Solve the puzzle as you would a crossword, working clockwise and counterclockwise instead of "down and across." The first clockwise answer is provided as an example.

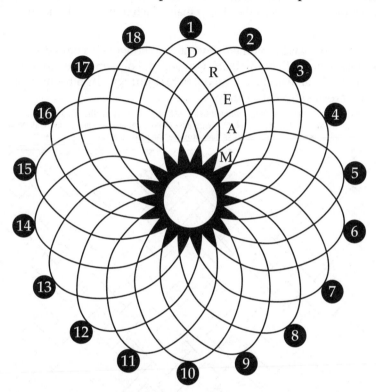

Clockwise
1 "Old man's" prophetic tool
2 Pulsating ache
3 West Point trainee
4 Concrete, steady
5 Luxurious fur animal
6 Summit or toothpaste
7 Lubricated
8 Tale or legend
9 Last's opposite
10 Morning bread slice
11 Large sea mammal
12 Category
13 Some will wear his mark (Revelation 13:16–17)
14 Hum, buzz
15 Thrill, exhilarate
16 Wine and jelly source
17 Snatches
18 People of the "Emerald Isle"

Counterclockwise
1 Swag window covering
2 Israel had twelve of these (sing.)
3 "Royal" board game
4 Prophecy of a son made her laugh
5 A city whose doom was foretold
6 Israelite general of note
7 Trajectory
8 As prophesied, Judas's thirty pieces of silver bought the potter's _____
9 The Bible warns *against* _____ prophets
10 Yak's home
11 God so loved the _____
12 Pursue
13 Explosion
14 Bargained or dispensed
15 Wipe out
16 Sheen
17 Endowment
18 Angry

Jacob's Return

*I*n Genesis 25, we find the story of two brothers so different that conflict was the constant theme of their life together. Esau, the elder brother, was his father Isaac's favorite son. Large and bronzed from his days hunting in the fields, Esau is described as hairy. He was probably considered a "man's man." As the older brother, he was more than likely a take-charge man which fit him well since he had the right to inherit all his father's holdings.

But the younger brother Jacob was his mother's favorite and he spent his days doing as she instructed him. By using these skills along with his mother's cunning and determination to secure the inheritance for her favorite son, Jacob was able to cheat Esau out of his birthright. As a result Jacob had to flee for his life and spent many years exiled from his family.

Jacob wants to return to his father's tent without being killed by his angry brother Esau. Armed with a bow and arrow, Esau can see all the way to the end of each path where he stands, but he can see only in the direction in which he is looking. He cannot see the paths that cross over or under the path he is on.

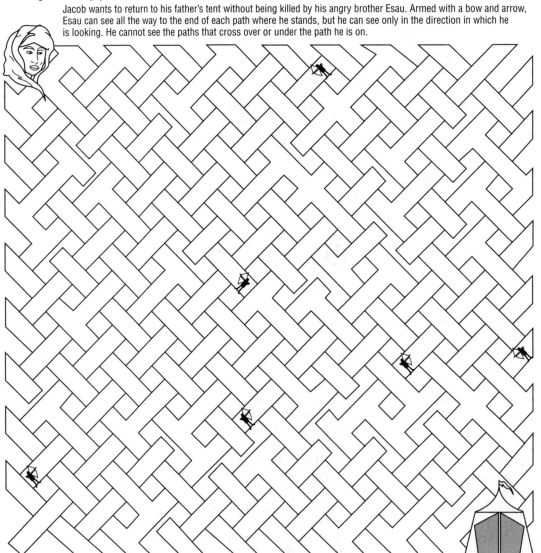

The Bible has a number of stories about people who gave to others—either freewill gifts or tribute. Find the names of twelve of these "givers" in the box of letters below. See how many you can find before consulting the Scripture Pool.

```
N  M  O  A  B  J  E  H  T  M  A  R  J  R  C  Z  T
E  H  O  R  I  T  S  O  O  I  H  S  E  U  Z  R  H
B  W  L  Y  T  A  H  A  T  A  S  E  B  A  I  S  A
U  I  N  S  O  S  B  P  H  A  B  H  O  P  I  H  D
C  D  E  P  E  I  W  R  O  R  N  E  S  H  E  E  N
H  A  M  I  T  C  N  C  A  I  L  E  S  Z  C  B  M
A  M  E  E  I  H  E  S  U  H  T  R  W  Z  O  A  O
D  S  S  O  R  H  B  E  J  T  A  Z  I  A  R  N  A
N  H  I  M  I  Z  U  M  E  T  I  M  D  R  N  E  B
E  A  W  M  P  T  A  H  P  A  H  S  O  H  E  J  S
Z  P  W  N  S  O  E  L  I  W  R  P  W  O  L  Z  E
Z  H  A  E  I  D  N  Z  Z  U  C  I  S  C  I  T  B
A  M  M  O  N  I  T  E  S  O  A  B  I  O  U  Y  I
R  A  T  N  C  O  R  E  N  M  S  E  T  R  S  W  S
E  M  D  A  H  C  U  B  T  U  I  L  E  N  D  I  E
```

Scripture Pool

GENESIS 25:6 2 SAMUEL 8:2 1 KINGS 10:10 2 CHRONICLES 21:1–3; 26:8
PSALM 72:10 DANIEL 2:1, 6, 48 MATTHEW 2:1,11 LUKE 21:1–4
ACTS 10:1-2 1 CORINTHIANS 12:4, 7

Caleb, Israel's mighty military leader, has an important meeting with Moses in the tent at the center of the maze. On the way, however, he must pass *through* twenty of his captain's tents without passing through any part of the maze twice.

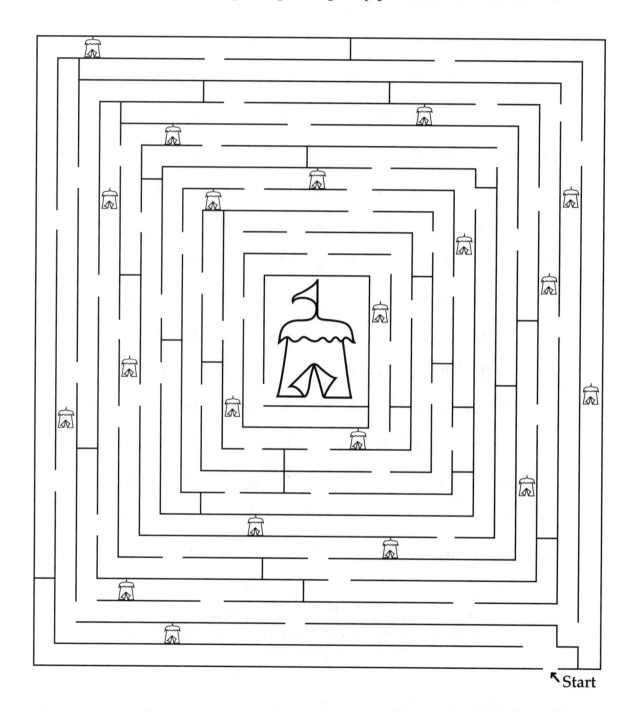

Start

*F*ind an important message in the box of letters below, and when you do, circle the letters that spell out the message!

X	Y	Z	U	Z	Y	Y	Z	U	Z	U	X	U	X	Y	Z
U	I	T	I	Z	U	S	X	G	Y	O	Y	R	E	C	U
Y	S	Z	Y	X	X	E	Y	I	X	T	Z	E	Y	Z	X
Z	M	U	E	S	U	D	Z	V	U	N	U	I	V	X	Z
U	O	X	L	Z	Z	T	U	E	T	A	X	E	U	Z	U
X	R	E	B	Z	Y	O	X	Y	H	Z	Y	ACTS 20:35
Z	Y	U	X	Y	X	Z	Z	U	X	Y	Z	U	X	Y	Z

*E*verything old was new again, when Jesus said, "It is written . . ."

Across

1 The rejected stone became the "main" cornerstone (Matthew 21:42)

6 Israel will say to these "small mountains," "Cover us!" (Luke 23:30)

7 Whoever commits this will be in danger of judgment (Matthew 5:21)

9 Science fiction (abbr.)

13 "A man's enemies will be those of his own 'home'" (Matthew 10:36)

15 Each (abbr.)

16 Isaiah said the people honored God with their "mouths," but not their hearts (Mark 7:6)

17 Road (abbr.)

18 If this sibling won't make amends, confront him with two or three witnesses (Matthew 18:15–16)

20 Jesus cited the "abomination of desolation" spoken of by this prophet (Matthew 24:15)

21 God desires this, not sacrifice (Matthew 9:13)

23 Like

24 Doctor (abbr.)

25 Judas ate this with Jesus, then betrayed Him (John 13:18)

26 They hated Him without a "reason" (John 15:25)

27 A house of prayer became a _____ of thieves (Matthew 21:13)

Down

2 The corpses of unrepentant sinners: Their "flame" is not quenched (Mark 9:48)

3 These members of the flock were scattered (Matthew 26:31)

4 "And the two shall become one _____" (Matthew 19:5)

5 "And He was numbered with the 'sinners'" (Luke 22:37)

8 Man doesn't live by this alone (Matthew 4:4)

10 Echoing David, Jesus asked, "Why have You _____ Me?" (Matthew 27:46)

11 "Respect" your father and mother (Matthew 15:4)

12 Looking on a woman with lust is the same as committing this, Jesus said (Matthew 5:27–28)

14 Satan couldn't tempt Jesus to "wait on" him instead of God (Matthew 4:10)

18 David was the first to say, "Out of the mouth of _____" (Matthew 21:16)

19 He *is* — not *was*— the God of Abraham, Isaac, and _____ (Matthew 22:32)

21 In the beginning, He "created" them male and female (Matthew 19:4)

22 God couldn't "restore" the people whose ears and eyes were closed (Matthew 13:15)

24 The hearts of the people, as Isaiah prophesied, had grown "blunt" (Matthew 13:15)

*R*eady for a mountaintop experience? Find the names of sixteen mountains named in the Bible. (See how many you can find before consulting the Word Pool.)

```
G  Z  I  O  L  I  B  A  L  I  G  O  B  H  B  A
I  S  O  S  B  E  O  D  E  A  M  E  R  O  N  L
L  E  N  I  A  T  A  A  B  E  D  T  L  I  A  E
B  V  L  N  R  H  L  O  M  O  R  I  A  S  I  B
A  I  A  A  E  O  I  A  V  S  G  O  I  G  O  L
L  C  R  L  C  R  C  R  E  G  E  R  I  Z  I  M
E  B  I  O  A  E  L  M  I  Z  A  R  E  P  V  S
A  G  C  L  M  B  E  L  A  I  G  B  Z  I  A  R
L  A  A  I  S  S  E  I  R  L  O  D  R  S  P  E
R  I  R  V  E  A  B  A  A  B  A  E  A  G  I  P
M  O  M  N  D  I  N  M  R  D  A  A  N  A  G  I
P  I  E  O  L  S  E  R  A  O  L  O  N  H  M  R
E  Z  L  I  R  O  B  A  T  V  M  B  M  E  N  O
R  A  O  Z  A  I  L  Z  S  R  A  L  A  B  B  M
A  L  M  C  R  M  A  I  E  E  N  I  Z  I  G  O
M  B  R  O  L  E  N  H  V  S  I  G  T  E  T  H
E  E  A  M  E  A  L  E  M  E  S  B  A  S  A  E
R  A  H  N  I  S  A  D  O  R  S  O  R  H  R  R
A  E  R  I  O  L  I  G  L  I  A  C  I  A  S  M
T  E  V  R  L  C  M  O  I  Z  V  E  R  O  R  O
```

Word Pool
ARARAT CARMEL EBAL GERIZIM GILBOA GILEAD HERMON
HOREB MORIAH NEBO OLIVES PISGAH SEIR SINAI TABOR ZION

THE RETURN HOME

*T*he life of the prodigal son that Jesus told about in a parable in Luke 15:11–32, is filled with difficult twists and turns. The young son pressured his father for his inheritance and then set out on a wild life of pleasure and excess that cost him everything he had inherited.

The young son was lost in his waywardness as his wanderings led him to the "pits" of the pig sty. There he determined to return home to become his father's sevant. But instead of servanthood, he was welcomed back by his father with a great feast as a beloved son. The older son, who had conducted his life in a much wiser manner, was angered by the celebration and confronted his father. The father declared that nothing had been taken away from the older son and everything that the father had belonged to him. What had been dead was now alive, and what was lost had been found. And so the father rejoiced.

Start ↓

End ←

Some fatherly advice goes a long way.

Clue: MESSIAH *is* BROOJZL

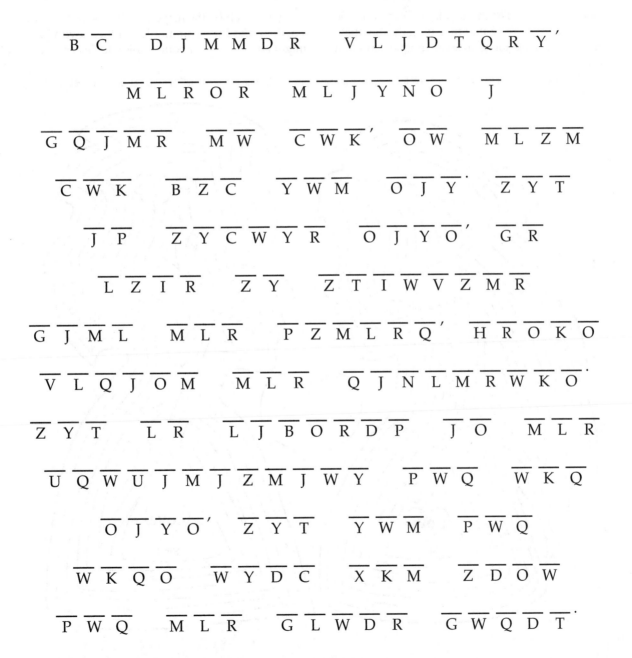

BC DJMMDR VLJDTQRY'

MLROR MLJYNO J

GQJMR MW CWK' OW MLZM

CWK BZC YWM OJY. ZYT

JP ZYCWYR OJYO' GR

LZIR ZY ZTIWVZMR

GJML MLR PZMLRQ' HROKO

VLQJOM MLR QJNLMRWKO.

ZYT LR LJBORDP JO MLR

UQWUJMJZMJWY PWQ WKQ

OJYO' ZYT YWM PWQ

WKQO WYDC XKM ZDOW

PWQ MLR GLWDR GWQDT.

RUTH AND BOAZ

*I*n addition to being a beautiful love story, the book of Ruth is an example of the fact that love will find a way to communicate even when communication is difficult. Ruth, a young widow, elected to leave the land of her birth to accompany her much-loved mother-in-law Naomi to the land of Naomi's birth. In doing this, Ruth committed herself to help support Naomi in a land where Ruth knew no one and, perhaps, did not even speak the language.

But God honored Ruth's loyalty to Naomi. While gathering grain left by the reapers in Boaz's fields, Ruth caught his eye. From that time until the day they married, Boaz and Ruth communicated their love and respect for one another in some unique ways that you might enjoy reading about in this Old Testament book.

This maze has two starting points, but they both end up in the same place. Help Ruth and Boaz "tell" one another what is in their hearts.

As you complete the words to one of the most famous Christmas carols in the world—"O Come, All Ye Faithful"—you'll have the clues you need to complete this crossword grid.

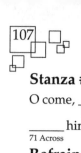

Stanza #1:

O come, _____ ye _____, _____ and _____, O come _____, O come ye _____ _____; Come _____
  4 Down   18 Down 31 Across 21 Across   61 Across   39 Across 6 Down   35 Down
_____ him, born the _____ of _____;
71 Across   52 Down   63 Across

Refrain:

O come, let _____ adore him, O _____, let us _____ him, O come, _____ us adore _____, _____
            32 Across   7 Down   16 Down   38 Across   46 Across 12 Down
_____ Lord.
34 Down

Stanza #2:

God of God, Light of _____, _____! _____ _____ not the _____ womb; Very God, _____, not
                      9 Across 60 Down 23 Across 45 Down   54 Across   26 Across
_____;
56 Down

Stanza #3:

Sing, _____ of angels, _____ _____ _____, _____, _____ ye _____ of heav'n _____; Glory to
      14 Across   41 Down 67 Down 44 Across 72 Across 27 Across 43 Down   8 Across
_____, in the _____;
51 Across   13 Down

Stanza #4:

_____ how the _____, _____ to _____ _____, Leaving their _____, draw _____ to _____; _____ too
47 Across   3 Down 30 Down 19 Across 24 Down   2 Down   17 Across 33 Down 25 Across
_____ thither, _____ _____ joyful _____;
25 Down   53 Down 42 Down   40 Down

Stanza #5:

_____, for us _____, _____ and _____ the _____, We would _____ thee, with _____ and _____;
29 Across   69 Across 22 Down 20 Down 15 Across   5 Across   64 Down   49 Across
Who would _____ love _____, _____ us _____ _____?
          70 Down   66 Across 28 Down 3 Across 48 Down

Stanza #6:

_____, _____, _____ _____ thee, Born _____ happy _____; _____, to thee _____ all _____
36 Across 65 Down 1 Down 33 Across   21 Down   37 Across 62 Down   11 Across 59 Across
_____; _____ _____ the _____, _____ in 40 Across 55 Across;
10 Down 50 Down 57 Across 58 Down 68 Across

*W*as Jesus the first to say, "actions speak louder than words"?

Clue: MESSIAH *is* RPIIEOU

U P   H U Y   T Y P I   G Y X

F Y Q P   R P   T Y P I   G Y X

A P P D   R Z   H Y K T I'   O G T ;

X U P   H Y K T   H U E M U   Z Y B

U P O K   E I   G Y X   R E G P

L B X   X U P   S O X U P K I'

H U Y   I P G X   R P .

UP TO JERUSALEM

*I*n New Testament times, the Jews celebrated Passover in Jerusalem. Who among them could forget the long-ago enslavement of God's people by Pharaoh . . . the plagues that befell the Egyptians as Pharaoh ignored Moses' entreaties . . . and finally, the most devastating plague of all: death of the firstborn child and animal in every Egyptian household?

But the children of Israel were spared. Following Moses' orders, they ate the first Passover meal, put the blood of the lamb on their doorposts, and avoided the fate of their earthly masters. And Pharaoh let God's people go.

Beginning on the bottom line, connect a string of letters that form a three-word phrase telling us what Passover symbolizes.

↙ End

S	A	L	J	E	R	U	S	A	L	E	M	J	E	R	U	S	E	A	L	E	M	J	E	R
J	E	R	U	S	J	E	R	U	S	A	L	E	M	S	A	G	L	E	M	J	E	R	U	S
S	A	L	E	J	E	R	U	J	E	R	U	S	R	U	A	S	A	L	E	M	J	E	R	U
J	E	R	J	E	R	U	S	A	L	E	J	E	R	D	U	S	J	E	R	U	S	A	L	E
L	E	M	S	A	J	E	R	U	S	A	L	E	E	R	N	U	S	A	L	E	M	J	E	R
R	U	S	A	L	E	M	J	E	J	E	R	U	S	J	E	O	R	U	S	A	L	E	M	U
S	A	L	J	E	R	U	S	A	L	E	J	E	R	M	B	J	E	R	U	S	A	L	J	E
M	J	E	R	U	S	J	E	R	U	S	U	S	O	A	L	E	M	J	E	R	U	S	A	L
A	L	J	E	R	U	S	J	E	R	U	F	R	S	A	L	E	M	U	S	A	L	E	M	J
J	E	R	U	J	S	A	L	J	U	E	J	E	R	U	S	A	L	E	M	J	E	R	U	S
A	L	E	M	J	E	J	E	R	C	U	S	J	E	R	U	S	A	L	J	E	R	S	A	L
M	J	E	J	E	R	U	S	A	J	N	E	R	U	S	J	E	R	U	S	A	L	J	E	R
A	J	E	R	U	S	J	E	R	A	U	S	A	L	J	E	R	U	S	J	E	R	U	S	A
J	E	R	U	J	E	R	U	R	S	A	L	E	R	U	S	A	L	E	M	E	M	J	E	R
L	E	M	J	E	J	E	R	U	E	S	A	J	E	R	U	S	A	L	E	M	S	A	L	E
S	J	E	R	U	S	A	J	V	J	E	R	U	A	L	E	M	R	J	E	R	U	S	A	L
A	L	E	J	E	R	U	I	A	L	E	S	A	L	E	M	J	E	R	U	S	A	L	E	M
M	J	E	R	U	J	L	E	R	U	S	A	L	E	M	E	R	U	S	A	L	E	M	J	E
S	A	J	E	R	U	S	E	A	L	E	M	J	E	R	U	S	A	L	E	M	J	E	R	U
J	E	R	U	S	A	D	J	E	M	A	L	E	M	J	E	R	U	S	A	L	E	M	J	E

Start ↗

These words have been a constant source of comfort and reassurance to Christians since the moment Christ spoke them.

Clue: MESSIAH *is* GQUUKCI

Y Q V   R F V   L F S E

I Q C E V   Z Q   V E F S Z Y Q H ;

L F S   Z Q Y K Q P Q   K R

X F H '   Z Q Y K Q P Q

C Y U F   K R   G Q .

111

Next to the name of each of these Bible figures is the jumbled name of his mother. Write the mothers' names in the blanks of the grid, and you'll discover a message each of these sons could have given to his mother. (A Scripture reference is provided if you need it.)

1. SOLOMON	B H T A E B H S A	(1 Kings 1:15–17)
2. JOSEPH	L A C E R H	(Genesis 35:24)
3. GERSHOM	Z I O A P R H P	(Exodus 2:21–22)
4. GAD	H I A Z L P	(Genesis 30:9–11)
5. JESUS	R A Y M	(Luke 2:4–7, 21)
6. REUEL	B A M T S E A H	(Genesis 36:10)
7. MOSES	E C B O H J E D	(Exodus 6:20)
8. OBED	U T R H	(Ruth 4:13, 17)
9. REUBEN	E H L A	(Genesis 29:32)
10. CAIN	V E E	(Genesis 4:1)
11. ISHMAEL	G A R A H	(Genesis 16:15)
12. ISAAC	H A S R A	(Genesis 21:2–3)
13. ELIPHAZ	D H A A	(Genesis 36:10)
14. SAMUEL	A N H N H A	(1 Samuel 1:20)
15. JOHN MARK	A Y R M	(Acts 12:12)

1 — — — — — — — — —

2 — — — — — —

3 — — — — — — —

4 — — — — — —

5 — — — —

6 — — — — — — —

7 — — — — — — —

8 — — — —

9 — — — —

10 — — —

11 — — — —

12 — — — —

13 — — — —

14 — — — — —

15 — — — —

*H*ave you ever had a perfect day? Isn't it nice to know that eternity is going to be just one perfect day after another, after another . . .

Bonus:

Unscramble the circled letters to reveal our "perfect home."

— — — — — —

112

Across

4 The perfect "statute" of the Lord converts the soul (Psalm 19:7)

7 When the perfect comes, the "portion" will be done away with (1 Corinthians 13:10)

8 No "untruth" was found in Jesus' mouth (1 Peter 2:22)

10 Be perfect as your _____ in heaven is perfect (Matthew 5:48)

11 This apostle wasn't perfected, but he pressed on (Philippians 3:1, 12)

13 Preposition

14 The faithful didn't receive the "pledge" and won't be made perfect apart from us (Hebrews 11:39–40)

16 Regarding (abbr.)

17 After we've "endured pain" a while, God will perfect us (1 Peter 5:10)

19 "Let _____ have its perfect work, that you may be perfect . . ." (James 1:4)

21 A peace offering could have no "fault" (Leviticus 22:21)

23 This bondservant of Christ prayed that the Colossians would stand perfect in God's will (Colossians 4:12)

27 If we say we have no sin, the _____ is not in us (1 John 1:8)

28 Abraham's faith, combined with his "actions," perfected his faith (James 2:21–22)

29 Christ was a Lamb without _____ or spot (1 Peter 1:19)

30 God told Abram, "Walk before Me and be 'without culpability'" (Genesis 17:1)

35 The perfect Son became the "writer" of eternal salvation (Hebrews 5:9)

36 Scripture was given to make us "whole" (2 Timothy 3:16–17)

37 Perfect love casts out _____ (1 John 4:18)

Down

1 The "commander" of our salvation was made perfect through sufferings (Hebrews 2:10)

2 After the "exam," Job would come forth as gold (Job 23:10)

3 David's wasn't broken; it would be perfect, he told God in Psalm 101:2

5 Not B.C., but _____

6 We're glad you're strong when we're _____, Paul told the Corinthians, that they may be made complete (2 Corinthians 13:9)

7 God keeps us in perfect _____ when our minds are stayed on Him (Isaiah 26:3)

9 The king of _____ (not Sidon) was the seal of perfection (Ezekiel 28:12)

10 Cleansing all filthiness of the _____ and spirit would perfect holiness in the Corinthians (2 Corinthians 7:1)

11 Not A.M., but _____

12 You and me

14 "Out of the mouth of babes . . . you have perfected _____ " (Matthew 21:16)

15 Everyone who is perfectly trained will be like his "instructor" (Luke 6:40)

18 "He is the 'Refuge,' His work is perfect" (Deuteronomy 32:4)

20 A just man, perfect in his generations (Genesis 6:9)

22 Paul wanted to perfect what the Thessalonians' "trust" lacked (1 Thessalonians 3:9–10)

24 Our High Priest is "hallowed" (Hebrews 7:26)

25 Was the flesh making the Galatians perfect, and not the _____ ? (Galatians 3:3)

26 God's _____ is made perfect in weakness (2 Corinthians 12:9)

28 "Prove what is that good and acceptable and perfect _____ of God" (Romans 12:2)

31 "Charity" is the bond of perfection, says Paul (Colossians 3:14)

32 Jesus was tempted as we are, but was without "transgression" (Hebrews 4:15)

33 God made David's "path" perfect (Psalm 18:32)

34 To be perfect, Jesus told the rich man, sell your possessions and give to the _____ (Matthew 19:21)

CROWN OF LIFE

*I*n Revelation 2:10, the angel to the church of Smyrna spoke these words of the Lord, "Do not fear any of those things which you are about to suffer. Indeed, the devil is about to throw some of you into prison, that you may be tested, and you will have tribulation ten days. Be faithful until death, and I will give you the crown of life."

Crowns have always been symbols of royalty. The cross is frequently combined with the crown to create a church symbol. It represents the reward of everlasting life given to those who accept the sacrifice of Jesus and believe in Him as their Savior.

Start →

← End

*W*hat is God like? Find twenty attributes of God in the letter box below.

P	X	L	T	F	R	T	N	E	I	T	A	P
S	O	G	R	A	C	I	O	U	S	N	T	L
L	I	O	R	I	A	S	E	J	O	E	N	O
U	R	O	E	T	E	R	N	A	L	T	S	V
F	A	D	U	H	H	R	R	X	G	O	P	T
I	W	L	A	F	C	G	O	R	E	P	V	N
C	O	U	B	U	R	O	I	L	W	I	S	E
R	D	O	Y	L	O	H	X	L	T	N	P	I
E	T	A	N	O	I	S	S	A	P	M	O	C
M	R	O	S	T	N	W	I	C	X	O	R	S
J	U	S	T	E	L	B	A	T	U	M	M	I
S	E	T	R	I	G	H	T	E	O	U	S	N
B	N	G	I	E	R	E	V	O	S	H	S	M
U	L	T	N	E	S	E	R	P	I	N	M	O

Word Pool

COMPASSIONATE ETERNAL FAITHFUL GOOD GRACIOUS HOLY
IMMUTABLE JUST LIGHT LOVE MERCIFUL OMNIPOTENT
OMNIPRESENT OMNISCIENT ONE PATIENT RIGHTEOUS
SOVEREIGN TRUE WISE

Many clues relate to the Sabbath.

Unscramble the circled letters
to reveal a phrase related to the Sabbath.

__ __ __ __ __ __ __   __ __ __

Across

1 High school organization for tomorrow's teachers (abbr.)
2 Mercy _____ (part of the ark of the covenant) (Leviticus 16:2)
7 Roman garb
11 The disciples did this to heads of grain on the Sabbath (Matthew 12:1)
13 Deliriously happy
15 Sound of discovery
16 Masculine, objective case
17 Quote
18 A man was stoned for doing this on the Sabbath (2 words) (Numbers 15:32–36)
23 Initials of a television evangelist
24 Truly, indeed
25 "_____ _____ little teapot, short and stout . . ."
28 Pedro's sun
29 Stitching
31 Affirmative
34 First lady
35 Home for #34 Across
36 Single word title for popular song about Him
38 King James English for #31 Across
40 Its yield depends on the soil it's in
41 Instructor
43 "Love one another; _____ I have loved you" (John 13:34)
44 Jesus did this as He taught in the temple (John 8:20)
46 "Gimme that _____' time religion"
47 Pie _____ mode
48 "Did _____ not know that I must be about My Father's business?" (Luke 2:49)
50 A king of Judah; Jehoshaphat's father (1 Kings 22:41)
51 Not refuted
55 Grill in the oven
58 Yard worker
60 Quarrel
61 Between la and do
62 Reply
64 Remorseful
65 Proclaim

Down

1 Horizontal
2 You, to Caesar
3 Pain
4 Prefix for half
5 Nickname for Queen Elizabeth's youngest son
6 Razz
7 Garish
8 Name in an elevator
9 "_____ along, lil' dogie"
10 Passes with flying colors (as a test)
11 Jesus' Sabbath critics (Luke 14:1)
12 Captain of the *Enterprise*
14 A "good" place for seed
15 Long time _____
19 Jesus did this for the man with a withered hand on the Sabbath (Luke 6:6–10)
20 Jesus' disciples were criticized for rubbing this between their hands on the Sabbath (Luke 6:1)
21 Jesus did this in the synagogue on the Sabbath (Mark 1:21)
22 Jesus healed a man's eyes with this on the Sabbath (John 9:14)
26 Relocate
27 Sabbath command: "Take up your _____ and walk" (John 5:11)
29 Ooze
30 The Sabbath is the seventh day of this
32 Apostles' Sabbath location (Acts 13:42)
33 Jesus spoke in these on the Sabbath (Luke 14:7)
37 One kind of love
39 Electric fish
40 Foolish place to build a house (Matthew 7:26)
42 Mississippi neighbor
44 Christian "Sabbath"
45 Baking places
49 "_____ Father in heaven, hallowed be . . ."
50 Tally
52 Daniel shared the lions'
53 Modern
54 Angered
56 Sign at a crossing
57 A, e, _____ , o, _____
58 Popular Ford model of 60s song
59 Atmosphere
63 Between do and mi

Unscramble the names of these twenty-three people mentioned in the New Testament, and discover in the process what they had in common. (Check the Scripture Pool for help.)

SISLA   — — — — —

RAKM   — — — —

ITHOMTY   — — — — — — —

ARNYNTSU   — — — — — — — —

AGBUAS   — — — — — —

UHTUCEYS   — — — — — — — —

YTHICSCU   — — — — — — — —

ANEASE   — — — — — —

KUEL   — — — —

ASGIU   — — — — —

MIARDAS   — — — — — — —

DAYLI   — — — — —

RMYA   — — — —

ISRPICLAL   — — — — — — — — —

ORPTUHSIM   — — — — — — — — —

RASETUS   — — — — — — —

QIAAUL   — — — — — —

ARIRASUTCSH   — — — — — — — — — — —

TIAHBTA   — — — — — — —

ASVISLNU   — — — — — — — —

OSAPRTE   — — — — — — —

LIOCNREUS   — — — — — — — — —

EINOSUMS   — — — — — — — —

Scripture Pool

ACTS 9:33, 36; 10:1; 11:28; 12:12; 16:14, 25; 17:34; 18:18; 19:9, 22, 29; 20:4, 9
COLOSSIANS 4:9, 14   1 THESSALONIANS 1:1

In John 14:6, Jesus gives us instruction as to how we are able to approach God. To reveal Jesus' words, begin with the circled letter and trace from letter to letter, until you have spelled out each word of the scripture. You may move in any direction, but only move to adjacent squares. Do not use any letter twice. When you finish, you will have used every letter in the puzzle. The first two moves are done for you.

N	E	F	I	L	W	A
O	O	N	E	H	E	Y
C	E	H	(I)	T	M	T
M	O	T	D	A	T	H
S	E	N	A	U	R	E
T	O	T	H	T	O	R
T	H	A	G	U	T	H
H	F	E	H	C	E	T
E	R	E	X	M	E	P

Overflowing Cup

*I*n Psalm 23:5, David joyfully exclaims, "My cup runs over." The cup pictured in the maze is a communion cup bearing two important Christian symbols. The first, the fish, is widely used to represent the same thing that it did to the early Christians who used it as a secret symbol to identify themselves to one another as followers of Christ at a time when open confession of one's faith was dangerous.

The second symbol, the letters IHS, is frequently used on sacred objects among Christian churches of all denominations. Often misinterpreted to mean "in His service," the letters are actually the first three letters of Jesus' name spelled IHSOUS in Greek.

*H*idden in the letter box below are names of sixteen false gods and idols mentioned in the Bible. Circle each one as you find it. After you have found the names, read the remaining letters left to right to find out what the apostle Paul wrote to the church at Corinth about false gods.

F	L	E	E	F	R	A	O	M	I	D	O	L	A	T
R	Y	I	D	N	O	N	N	O	M	T	W	A	N	T
Y	O	U	T	I	O	A	H	M	O	L	E	C	H	A
V	E	D	F	S	E	M	L	L	C	O	W	S	H	I
P	W	A	D	R	A	M	M	E	L	E	C	H	I	T
H	D	G	E	O	M	E	O	N	I	S	Y	O	U	C
A	N	O	N	C	O	L	T	D	M	R	I	L	N	K
T	H	N	E	H	T	E	R	O	T	H	S	A	C	L
U	P	O	T	F	T	C	H	E	L	O	R	A	E	D
A	N	D	A	T	N	H	H	E	C	U	S	B	P	O
F	D	E	M	O	B	E	E	L	Z	E	B	U	B	M
O	N	S	M	Y	O	M	U	C	M	A	N	N	O	T
P	A	M	U	R	T	O	A	R	K	E	O	F	T	H
E	I	L	Z	E	U	S	E	O	R	O	B	E	N	D
R	S	T	A	B	L	H	E	A	N	D	O	F	T	H
E	T	A	B	L	E	O	F	D	E	M	O	N	S	✐

Word Pool

ADRAMMELECH ANAMMELECH ASHTORETH BAAL BEELZEBUB BEL
CHEMOSH DAGON HERMES MILCOM MOLECH NEBO NISROCH
RIMMON TAMMUZ ZEUS

*A*ll chapter and verse references in these clues are from 2 Kings, unless stated otherwise. Many of the clues have to do with Elisha and his prophetic mission.

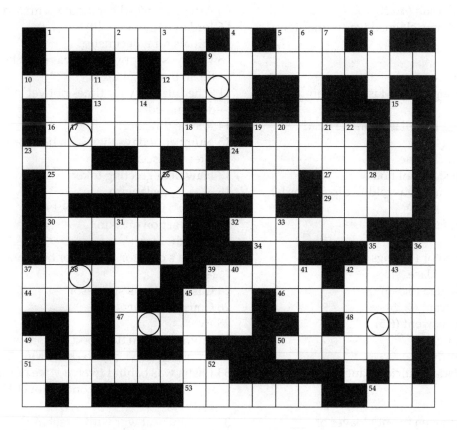

Bonus:

Unscramble the circled letters to reveal
the name of the prophet who anointed Elisha.

_____ _____ _____ _____ _____ _____

Across

1 City of famine rescued by four lepers (7:1, 3)
5 Peaches _____ cream
9 _____ woman—for whom Elisha prophesied a son (4:12)
10 What the diners claimed was in the stew pot (4:40)
12 Region
13 Finest
16 Wall coverings or old-fashioned ointment bandages
19 What Elisha had placed on the dead child's face (4:29)
23 Lincoln's nickname
24 Fashion designer of note
25 Where Naaman was told to dip (2 words) (5:10)
27 Prominent facial feature
29 Adorable
30 Elisha's mentor (1 Kings 19:19–21)
32 Collar or necklace
34 Its head floated (6:5–6)
37 Elisha's servant (4:25)
39 Where the ax went (6:5)
42 Sunday song
44 Mining product
45 _____-Hadad; suicidal king of Syria (8:7–15)
46 Organic
47 Elisha was given twenty loaves of _____ bread with which he fed one hundred people (4:42–44)
48 Wee
50 Rouge kitty (2 words)
51 How Elijah left (2:11)
53 City surrounded by chariots of fire (6:13–17)
54 Elisha prayed, "LORD, open the eyes of these _____ , that they may see" (6:20)

Down

1 Mutton/lamb producer
2 Evidence of fire
3 Angry
4 Mortgage loan type
5 Article for word beginning with a vowel
6 Jordan bather (5:9–10)
7 Initials for a decimeter
8 Widow's supply of this was stretched to fill all the jars (4:2)
11 Schedule entry for times not yet determined
14 Recipe direction
15 Number of days they searched for Elijah after his ascent (2:17)
17 Hawaiian greeting token
18 _____ de Janeiro
19 Elisha's father (1 Kings 19:19)
20 Sun's action on skin
21 Yard divider
22 Elisha's cure for the poisonous stew (4:40–41)
24 Cassette tape's successor
26 Cousin of Jesus
28 Ave.
31 From queen to dog food—Elisha's prophecy came true for her (9:36–37)
33 Elisha was behind twelve yoke of these when Elijah commissioned him (1 Kings 19:19)
35 A country at war with Israel (6:8)
36 Solely
37 "_____ into all the world and preach the gospel" (Mark 16:15)
38 Abdominal rupture
39 Tiny
40 One or another
41 Fury
42 Boxlike pen for rabbits
43 Elisha inherited Elijah's (2:13)
45 Insipid
49 Number of widow's sons (4:1)
52 "_____ good to those who hate you" (Matthew 5:44)

*S*tring together the letters below to reveal one of the Bible's most famous verses about love.

RAHAB'S ESCAPE ROUTE

*W*hen Joshua sent spies into the city of Jericho, they were aided in their escape by a woman named Rahab. Rahab was a prostitute, but she had heard about the power of the true God of the Israelites. She believed that Jericho, though surrounded by a high wall, would be conquered by Israel. She offered to help the spies in exchange for safety for her and her family when the Israelites invaded Jericho.

Rahab's house was actually on the wall. After hiding the spies on the roof while her house was searched, she let them down the side of the wall by a rope and they made good their escape in the darkness. When the walls of Jericho fell, Rahab and her family were the only ones left alive.

Beginning at Rahab's window, travel only on stones that are touching. Exit anywhere on the ground as long as the last stone touches the ground.

Start

*A*fter leaving Egypt, the Israelites needed the discipline of a godly life. So God gave them specific rules to follow to help them stay on track. This puzzle is based on the book of Deuteronomy.

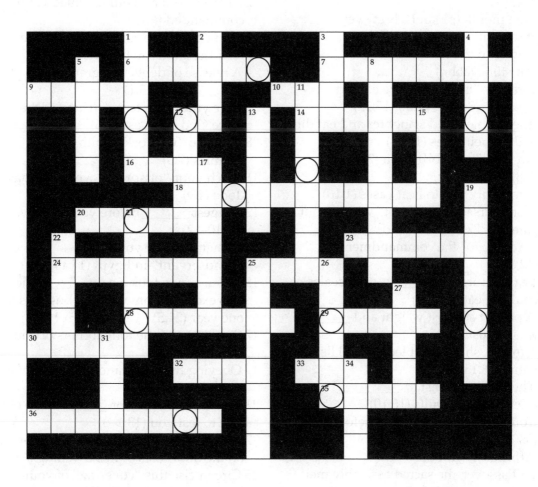

Bonus:

Unscramble the circled letters to reveal the place
where the Israelites were about to enter when
the message of Deuteronomy was given to them.

___ ___ ___ ___ ___ ___ ___   ___ ___ ___ ___

Across

6 Don't take God's name this way (2 words) (5:11)

7 And "don't forget" the Lord your God (8:18)

9 First month (pl.) in Hebrew year; observe it! (16:1)

10 Comes in cubes

12 Part-time (abbr.)

14 A fellow "Israelite" slave earned freedom after six years (15:12)

16 The people could slaughter and eat this within their gates (12:15)

18 An "idol" was forbidden (2 words) (5:8)

20 Their duty was to hear cases (1:16)

23 Don't forsake the "priest" within your gates (14:27)

24 "Adhere to" the commandments (12:32)

25 Sea creatures with _____ and scales could be eaten (14:9)

28 A perfect and just weight and _____ was a must (25:15)

29 "You . . . shall take 'pledges' in His name" (6:13)

30 The required Feast of _____ celebrated firstfruits (16:10)

32 You shall have none other before Him (5:7)

33 Affirmative response

35 At Passover, the sacred assembly met on day _____ (16:8)

36 The third-generation Edomite and _____ could enter the Lord's assembly (23:7–8)

Down

1 Following God's statutes was the Israelites' "knowledge" and understanding (4:6)

2 "Throw" out all your enemies, God commanded (6:19)

3 Don't plant one as a wooden image near the altar you build (16:21)

4 A release of debts was granted every _____ years (15:1)

5 Take your "one-tenth" (sing.) to the place God chooses (12:6)

8 Enter no "wedlocks" with your enemies (7:3)

11 Teach your "offspring" what God has done (4:9)

12 Suggest _____ before you make war (20:10–12)

13 Remember that you were a "bondservant" in Egypt (15:15)

15 When a man took a new _____ , he was excused from war and business for one year (24:5)

17 Sew these on the four corners of your clothing (22:12)

19 Obeying the commandments meant a "benefit" (11:27)

21 Beware a dreamer of _____ ; God uses him to test you (13:1–3)

22 The commandments should be written on the doorposts of this dwelling (6:9)

25 Circumcise this "covering" of your heart, Moses said (10:16)

26 If someone close to you encourages you to worship false gods, throw these at him until he dies (13:10)

27 Don't do a close one to the front of your head for the dead (14:1)

31 "Hang onto" the commandments (4:2)

34 Don't forget, children of Israel, what your eyes have _____ God do (4:9)

All adult Jewish males were required to go "up to Jerusalem" for the three major feasts of the year: the Feast of Passover, the Feast of Weeks, and the Feast of Tabernacles. Help the sojourners below get to Jerusalem in record time.

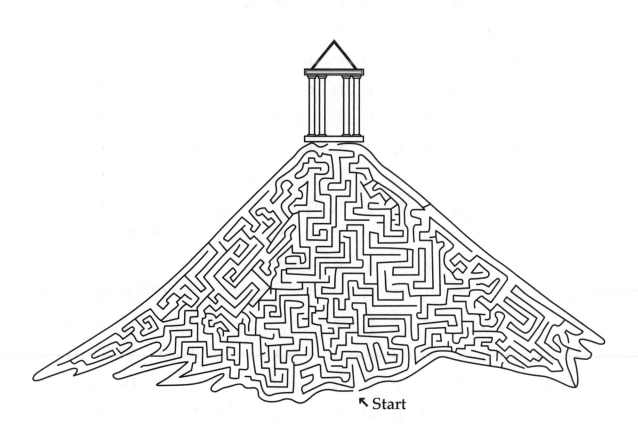

↖ Start

Galatians 5:19–21 lists seventeen specific "works of the flesh" that are contrary to the work of the Holy Spirit in a person's life. Paul warns that "those who practice such things will not inherit the kingdom of God." See how many of these fleshly sins you can find in the letter box below before consulting the Scriptures.
(Note: Two of the "works" have more than one word.)

```
L  C  N  T  U  S  N  O  I  T  N  E  T  N  O  C  I  E  E
E  L  E  R  N  S  Y  M  O  I  S  R  S  S  M  R  B  W  A
N  N  A  E  O  E  R  F  U  N  S  O  O  U  T  M  C  D  B
V  E  R  C  T  N  M  O  U  R  E  R  R  N  K  E  N  E  U
E  S  E  I  A  N  U  R  D  C  D  D  U  C  S  S  E  N  R
R  S  V  O  L  E  L  N  E  I  E  D  R  I  E  H  A  H  S
E  H  E  N  O  K  E  I  S  R  F  I  S  H  A  R  D  T  T
H  O  L  S  D  N  W  C  S  A  O  D  Y  S  E  E  Y  A  S
E  D  R  I  A  U  D  A  H  T  R  E  R  V  R  Y  V  R  S
W  U  I  T  Y  R  E  T  L  U  D  A  T  T  N  D  N  W  E
U  T  E  S  R  D  F  I  B  F  N  N  A  R  I  E  E  F  C
B  B  S  J  S  W  O  O  U  L  I  H  L  S  W  I  S  O  L
T  U  R  S  T  E  S  N  R  E  C  N  O  T  E  N  N  S  F
U  O  S  L  E  A  N  T  S  S  A  S  D  V  Y  T  O  T  H
E  E  S  E  L  F  I  S  H  A  M  B  I  T  I  O  N  S  E
R  S  I  W  L  O  E  U  I  O  T  O  S  O  D  I  S  R  R
I  D  E  D  M  I  W  S  I  O  I  S  N  W  B  T  E  U  L
S  Y  N  N  S  E  D  S  R  S  N  S  T  A  M  S  E  B  S
I  V  L  E  L  U  O  L  A  E  J  S  H  S  I  E  S  T  W
D  S  R  S  S  I  D  S  S  E  N  N  A  E  L  C  N  U  D
S  E  E  S  N  J  E  A  L  O  U  S  I  E  S  T  N  O  C
H  N  N  A  I  O  N  S  S  E  M  U  R  U  N  C  O  L  E
```

*Y*ou may find the *WAY* to work this puzzle in the *TRAIL* of scriptures given . . . all of which trace a *PATH* to a better life.

Across

1 A military address
4 On's opposite
6 Initials of *The Lion, the Witch, and the Wardrobe* author
10 Illustration
12 "_____ for yourselves this day whom you will serve" (Joshua 24:15)
14 British slang for "thanks!"
15 Decipher
16 Small collie-like dog
17 "These men are the _____(s) of the Most High God, who #38 Across to us the way of #24 Down" (Acts 16:17)
19 "_____ is a way that #9 Down to a man" (Proverbs 14:12)
20 Comes between K and N
21 Despised
22 Wise men went another way to avoid seeing him (Matthew 2:12)
24 International signal of distress
25 Earthy red or yellow color (British spelling)
26 What Miss Muffet was eating with #27 Across
27 See #26 Across
28 Large Hawaiian thistle flower
29 Hawaiian welcome token
30 Maine's southern neighbor (abbr.)
32 Regarding flight (combined form)
35 Crush
38 See #17 Across
40 Early religious song form
41 What your bread is doing in the morning
43 Destination for Paul and Sopater (Acts 20:4)
44 Paul's home for three months until he fled the Jews who plotted against him (Acts 20:2)
45 The losers: "_____-rans"
46 Charley-horse
47 Pilfer
48 "_____ stands in the path of sinners" (Psalm 1:1)

Down

1 What Elisha caused to float
2 Procession
3 Sign
4 "The _____ Rugged Cross"
5 Symbol for iron
6 Sonny's "ex"
7 Favored filet fish
8 He found a way out of Sodom and Gomorrah
9 See #19 Across (2 words)
10 Terra cotta container (2 words)
11 "#14 Down me Your way, O LORD, and lead me in a smooth _____ " (Psalm 27:11)
12 A yellow cheese
13 Farm structure
14 See #11 Down
16 Beach
17 "And yet I _____ you a more excellent way" (1 Corinthians 12:31)
18 Extremely

19 "I am the way, the _____ , and the life" (John 14:6)
23 Science of commerce and exchange
24 See #17 Across
28 "But without faith it is impossible to _____ Him" (Hebrews 11:6)
31 Unlocks
32 Buzzer
33 Ritual
34 Droop
35 Petite
36 Tree's northern covering
37 Paul's frequent "escape route"
39 Parts of an interlocking wheel
42 An object made of mesh
45 Confidential rehab group for persons with a drinking addiction (abbr.)

THE NESTORIAN CROSS

*T*his cross design was used by Christians as early as A.D. 44. It was not called the Nestorian Cross, however, for four more centuries.

Nestorius was a monk who became presbyter at Antioch, and eventually, the Patriarch of Constantinople in A.D. 428. He became involved in a dispute between the Alexandrian and Antiochian schools of thought in what became known as the "Christological Controversy," and as a result, he was deposed at the Council of Ephesus in A.D. 431. He spent four years in Antioch, then was banished to upper Egypt, where he suffered great indignities before his death in A.D. 451.

His loyal followers, known as Nestorians, continued to preach the gospel in Persia and eventually took the message of Christ east to India and China. They carried with them this cross shape, and thus it became known as the Nestorian Cross. Historians believe it is the first cross ever taken to China, and several ancient examples of it are still found there.

Start ➜

← End

*P*ut the missing words from 1 Corinthians 13 in the acrostic grid on the next page . . . and you'll complete an important message about the theme of this chapter. (Note: The first part of the message has been provided for you.)

Though I speak with the tongues of men and of angels, but have not love, I have become sounding brass or a clanging cymbal. And though I have the gift of prophecy, and understand all mysteries and all knowledge, and though I have all faith, so that I could remove mountains, but have not love, I am nothing. And though I bestow all my goods to feed the poor, and though I give my body to be burned, but have not love, it profits me nothing.

Love _____ long and _____ _____ ; love does _____ _____ ; love does _____ _____ _____ , is
17   15   5   1
_____ _____ _____ ; does _____ _____ _____ , does _____ _____ _____ _____ , is _____ _____ ,
4   12   13   10
_____ _____ _____ ; does _____ _____ _____ _____ , but rejoices in the _____ ; _____ all
9   6   18   22
things, _____ all things, _____ all things, _____ all things.
8   16   3

Love _____ _____ . But whether there are prophecies, they will fail; whether there are tongues,
19

they will cease; whether there is knowledge, it will vanish away. For we know in part and we

prophesy in part. But when that which is _____ has come, then that which is in part will be done
20

away.

When I was a child, I spoke as a child, I understood as a child, I thought as a child; but when I

_____ _____ _____ , I put away childish things. For now we see in a mirror, dimly, but then _____
11

_____ _____ . Now I know in part, but then I shall know just _____ _____ _____ _____ _____ .
14   21

And now _____ faith, hope, love, these three; but the _____ of these is love.
2   7

128

1   _ _ _ P _ _ _ _ _ _ _ _ _

2   _ _ _ _ E

3   _ _ _ _ R _ _

4   _ _ _ _ _ F _ _ _ _

5   _ _ _ E _ _ _

6   _ _ _ _ _ _ _ C _ _ _ _ _ _ _ _ _

7   _ _ _ _ T _ _ _

8   _ _ L _ _ _ _

9   _ _ _ _ _ _ _ O _ _ _ _

10   _ _ _ _ _ _ V _ _ _ _

THERE IS NO FEAR IN LOVE, BUT . . .

11   _ _ C _ _ _ _ _ _ _

12   _ _ _ _ _ _ A _ _ _ _ _ _ _

13   _ _ _ S _ _ _ _ _ _ _ _

14   _ _ _ T _ _ _ _ _

15   _ S _ _ _ _

16   _ O _ _ _

17   _ U _ _ _ _

18   T _ _ _ _

19   _ _ _ _ F _ _ _

20   _ E _ _ _ _

21   _ _ _ A _ _ _ _ _ _ _ _

22   _ _ _ R _

King Solomon reigned over all Israel—but not without the help of officials and governors. Below is an organizational chart of Solomon's administrators as they are named in 1 Kings 4:1–19. Administrators, of course, must interact with one another in order for a kingdom to function smoothly. Your goal is to place these names (not titles) in the crossword grid . . . we've given you a few letters as a start.

KING
Solomon

OFFICIALS

Azariah
Priest

Elihoreph and Ahijah
Scribes

Jehoshaphat
Recorder

Zadok and Abiathar
Priests

Zabud
Priest and Friend

OFFICERS

Benaiah
Army

Azariah
Officers

Ahishar
Household

Adoniram
Labor Force

GOVERNORS

Ben-Hur
Mountains of Ephraim

Ben-Deker
Makaz, Shaalbim, Beth Shemesh, Elon Beth Hanan

Ben-Hesed
Arubboth

Ben-Abinadab
Dor

Baana
Taanach, Megiddo, Beth Shean

Ben-Geber
Ramoth Gilead

Ahinadab
Mahanaim

Ahimaaz
Naphtali

Baanah
Asher, Aloth

Jehoshaphat
Issachar

Shimei
Benjamin

Geber
Gilead

*D*iscover three of the most potent Bible verses for those who are under a great deal of stress!

Clue: MESSIAH *is* MSOOCIT

A E M S   X E   M S '   I D D   Q E G

Y T E   D I R E F   I V J   I F S

T S I P Q   D I J S V '   I V J   C

Y C D D   K C P S   Q E G   F S O X.

X I U S   M Q   Q E U S   G N E V   Q E G

I V J   D S I F V   B F E M   M S '   B E F

C   I M   K S V X D S   I V J   D E Y D Q

C V   T S I F X '   I V J   Q E G   Y C D D

B C V J   F S O X   B E F   Q E G F

O E G D O.   B E F   M Q   Q E U S   C O

S I O Q   I V J   M Q   R G F J S V

C O   D C K T X.

*A*ll of the words below describe a key figure in the Bible. The vowels of the words are missing, however. When you add the vowels and fit the words into the grid, the name of this famous Bible person will be revealed.

J S T N (2 words)

W N D R F L

S R V N T

R R G H T S N S S (2 words)

C N S L R

K N G F T H J W S (4 words)

C H R S T

V N

L P H N D M G (3 words)

P R N C F P C (3 words)

M N F S R R W S (3 words)

D Y S P R N G

M D T R

B R G H T N D M R N N G S T R (4 words)

S H P H R D

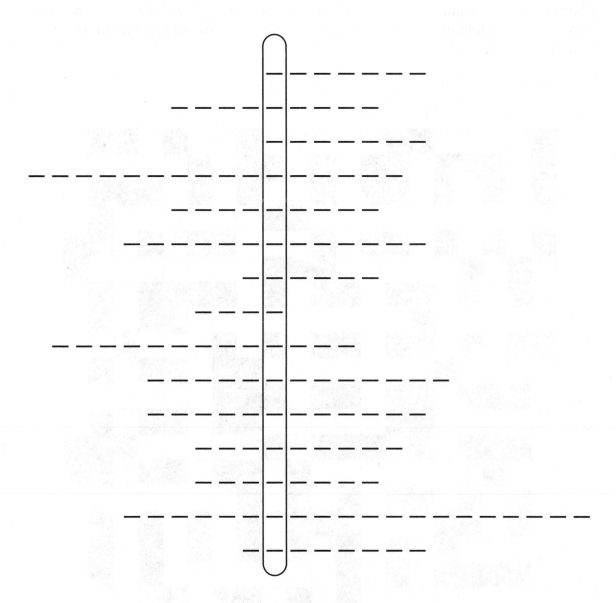

Scripture Pool

PSALM 80:1   ISAIAH 9:6; 52:13; 53:3   JEREMIAH 23:6   MATTHEW 2:2
LUKE 1:78   JOHN 15:5   ACTS 7:52   1 TIMOTHY 2:5   1 JOHN 5:1
REVELATION 22:13, 16

*T*he church is the community of Christian believers throughout all the world—and throughout all generations. Most of the clues in this crossword have to do with the church of Jesus Christ.

Across

1 "Enter by the narrow _____ " (Matthew 7:13)

2 The Greek term for *hell* (Matthew 16:18)

5 You and I

9 "The _____ , the Lamb's wife" (Revelation 21:9)

11 Extraterrestrial (abbr.)

12 "A holy _____ , to offer up spiritual sacrifices acceptable to God through Jesus Christ" (1 Peter 2:5)

13 The chief cornerstone of the church (Ephesians 2:20)

15 Before now

18 Disciples met together to "break _____ " (Acts 20:7)

20 "We are members of His body . . . This is a great _____ " (Ephesians 5:30, 32)

23 These people became members of the church (Acts 2:47)

24 Christians are members of the _____ of God (Ephesians 2:19)

26 The sick are instructed to call the leaders of the church for prayer and anointing with _____ (James 5:14)

27 Great persecution rose against the church which was "_____ Jerusalem" (Acts 8:1)

28 Stephen, one of the first deacons, was a man " _____ of faith and the Holy Spirit" (Acts 6:5)

29 Where disciples were first called Christians (Acts 11:26)

32 House of the Lord (Ephesians 2:21)

33 Husbands should love their wives as Christ _____ the church (Ephesians 5:25)

34 Paul admonished Christians to seek to "be skilled" in spiritual gifts for the edification of the church (1 Corinthians 14:12)

36 A righteous person (Ephesians 2:19)

37 " _____ this rock I will build My church" (Matthew 16:18)

38 "Individuals" who belong to the body of Christ (1 Corinthians 12:27)

44 Give praise (1 Corinthians 12:26)

47 When the church gathered together, they "reported all that _____ had done with them" (Acts 14:27)

48 The church should be " _____ and without blemish" (Ephesians 5:27)

50 "Not having spot or _____ " (Ephesians 5:27)

52 One of the offices of the church; these people had a special word from God for a particular circumstance (1 Corinthians 12:28)

53 The church met together to _____ (Acts 2:42)

Down

1 Honor and praise; the churches are the " _____ of Christ" (2 Corinthians 8:23)

3 Agreement (Acts 2:1)

4 "The _____ cannot say to the hand, 'I have no need of you'" (1 Corinthians 12:21)

5 " _____ one accord" (Acts 2:46)

6 "Where two _____ three are gathered together" (Matthew 18:20)

7 Authority (Colossians 2:19)

8 One of the apostles, his name means "Rock" (Matthew 16:18)

9 Jesus, the Cornerstone, and Christians, the living stones, are being _____ up into a spiritual house (1 Peter 2:5)

10 Allow (Colossians 3:15)

13 Early Christians "had all things in _____ " (Acts 2:44)

14 Christ is present where #49 Down or _____ meet in His name (Matthew 18:20)

16 "We are members of _____ body, of _____ flesh and of _____ bones" (Ephesians 5:30)

17 A bishop must have a good testimony "lest he fall into . . . the snare of the _____ " (1 Timothy 3:7)

18 "His _____ , which is the church" (Colossians 1:24)

19 One sent forth (1 Corinthians 12:28)

21 One who instructs (1 Corinthians 12:28)

22 "Assemble" together (Matthew 18:20)

25 Belief (Acts 2:42)

28 Koinonia, in Greek (Acts 2:42)

30 Inclined

31 "Believers were increasingly _____ to the Lord" (Acts 5:14)

35 Citizens' band (abbr.)

39 Spiritual leaders of the church (1 Timothy 5:17)

40 "Exalt Him al_____ in the assembly of the people" (Psalm 107:32)

41 "For by one _____ we were all baptized into one body" (1 Corinthians 12:13)

42 "The church of the living God, the _____ and ground of the truth" (1 Timothy 3:15)

43 "If one member suffers, _____ the members suffer with it; or if one member is honored, _____ the members rejoice with it" (1 Corinthians 12:26)

44 Petra, in Greek (Matthew 16:18)

45 This twenty-sixth book of the New Testament tells believers to "contend earnestly for the faith"

46 Build up; " _____ one another" (1 Thessalonians 5:11)

47 "Christ also loved the church and _____ Himself for her" (Ephesians 5:25)

49 See #14 Across

51 Behold (Revelation 7:9, KJV)

*P*haraoh's refusal to allow the children of Israel to return to the promised land led to great misery for the Egyptian people. Below is a list of the ten plagues that fell on the Egyptians as a result of Pharaoh's stubbornness. After unscrambling the words, unscramble the circled letters to find out why Pharaoh refused to let the Israelites go.

LODOB _ _ _ _ Ⓞ

GORFS _ Ⓞ _ _ _

CILE _ _ _ Ⓞ

LIFES _ _ _ Ⓞ _

LICENSEPET _ Ⓞ _ _ _ _ Ⓞ _ _

SOLIB _ _ _ _ _ _

LAHI Ⓞ Ⓞ _ _

CUTLOSS _ _ _ _ _ Ⓞ _

DRSNAKES _ Ⓞ Ⓞ _ _ _ _ _

HATED Ⓞ _ _ _ Ⓞ

Scrambled letters:

_ _ _ _ _ _ _ _ _ _ _ _ _ _

Unscrambled letters:

_ _ _ _ _ _ _   _ _ _ _ _

Scripture Pool
EXODUS 7:17; 8:2, 16, 21; 9:3, 9, 18; 10:4, 21; 11:5

Work the clues about the building of Solomon's temple to find the number of years it took to complete the temple. The answers are found in the book of 1 Kings in the chapter and verse at the end of each clue.

The number of Israelites in the labor force (5:13) $=$ _____

Multiplied by . . .
The part of the wall that was the door
of the sanctuary (6:33) $\times$ _____

Divided by . . .
The number of years after the children of Israel
left Egypt before Solomon began building the
temple (6:1) $\div$ _____

Multiplied by . . .
The year of Solomon's reign when work on
the temple began (6:1) $\times$ _____

Multiplied by . . .
The length of the temple in cubits (6:2) $\times$ _____

Divided by . . .
The number of rows of hewn stone in the
inner court (6:36) $\div$ _____

Multiplied by . . .
The width in cubits of the inner sanctuary (6:20) $\times$ _____

Minus . . .
The number of construction supervisors (5:16) $-$ _____

Divided by . . .
The width of the temple in cubits (6:2) $\div$ _____

Multiplied by . . .
The number of cherubim in the inner sanctuary (6:23) $\times$ _____

Minus . . .
The number of baths in the Sea (7:26) $-$ _____

Plus . . .
The number of years that Solomon reigned
as king (11:42) $+$ _____

Divided by . . .
The height in cubits of the temple (6:2) $\div$ _____

Equals . . .
The number of years it took to build the temple (6:38) $=$ _____

135

*F*ools have a lot to learn.

Across

1 God chose foolish things to shame the _____ (1 Corinthians 1:27)

4 Did the Corinthians think him a fool? (2 Corinthians 11:16)

6 A foolish woman is "loud" (Proverbs 9:13)

9 A foolish son is the "downfall" of his father (Proverbs 19:13)

11 Sixteenth U.S. President, for short

13 God knew this psalmist's foolishness (Psalm 69:5)

14 The "seer" is a fool, said Hosea, because of Israel's great sin (Hosea 9:7)

15 Foolish "desires" (1 Timothy 6:9)

18 Doing "wickedness" is sport to a fool (Proverbs 10:23)

19 A fool's "speaking tool" is near destruction (Proverbs 10:14)

21 God told Zechariah: Take the implements of a foolish "lamb leader" (Zechariah 11:15)

24 A foolish man "wastes" treasure (Proverbs 21:20)

28 Foolish for them to risk Eden's loss (3 words)

29 Saying, "You fool," brings danger of this fire (Matthew 5:22)

30 Shame is the "inheritance" of fools (Proverbs 3:35)

33 Storing up crops didn't save the rich man's _____ (Luke 12:20)

34 Doing this silences the ignorance of foolish men (1 Peter 2:15)

35 Would *you* build a house on this? (Matthew 7:26)

Down

2 Devising foolishness is "impiety" (Proverbs 24:9)

3 His wife spoke like a foolish woman (Job 2:10)

4 Postscript (abbr.)

5 Wisdom is too "high" for a fool (Proverbs 24:7)

7 This writer sought to know the wickedness of foolishness and "lunacy" (Ecclesiastes 7:25)

8 Don't make me the "disgrace" of the foolish, David said (Psalm 39:8)

10 God was angered by foolish "graven images" (Deuteronomy 32:21)

12 Foolish "purists" left inward parts dirty (Luke 11:39–40)

13 Avoid foolish "arguments" (2 Timothy 2:23)

16 Foolish Jacob and Judah, with eyes that couldn't _____ (Jeremiah 5:20–21)

17 A foolish man "hates" his mother (Proverbs 15:20)

20 Spreading "defamation" makes one a fool (Proverbs 10:18)

22 Foolishness "dirties" a man (Mark 7:20–23)

23 Men's foolish _____ were darkened (though still beating) (Romans 1:21)

25 Any fool can start a "fight" (Proverbs 20:3)

26 He's the biggest fool of all

27 This king played the fool with David (1 Samuel 26:21)

31 The fool doesn't believe in Him (Psalm 14:1)

32 No's antonym

There are twelve people named in this puzzle who are related in some way to Aaron, Israel's first high priest. Find the names of Aaron's great-grandfather, grandfather, father, mother, brother, sister, wife, sons, and grandson.

```
E  L  E  A  Z  P  H  I  M  A  R  M  A  K  O  L
R  O  M  I  R  I  A  M  A  M  R  J  O  C  R  E
D  O  J  R  A  H  I  H  M  A  I  A  M  V  A  V
E  K  O  H  A  V  T  O  R  T  B  B  I  E  M  O
B  O  C  A  E  M  S  A  A  E  Z  I  R  L  A  S
E  B  H  L  P  E  H  A  H  A  P  H  I  N  H  A
H  H  A  M  S  O  R  S  D  O  A  U  A  A  T  M
C  S  B  D  I  M  I  A  H  O  K  E  N  B  I  H
O  I  E  A  A  L  N  S  O  M  O  S  E  I  D  I
J  L  D  H  E  N  V  E  L  E  B  E  H  C  O  J
B  E  A  T  S  R  A  Z  A  E  L  E  L  H  A  R
O  P  H  I  N  E  H  A  S  R  I  M  E  U  N  I
M  I  R  I  A  D  A  N  B  E  H  S  I  L  E  A
```

Scripture Pool
EXODUS 6:16, 18, 20, 23, 25 (KJV); 7:1; 15:20

TO TOUCH JESUS

*O*ne can imagine the crowds of people that followed and surrounded Jesus as He taught and healed those who came to Him. A person probably had to be rather able-bodied to even get close to Him. But a woman who had been ill for twelve years would have to be even more determined.

Apparently having given up any hope of encountering Jesus face to face, this sick but unwavering woman believed that if she could just touch the hem of His garment, she would be healed. So that is what she decided to do. But getting to Jesus was not easy. She maybe even had to crawl along the ground around and between the feet of those standing between her and her Master. Her faith and persistence were rewarded when she touched Jesus' garment. Jesus turned to her and said, "Daughter, be of good cheer; your faith has made you well." (See Luke 8:43-48.)

Unable to fight the crowd, a certain woman crawled along the ground to touch the hem of Jesus' garment. Find the path to Jesus without stepping on any feet.

*W*e are told to fear God—to respect and acknowledge who He is. But we really don't have to be afraid.

Across

1 Fearing Jezebel, he ran (1 Kings 19:1–3)

6 "Only fear the LORD, and serve Him in 'honesty'" (1 Samuel 12:24)

8 Fearing the approaching Moabites and Ammonites, this king of Judah proclaimed a fast (2 Chronicles 20:1–3)

9 "The fear of the LORD is a fountain of 'being'" (Proverbs 14:27)

11 Fear not, Jacob; God pours _____ on the thirsty (Isaiah 44:2–3)

13 God said not to fear the gods of these "mountain dwellers" (Judges 6:10)

15 Joshua wasn't to fear this royal city of Canaan (Joshua 8:1)

16 Peter feared the "rambunctious" wind (Matthew 14:29–30)

17 "Reprimand" sinners publicly, that others may also fear (1 Timothy 5:20)

19 Walking in the fear of the Lord, the churches "increased" (Acts 9:31)

21 _____ Shaddai

24 Jacob feared an encounter with him (Genesis 32:11)

25 Even these obeyed Him, though the Twelve feared them (3 words) (Mark 4:40–41)

29 The angel told Paul not to fear, that he must appear before this emperor (Acts 27:24)

30 God parted the Red Sea so the Israelites would fear God "through eternity" (Joshua 4:23–24)

31 The blind man's parents feared being put out of this place (John 9:22)

32 When Benjamin's mother was in hard labor, the midwife told her not to fear (Genesis 35:16–17)

Down

2 Wonder, reverence (Psalm 119:161)

3 "He will fulfill the 'longing' [pl.] of those who fear Him" (Psalm 145:19)

4 Did the people not fear God because He held His _____ ? (Isaiah 57:11)

5 Fear is due the King of the "republics" (Jeremiah 10:7)

6 A man who fears God isn't afraid of evil "news" (sing.) (Psalm 112:7)

7 They were afraid of the notorious Saul when he tried to join them (Acts 9:26)

8 Shutting the doors for fear of these people, the disciples met and had a surprise visit from Jesus (John 20:19)

10 The scribes and chief priests feared Jesus because His "instruction" amazed the people (Mark 11:18)

12 "Let not your heart be _____ " (John 14:27)

14 "The fear of the LORD is the beginning of _____ " (Proverbs 9:10)

18 Another word for #14 Down, from Proverbs 1:7

20 David was afraid to move the ark after God struck down this man (2 Samuel 6:6–10)

22 Don't be afraid, said Jesus; "I am the First and the _____ " (Revelation 1:17)

23 Those who feared death were subject to "enslavement" (Hebrews 2:15)

24 Fear of the Lord is to hate "wickedness" (Proverbs 8:13)

26 Fear of being killed made Abraham claim she was only his sister (Genesis 20:2, 11)

27 "So great is His _____ toward those who fear Him" (Psalm 103:11)

28 "Fear God. Honor the _____ ." (1 Peter 2:17)

30 The subject of this puzzle

139

Unscramble the names of these Bible people, and then unscramble the circled letters to reveal what they had in common. (See how many you can unscramble before consulting the Scripture Pool.)

B O A C J   _ Ⓞ _ _ _

O N H A   _ _ _ _

B R A A M A H   Ⓞ _ _ _ _ _ _

S E M O S   _ _ _ _ _

J I L H E A   _ Ⓞ _ _ _ _

children of
E B R U N E / D G A   Ⓞ _ _ _ _ _ / _ _ _ (2 words)

V E L T I S E   _ _ _ _ Ⓞ _ _

Unscrambled letters:

_ _ _ _ _

Scripture Pool
GENESIS 8:20   GENESIS 22:9   GENESIS 33:18, 20   GENESIS 35:6–7
EXODUS 17:15   JOSHUA 22:34   1 KINGS 18:30–32   EZEKIEL 43:19–20

*D*ecipher the message below to see what the Lord had to say in relation to the object of puzzle #50!

Clue: MESSIAH *is* GCJJEAQ

E T   C X C V M   U S A B C

L Q C V C   E   V C B H V O

G M   T A G C E

L E S S   B H G C   W H

M H K ' A T O E   L E S S

N S C J J   M H K.

C Y H O K J   20:24

*T*he apostle Peter was not a man without problems!

Across

3 Where Peter found money (Matthew 17:27)

5 Rose of _____ (Song of Solomon 2:1)

7 "It is hard for a _____ man to enter the kindgom of heaven" (Matthew 19:23)

8 Nickname for a physician

9 Peter's other name (Matthew 10:2)

11 _____ California; Mexican peninsula

13 Christ built this "on this rock" (Matthew 16:18)

15 Preposition

16 Either's partner

17 A direction for the wind to blow (abbr.)

18 Where Herod put Peter (Acts 12:5)

21 Peter's liberator (Acts 12:7)

23 Sweet potato

25 Number of times Peter denied Christ (Luke 22:61)

26 "Come unto _____ "

27 " _____ who believes and is baptized will be saved" (Mark 16:16)

29 Loaves and fishes containers (Matthew 14:20)

30 Occupation of Peter's Joppa host (Acts 9:43)

33 "In the beginning was the ____" (John 1:1)

34 "Behold, I stand at the ____ and knock" (Revelation 3:20)

36 Spirit of a person

38 When Peter escaped from prison, she got so excited that she forgot to answer the door (Acts 12:13)

39 Number of times the cock crowed (Mark 14:72)

42 Maryland neighbor (abbr.)

43 Stay

45 "And by His ____ we are healed" (Isaiah 53:5)

48 Easter exultation: "He is ____!"

49 John 7:24: "Do not judge according to ____, "

52 Hospital's life-sustaining tube (abbr.)

53 Manhattan's home state (abbr.)

54 Twelve hours past midnight

55 Tidings

56 Gratuity, lead, or topmost part

57 He crowed twice (Mark 14:72)

Down

1 Wealthy

2 Here and ____

3 Peter's occupation (John 21:3)

4 Some of the animals in Peter's vision had this kind of foot

5 Multiplied by itself

6 Close by

7 "And on this ____ I will build My church" (Matthew 16:18)

10 What Peter found in the mouth of the fish (Matthew 17:27)

12 What an Old Testament fish found in his mouth!

14 What Peter called the animals in his vision (Acts 10:14)

19 Animal-holder in Peter's vision (Acts 10:11)

20 "____ one of the least of these" (Matthew 25:40, KJV)

22 Christ, the ____ of God (John 1:29)

24 Size up

27 He put Peter in prison (Acts 12:1–4)

28 "Many are called, but ____ are chosen" (Matthew 20:16)

30 "One" follower

31 Tuber

32 One of Peter's fellow sleepers at Gethsemane (Mark 14:33)

34 Creed

35 Desert garden

36 Occupation of Peter's accuser (Mark 14:69)

37 Yeast

40 Victor

41 Popular crunchy cheese snack (sing.)

42 Jesus predicted Peter would do this to Him (Mark 14:72)

44 Location of Dan's tribe in relationship to the tabernacle (Numbers 2:25)

46 Body of flowing water

47 Pig places

50 Hawaiian root-paste dish

51 Nickname for Dad

LITTLE CHILDREN

Matthew 19:13–15 gives us an account of Jesus' relationship to children. One can imagine that a young mother must have ventured forth with a small child to seek Jesus' blessing . . . and then perhaps another and another until Jesus was surrounded by the little ones. His disciples, seeking to protect Him from the "annoyance" of so many children, rebuked them and shooed them away. But Jesus said, "Let the little children come to Me, and do not forbid them; for of such is the kingdom of heaven" (v.14).

Gather all the children and take them to Jesus. Travel each path only once, and do not cross over your own path.

Hearing with the Heart

*M*atthew 13:10–17 gives us an indication of the importance Christ placed on *hearing* the Word of God. In this passage, Jesus' disciples ask why He speaks to the people in parables. He responds that the people have heard the Scriptures but do not understand them. He speaks to them in a way that they both hear and understand *in their hearts*. Hearing the Word is important for convincing the heart of truth.

Start at the top left corner and go to the heart at the bottom of the page. To get there, cross through words only having to do with sounds, hearing, or messages. Do not cross through corners. Move only to a word that shares a line with the current word.

(puzzle grid of words)

*M*any of the clues for this puzzle relate to the third personage of the Trinity.

Across

1 Two regions where "you shall be witnesses to Me" (use *and* between) (Acts 1:8)

11 Angel's hat

12 What the Holy Spirit gives (Acts 1:8)

14 Another name: Holy ____

18 Author Eliot's first two initials

19 What sat upon the Upper Room occupants (3 words) (Acts 2:3)

24 Get up

25 Entice

26 Govern

27 Comes before "dos"

28 Speechless

30 Not false

31 Bride and groom's word

33 Initials of the light-bulb man

34 Had dinner

35 Hear-piece

36 Holy Spirit came to Jesus in this form (Luke 3:22)

37 John the Baptist baptized Him (Luke 3:21)

40 Name for a Norseman

42 Salem, Eugene, and Portland state (abbr.)

43 Bean's cousin

47 Place for pigs

48 Soft, light metal

49 "For God so ____ the world" (John 3:16)

51 Him's counterpart

52 What the Holy Spirit makes us (Acts 1:8)

54 Bond

57 Name of a false god; an Olympian

59 Attorney's professional group

60 Day of Pentecost preacher (Acts 2:14)

61 He will also be the reaper (2 Corinthians 9:6)

Down

2 Sound of pleasure

3 Chart

4 Paraclete: One who comes ____ to help

5 Continuous succession

6 Free-floating gas

7 Old's opposite

8 Earthenware container of liquid

9 Pair (slang)

10 Biblical location of day of Pentecost account (2 words)

13 Twilight time of day

15 Rabbit

16 Frequent designation for early Christians (sing., abbr.) (Romans 1:7)

17 Another name for the Holy Spirit (John 14:26, KJV)

20 Circles result if both aren't in the water

21 What the Spirit produces in Christians (Galatians 5:22)

22 "But be ____ with the Spirit" (Ephesians 5:18)

23 "I once was blind, but now ____ ____ " (2 words) "Amazing Grace"

27 "As the Spirit gave them ____" (Acts 2:4)

29 Main part of the church sanctuary

32 Horse's favorite type of bran

37 Peter quoted this prophet in his sermon (Acts 2:16)

38 They were awaiting the Holy Spirit in the ____ Room (Acts 1:13)

39 Plant starter

41 "Suddenly there ____ a sound from heaven" (Acts 2:2)

44 Article

45 John did this with water (present tense) (John 1:31)

46 Upper arm bone

50 Bible division

52 Put on

53 A special one appeared in the East

55 Opposite of down

56 Extraterrestrial of movie fame

58 "____ send I you" (John 20:21, KJV)

59 "To ____ or not to ____" (Shakespeare)

Connect the letters below into a word string to reveal one of Jesus' harshest sayings in the entire New Testament. See how many letters you can connect before consulting the reference at the base of the chalice, or "cup."

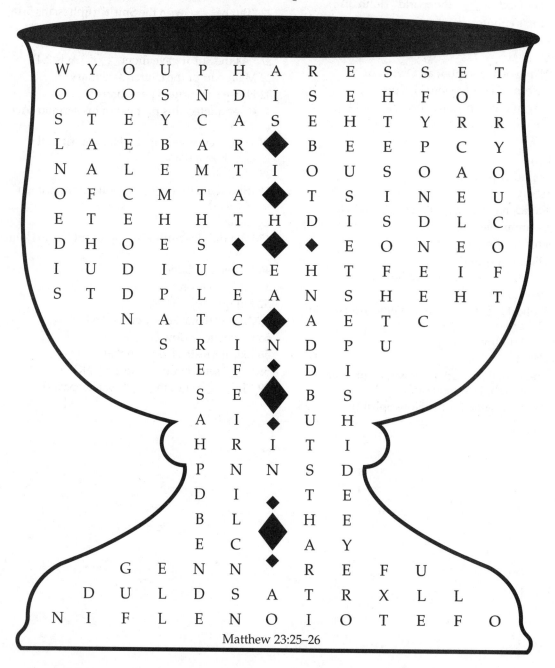

```
W  Y  O  U  P     H     A  R     E     S     S     E     T
O  O  O  S  N  D  I  S  E  H  F  O  I
S  T  E  Y  C  A  S  E  H  T  Y  R  I
L  A  E  B  A  R  ◆  B  E  E  P  C  R
N  A  L  E  M  T  I  O  U  S  O  A  Y
O  F  C  M  T  A  ◆  T  S  I  N  E  O
E  T  E  H  H  T  H  D  I  S  D  L  U
D  H  O  E  S  ◆  ◆  ◆  E  O  N  E  C
I  U  D  I  U  C  E  H  T  F  E  I  O
S  T  D  P  L  E  A  N  S  H  E  H  F
      N  A  T  C  ◆  A  E  T  C     T
      S  R  I  N  D  P  U
      E  F  ◆  D  I
      S  E  ◆  B  S
      A  I  ◆  U  H
      H  R  I  T  I
      P  N  N  S  D
      D  I  ◆  T  E
      B  L  ◆  H  E
      E  C  ◆  A  Y
   G  E  N  N  ◆  R  E  F  U
   D  U  L  D  S  A  T  R  X  L  L
N  I  F  L  E  N  O  I  O  T  E  F  O
```

Matthew 23:25–26

Good instructions for Christian living.

Clue: MESSIAH *is* COMMAND

P O Y U A W O   N B X N S M '

Z P N S   X A E D U L E

W O N M A H I '   A H

O G O P S E D A H I   I A G O

E D N H F M ;   Q U P   E D A M

A M   E D O   X A B B   U Q

I U R   A H   W D P A M E

Y O M L M   Q U P   S U L .

THE FIFTH DAY

*T*he maze depicts some of the things that God created on the fifth day. God's creation of the universe was a very orderly process. First He created the environment that the living creatures needed in order to survive and multiply. Then He created the creatures themselves.

On the fifth day the Lord made the creatures of the sky and the sea. The animals in this maze are an angelfish, whale, seahorse, bird, chick, frog, snail, starfish, and dove.

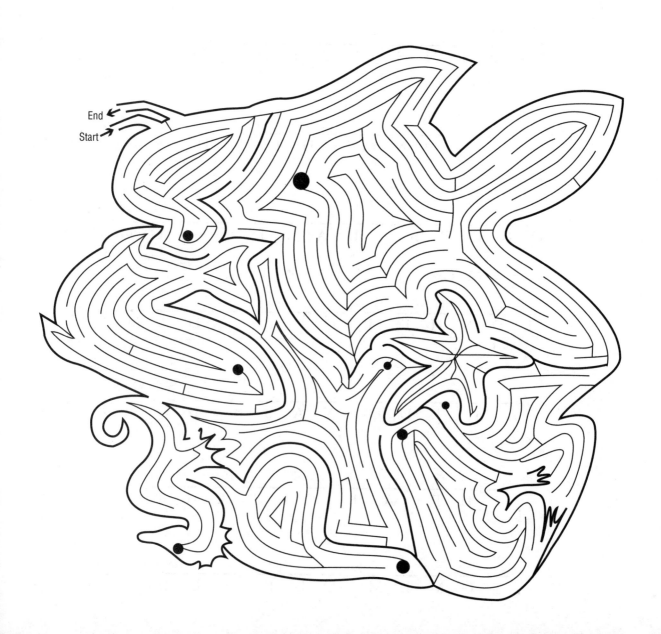

Revelation is a book in which numbers abound—frequently as symbols. Using the numbers indicated by the clues, work the equation to come up with the "perfect" answer. All the numbers are found in the book of Revelation. You may need your calculator for this one!

Number of Jews receiving the seal of the living God
(Revelation 7:4)   =   _____

Divided by . . .
Number equal to ten percent of the army of the horsemen
(Revelation 9:16)   ÷   _____

Multiplied by . . .
Number of men killed in the earthquake after the
murdered prophets ascended (Revelation 11:13)   ×   _____

Minus . . .
Number of living creatures (full of eyes) surrounding the
throne (Revelation 4:6)   —   _____

Divided by . . .
Number of edges on the sword coming from the Son of
man's mouth (Revelation 1:16)   ÷   _____

Multiplied by . . .
Number of months locusts were allowed to sting
(Revelation 9:5)   ×   _____

Plus . . .
Number of thrones around God's throne (Revelation 4:4)   +   _____

Divided by . . .
Number of lampstands (Revelation 2:1)   ÷   _____

Plus . . .
Number of pearls used for each gate in the New Jerusalem
(Revelation 21:21)   +   _____

Divided by . . .
Number of gates on each wall of New Jerusalem
(Revelation 21:13)   ÷   _____

Number of churches that received the Revelation from
John (Revelation 1:4)   =   _____

Not all the authors of the Bible are known for sure, but the ones that are known come from a wide variety of walks of life. They include a fisherman, poet, musician, prophet, priest, and king. Using your Bible and Bible concordance, find the answers to the clues in this crossword and fill in the grid.

Word Pool

AGUR AMOS ASAPH DANIEL DAVID ETHAN EZEKIEL EZRA HABAKKUK HAGGAI HEMAN HOSEA ISAIAH JAMES JEREMIAH JOEL JOHN JONAH JUDE SONS OF <u>KORAH</u> LEMUEL LUKE MALACHI MARK MATTHEW MICAH MOSES NAHUM NEHEMIAH OBADIAH PAUL PETER SOLOMON ZECHARIAH ZEPHANIAH

Across

2 He went naked to carry his prophetic message; a prophet from the town of Moresheth

4 A prophet of royal descent, he was the great-great-grandson of King Hezekiah

7 Priest, scribe, expert in the words of the commandments of the Lord

8 Son of Pethuel, author of one of the books of the minor prophets

9 Patriarch of the Exodus

10 Musician, shepherd, warrior, and king

11 A prophet, he wrote about the destruction coming to Edom

13 Tax collector and disciple

15 Physician and disciple

18 Contributor to the book of Proverbs

19 Son of Hilkiah, he was a prophet from Anathoth

20 Herdsman from Tekoa

23 Son of Berechiah and grandson of Iddo, he wrote a book of the minor prophets

26 Called "the Ezrahite," he wrote a psalm (1 Chronicles 15:19)

27 His name is mentioned only once in Scripture as the author of the last book in the Old Testament

28 This Ezrahite wrote a favorite psalm—"I will sing of the mercies of the LORD forever"

29 A prophet from Judah, the theme of his book is "the just shall live by his faith"

30 As a captive in Babylon, he was called Belteshazzar

Down

1 The brother of the Lord wrote this book as a letter to the "twelve tribes which are scattered abroad"

3 A priest in charge of the singers, he wrote several psalms (1 Chronicles 15:19)

5 Tentmaker and apostle to the Gentiles

6 Son of Beeri, faithful husband to Gomer, and father of Jezreel, Lo-Ruhamah, and Lo-Ammi

7 A priest, the son of Buzi

8 "Bondservant of Jesus Christ, and brother of James," he wrote a warning about false teachers

12 Fisherman and disciple

13 A Gospel writer, disciple, and missionary traveler with Paul and Barnabas

14 This son of Amoz wrote a book that bears his name; it records a vision from the Lord concerning Judah and Jerusalem

16 A music guild of singers and composers credited with writing ten psalms

17 An Elkoshite, this prophet foretold the fall of the city of Nineveh

19 The beloved disciple

21 Wise king

22 Cupbearer to Artaxerxes I

24 A king who contributed to the book of Proverbs

25 Son of Amittal, a prophet who was from Gath Hepher

26 Author of a book of the minor prophets, he prophesied of Joshua to Zerubbabel

God's encouraging word to Joshua is still a good word of encouragement to us today.

Clue: MESSIAH *is* CRIISTO

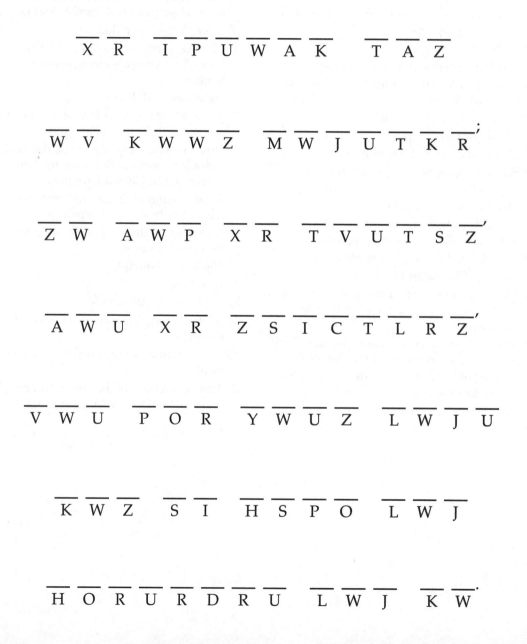

X R   I P U W A K   T A Z

W V   K W W Z   M W J U T K R ;

Z W   A W P   X R   T V U T S Z ,

A W U   X R   Z S I C T L R Z ,

V W U   P O R   Y W U Z   L W J U

K W Z   S I   H S P O   L W J

H O R U R D R U   L W J   K W .

THE OPEN WORD

*T*he Bible is the most widely read book in the world. It continues to appear on the list of best-selling books every year. Yet owning a Bible does not assure its owner of a relationship with God.

The book of John says, "In the beginning was the Word, and the Word was with God, and the Word was God. . . .And the Word became flesh and dwelt among us, and we beheld His glory, the glory as of the only begotten of the Father, full of grace and truth" (v. 1, 14).

The Word of God is not just a beautiful piece of literature or an historical account of our spiritual roots, it is literally the Word of God to us and our path to Him through Jesus Christ His Son.

Start at "In the beginning" and finish at "Amen."

*U*nscramble the words below, all of which have something in common.

TIHEW   __ __ __ ◯ __   (Revelation 6:2)

LABKC   __ __ ▢ __ __   (Revelation 6:5)

ERGNE   ▢ __ __ __ ◇   (Psalm 23:2)

RICOMSN   __ __ ◯ __ ◇ __ __   (Isaiah 1:18)

PULERP   __ ◯ __ __ __ __   (Judges 8:26)

LEBU   __ __ __ ◇   (Exodus 28:31)

ELAP   __ __ ▢ __   (Revelation 6:8)

ERD   __ ▢ __   (Revelation 6:4)

LERACST   ◇ ◯ __ __ __ __ ◇   (Nahum 2:3)

NOLGDE   __ ◇ __ __ __ __   (Exodus 28:34)

LEOYWL   __ ▢ __ __ __ __   (Leviticus 13:30)

OBRNW   __ __ __ __ ◯   (Genesis 30:32)

YGAR   __ __ __ __   (Deuteronomy 32:25)

Unscramble the marked letters above to reveal
three items the Bible describes as being of "many":

The CIRCLED letters   __ __ __ __ __   (Genesis 37:3)

The DIAMOND letters   __ __ __ __ __ __   (1 Chronicles 29:2)

The SQUARE letters   __ __ __ __ __   (Ezekiel 17:3)

"*H*e counts the number of the stars; He calls them all by name. Great is our Lord, and mighty in power; His understanding is infinite" (Psalm 147:4–5).

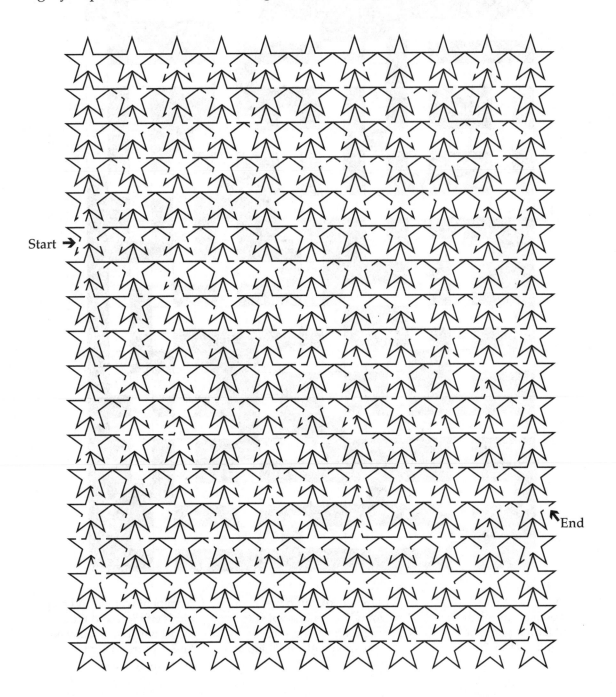

Start →

End

*P*eople and places of the early church form the words of this crossword grid. All of the references are from Acts.

Across

1 Lycaonian city where Paul and Barnabas "made many disciples" (14:6, 20–21)

2 Place where Philip was "found" when the Spirit caught him away after his discussion with an Ethiopian eunuch (8:39–40)

4 Prominent women and men in this city received the gospel when they searched the Scriptures daily with Paul and Silas (17:10–12)

9 Paul taught daily for two years in the one established by Tyrannus in Ephesus (19:9–10)

11 Paul preached to the people of this city while standing in the midst of the Aeropagus (17:22)

12 Place where disciples were first called Christians (11:26)

14 Region of a second "Antioch"; Paul and Barnabas shook the dust of this city from their feet when the people refused to accept the gospel (13:13–52)

15 Both Jewish and Greek communities were split over the gospel in this city; both Jews and Greeks attempted to abuse Paul and Barnabas (14:1–5)

18 Woman from Thyatira who opened her me to Paul in Philippi (16:11–15)

19 This city's rulers called Paul and Silas those "who have turned the world upside down" (17:1–9)

22 Apollos vigorously debated the Jews there and "greatly helped those who had believed" (18:24–28)

25 Philip's home city, where he lived with his four daughters who prophesied (21:8–9)

28 Crete or Malta, for example

29 Many in this city believed in the Lord after Peter raised Tabitha from the dead (9:36–42)

30 Paul met with James and the elders of this city about conformity by Gentiles to Jewish customs (21)

31 A slave, she was delivered by Paul from a spirit of divination (16:16–18)

32 The ruler of the synagogue in Corinth who became a believer (18:8)

35 Many were healed, including Publius's father, during Paul's shipwreck stay on this island (28:1–10)

37 Wife of Aquila, she worked with Paul and helped train Apollos (18:1–3, 26)

39 The people here turned to the Lord after seeing the healing of a paralyzed man (9:35)

40 Person Paul saw in a vision saying, "Come over to Macedonia and help us" (16:9)

42 Prophet from Judea who took Paul's belt and bound his hands and feet, prophesying Paul's arrest in Jerusalem (21:10–11)

43 A Greek believer in Athens called "the Areopagite" (17:34)

45 He fell from a third-story window while Paul was preaching and was restored to life (20:9–12)

46 Region in which Paul traveled, "strengthening all he disciples" (18:23)

Down

1 While on the road to persecute believers in this city, Saul heard the voice of the Lord in a blinding light (9:1–9)

3 The first place Paul, Barnabas, and John Mark preached the gospel in Jewish synagogues after being sent out from the Antiochian church (13:5)

5 The Lord "worked unusual miracles by the hands of Paul" in this city, even using Paul's handkerchiefs and aprons to heal the sick (19:11–12)

6 Believers met in her house in Jerusalem to pray for Peter's release from prison (12:12)

7 The rulers of this city asked Paul and Silas to leave after imprisoning them and then discovering they were Roman citizens (16:35–39)

8 A devout centurion in the Italian regiment, his conversion opened the gospel to the Gentile world in a dramatic way (10)

10 The Lord spoke to Paul in the night about this city and said, "Do not be afraid, but speak, and do not keep silent; for I am with you, and no one will attack you to hurt you; for I have many people in this city" (18:9–10)

13 Charitable woman also known as Tabitha, whom Peter raised from the dead (9:36–41)

16 Girl who forgot to open the gate for Peter in her excitement at hearing his voice (12:13–16)

17 Place where Paul was stoned and left for dead until "the disciples gathered around him" (14:19–20)

20 Disciple in Damascus who laid hands on Saul, praying his sight would be restored and he would be filled with the Holy Spirit (9:10–18)

21 After Paul cast out evil spirits in the name of Jesus, this Jewish priest's seven sons attempted to cast out a demon in the name of Jesus, but they were wounded and had to flee (19:14–20)

23 "Lame" man; his healing in Lystra nearly caused a riot (14:6–18)

24 Paul stayed seven days with believers there en route to Jerusalem; they warned Paul "through the Spirit" not to go (21:3–6)

26 Paul spent two years in this city, preaching and teaching those who came to his "rented house" (28:30–31)

27 A fellow tentmaker, Paul stayed and worked with him while he was in Corinth (18:1–3)

30 Believer with whom Paul and Silas stayed in Thessalonica (17:5–9)

32 Paul perceived his vision of a Macedonian man as this from the Lord (16:10)

33 A tanner in Joppa, he opened his home to Peter (10:6)

34 Athenian woman who believed the gospel after hearing Paul preach of the resurrection (17:31–34)

36 Paul preached there for seven days, and on the final day, preached to and talked with the disciples all night (20:6–11)

38 Believer from Berea who accompanied Paul on his journey to Asia (20:4)

41 Tychicus and Trophimus, who worked closely with Paul, were believers from this region (20:4)

44 Abbreviated name of a disciple in Lystra who became a "true son in the faith" to Paul (16:1; 1 Timothy 1:2)

The Embattled Cross

*T*his variation of the Greek cross (in which all four arms of the cross are equal in length) suggests the battlements of a fortress. It is an emblem of the Church Militant, a church ardently engaged in the defeat of the devil and his minions.

When used as part of liturgical vestments, the cross is worked in purple, indicating triumph through difficult times of battle.

The cross reminds us of Jesus' words to Peter: "On this rock I will build My church, and the gates of Hades shall not prevail against it" (Matthew 16:18).

Start

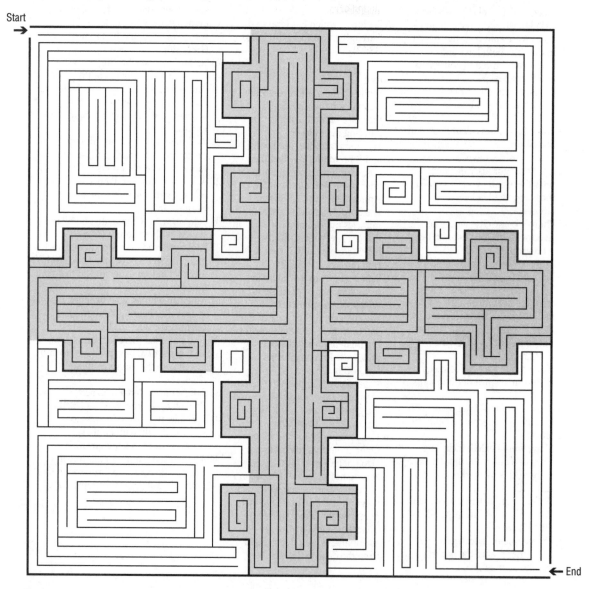

← End

*J*esus used these words to comfort His disciples.

Clue: MESSIAH *is* AYZZXNF

W Y U P K U I K R G

F Y N G U D Y

U G K R D W Y S ; I K R

D Y W X Y H Y

X P M K S ' D Y W X Y H Y

N W Z K X P A Y .

Can you hear the lion's roar?

Across

1 A young lion

3 When you make the Lord our refuge, "you shall ____ upon the lion and the cobra" (Psalm 91:13)

6 God replied to Jeremiah, "My ____ is to Me like a lion . . . it cries out against Me" (Jeremiah 12:8)

9 Prophet saved from a den of lions

10 "Blessed is he who ____ Gad; He dwells as a lion" (Deuteronomy 33:20)

14 The valiant are said to have the ____ of a lion (2 Samuel 17:10)

16 Lion's "crown"

17 Weapon of shepherd for fending off wild beasts

18 The Lord says of transgressors, "Your sword has ____ your prophets like a destroying lion" (Jeremiah 2:30)

19 "Judah is a lion's ____" (Genesis 49:9)

21 Hezekiah said of the Lord, "Like a lion, so He breaks all my ____" (Isaiah 38:13)

23 Sound a lion makes

24 The psalmist prayed for deliverance from persecutors "lest they ____ me like a lion" (Psalm 7:2)

25 "A swarm of bees and ____ were in the carcass of the lion" (Judge 14:8)

26 The psalmist prayed for deliverance from the lion's mouth and the ____ of wild oxen (Psalm 22:21)

28 The way a lion waits in his den (Psalm 10:9)

31 The one who enlarges ____ "dwells as a lion" (Deuteronomy 33:20)

33 A nearby lion's roar might make this seem to tremble

34 "The ____ man saith, 'There is a lion without, I shall be slain in the streets'" (Proverbs 22:13, KJV)

36 The king's ____ is described as being like the "roaring of a lion" (Proverbs 19:12)

38 Job said to God, "You hunt me like a ____ lion" (Job 10:16)

40 "Will a lion roar in the forest, when he has no ____?" (Amos 3:4)

42 Paul was delivered out of the ____ of the lion (2 Timothy 4:17)

43 "The lion has come up from his ____," says Jeremiah 4:7

Down

2 He killed a lion in a pit on a snowy day (2 Samuel 23:20)

3 Joel described the enemy as having the "____ of a lion" (Joel 1:6)

4 Peter wrote, "Your ____ the devil walks bout like a roaring lion" (1 Peter 5:8)

5 Lion's home

7 "The ____ are bold as a lion" (Proverbs 28:1)

8 Daniel saw four great beasts: the first was like a lion that had the wings of an ____ (Daniel 7:4)

9 "A living dog is better than a ____ lion" (Ecclesiastes 9:4)

11 The devil "walks ____ like a roaring lion, seeking whom he may devour" (1 Peter 5:8)

12 The Lord regarded His heritage as a "lion in the ____" (Jeremiah 12:8)

13 The remnant of this tribe is described as a lion among the Gentiles (Micah 5:8)

15 David slew a lion and a ____ before acing Goliath

20 Female lion

22 He posed a riddle about a lion (Judges 14:12–14, 18)

27 "The king's wrath is like the ____ of a lion" (Proverbs 19:12)

29 It housed a swarm of bees and honey (Judges 14:8)

30 Jesus was described as the ____ of the tribe of Judah

32 Paul said, "I was ____ out of the mouth of the lion" (2 Timothy 4:17)

35 Joel described the enemy as having the "fangs of a ____ lion" (Joel 1:6)

37 The lion is called "____ among beasts" in Proverbs 30:30

39 "The young lion and the ____ you shall trample underfoot" (Psalm 91:13)

41 A lion's search for food

Flight Across the City

"*T*hen all the disciples forsook Him and fled" (Matthew 26:56).

Jesus had been betrayed by Judas Iscariot. Equally painful for Him must have been the desertion by Peter, James, and John, the three disciples who were with Him that night in the Garden of Gethsemane. But He understood their confusion and fear, and knew they were running from the situation—not from Him. They had much to learn about the cost of discipleship.

Future events proved that Jesus' faith in them was not misplaced.

Peter, James, and John must cross the city without entering the sections where the chief priests and Pharisees wait.

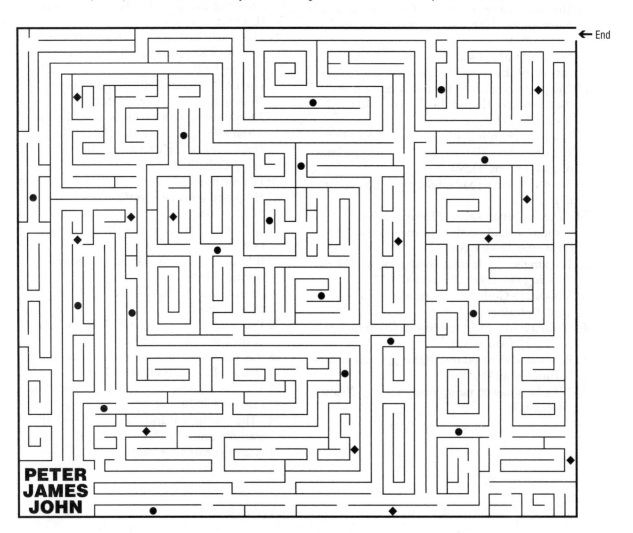

Confidence and assurance characterize the Christian faith.

Clue: MESSIAH *is* NRXXTEL

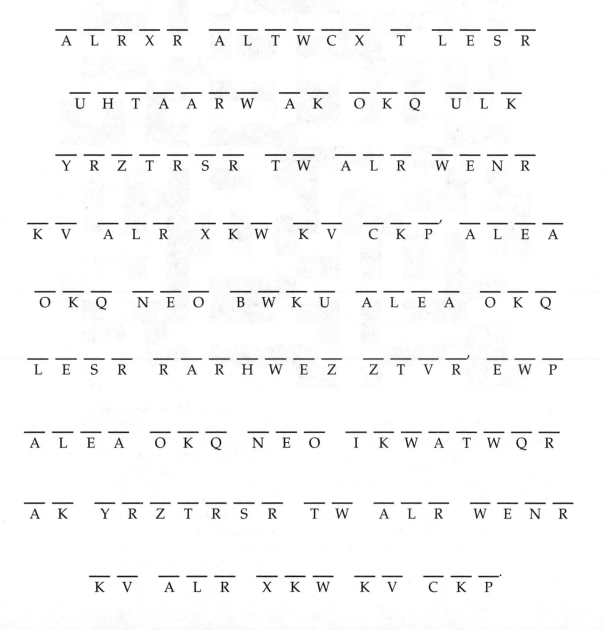

A L R X R   A L T W C X   T   L E S R

U H T A A R W   A K   O K Q   U L K

Y R Z T R S R   T W   A L R   W E N R

K V   A L R   X K W   K V   C K P' A L E A

O K Q   N E O   B W K U   A L E A   O K Q

L E S R   R A R H W E Z   Z T V R' E W P

A L E A   O K Q   N E O   I K W A T W Q R

A K   Y R Z T R S R   T W   A L R   W E N R

K V   A L R   X K W   K V   C K P.

Questions . . . the Gospels are full of them. The disciples asking sincere questions, the Sadducees and Pharisees trying to ask the trick questions, Jesus asking questions to teach and examine persons' hearts. If Jesus was physically present on earth and you could ask Him any question, what would it be? What would you answer if Jesus asked *you*, "What do you want Me to do?"

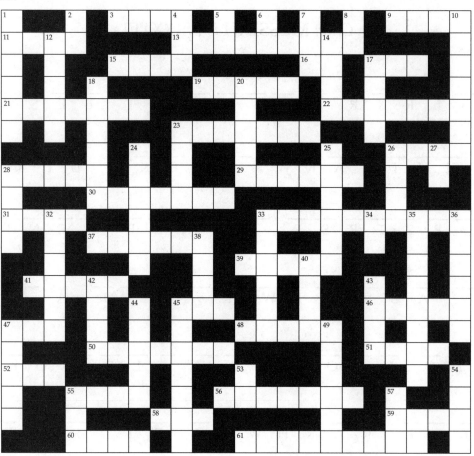

Across

3 "Do you ____ Me?" (John 21:16)

9 "Did you ____ anything?" (Luke 22:35)

11 "Lord, to whom shall we go? You have the words of eternal ____" (John 6:68)

13 "By what ____ are You doing these things?" (Matthew 21:23)

15 "Did you not know that I ____ be about My Father's business?" (Luke 2:49)

16 "Why do you seek to kill ____?" (John 7:19)

17 "____ can we know the way?" (John 14:5)

19 "Do You not know that I have ____ to crucify You, and ____ to release You?" (John 19:10)

21 "Did not He who made the ____ make the inside also?" (Luke 11:40)

22 "Who ____ Me?" (Luke 8:45)

23 "Why are you ____?" (Matthew 8:26)

26 "____ makest thou thyself?" (John 8:53, KJV)

28 "Have I been with you so long, and yet you have not ____ Me?" (John 14:9)

29 "Who ____, this man or his parents, that he was born blind?" (John 9:2)

30 "Which is ____, the gold or the temple that sanctifies the gold?" (Matthew 23:17)

31 "What is your ____?" (Luke 8:30)

33 "Is this not the ____ son?" (Matthew 13:55)

37 "Are you ____?" (John 1:21)

39 "Do you suppose that I came to give ____ on earth?" (Luke 12:51)

41 "What profit is it to a man if he gains the ____ world, and loses his own soul?" (Matthew 16:26)

45 "Whom ____ you seeking?" (John 18:4)

46 "Whose ____ and inscription is this?" (Matthew 22:20)

47 "____ do you sleep?" (Luke 22:46)

48 "What is ____?" (John 18:38)

50 "Is it lawful for a man to ____ his wife for just any reason?" (Matthew 19:3)

51 "What will be the ____ of Your coming?" (Matthew 24:3)

52 "How then does he now ____?" (John 9:19)

55 "Have you any ____ here?" (Luke 24:41)

56 "Do you ____ in the Son of God?" (John 9:35)

58 "Who ____ forgive sins but God alone?" (Mark 2:7)

59 "Do you believe that I am ____ to do this?" (Matthew 9:28)

60 "Why do you call Me ____?" (Matthew 19:17)

61 "Are You the ____, or do we look for another?" (2 words) (Matthew 11:3)

Down

1 "If the salt has lost its ____, how shall it be seasoned?" (Luke 14:34)

2 "Why, what evil has ____ done?" (Matthew 27:23)

4 "Why does your Teacher ____ with tax collectors and sinners?" (Matthew 9:11)

5 "Rabbi, is ____ I?" (Matthew 26:25)

6 "Why ____ you call Me 'Lord, Lord,' and not do the things which I say?" (Luke 6:46)

7 "Why could not we cast ____ out?" (Mark 9:28, KJV)

8 "If I cast out demons ____ Beelzebub, ____ whom do your sons cast them out?" (Matthew 12:27)

10 "How then will his ____ stand?" (Matthew 12:26)

12 "O you of little ____, why did you doubt?" (Matthew 14:31)

14 "Why do you ____ Me, you hypocrites?" (Matthew 22:18)

17 "Could you not watch with Me one ____?" (Matthew 26:40)

18 "Where then do You get that ____ water?" (John 4:11)

20 "What shall we do, that we may work the ____ of God?" (John 6:28)

23 "Lord, are You washing my ____?" (John 13:6)

24 "But if you love those who love you, what ____ is that to you?" (Luke 6:32)

25 "Does your Teacher not pay the ____ tax?" (Matthew 17:24)

26 "Do you ____ to be made well?" (John 5:6)

27 "Whom do you want me to release to you? Barabbas, ____ Jesus who is called Christ?" (Matthew 27:17)

28 "Are You the ____ of the Jews?" (Matthew 27:11)

32 "Where did this Man get this wisdom and these ____ works?" (Matthew 13:54)

33 "Is it lawful to pay taxes to ____, or not?" (Matthew 22:17)

34 "How is it that you have ____ faith?" (Mark 4:40)

35 "What will a man give in ____ for his soul?" (Matthew 16:26)

36 "Who is greater, he who sits at the table, or he who ____?" (Luke 22:27)

38 "Who is this of whom I ____ such things?" (Luke 9:9)

40 "Why could we not ____ it out?" (Matthew 17:19)

42 "Where have you ____ him?" (John 11:34)

43 "Are you betraying the Son of Man with a ____?" (Luke 22:48)

44 "Could this be the Son of ____?" (Matthew 12:23)

45 "Are You greater than our father ____?" (John 8:53)

47 "Why this ____?" (Mattthew 26:8)

49 "The baptism of John—where was it from? From ____ or from men?" (Matthew 21:25)

53 "What further need do ____ have of witnesses?" (Matthew 26:65)

54 "Who can this be, that even the winds and the sea ____ Him?" (Matthew 8:27)

55 "Do men gather . . . ____ [sing.] from thistles?" (Matthew 7:16)

57 "How can this be, since I do not know a ____?" (Luke 1:34)

FISHERS OF MEN

Matthew 4:18 tells us that Jesus found Simon Peter and his brother Andrew fishing in the Sea of Galilee. Peter and Andrew were professional fishermen when Jesus called them to be His disciples. Fishing was all that they had known; it was quite possibly the only way they knew to make a living.

Jesus said to them, "Follow Me, and I will make you fishers of men" (v. 19). Jesus spoke in terms that they would understand. Indeed, so strong was the analogy for them, that the fish became the secret symbol identifying the early persecuted Christians.

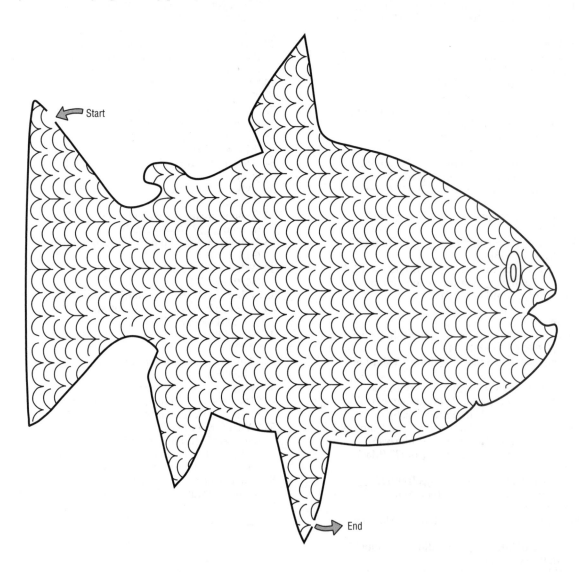

*W*hat is your first priority? What does the Scripture say it should be? To find out, unscramble the words and write them in the blank spaces.

ENTICINGARK — — — — — — — — — — — — (2 words)

IYOUTHWIN — — — — — — — — — (2 words)

SHAREENDUREDIT — — — — — — — — — — — — (2 words)

GRANTED — — — — — — —

WANDERLON — — — — — — — —

YJO — — —

ASSUMEDTRED — — — — — — — — — —

LAPPERFOGTARERICE — — — — — — — — — — — — — — — — — (4 words)

RAFASTERIMAGE — — — — — — — — — — — — (2 words)

SONGTHEUSESIR — — — — — — — — — — — — —

PETREN — — — — — —

CEPEA — — — — —

VALENE — — — — — —

WROPE — — — — —

INVITEGNRS — — — — — — — — — — (2 words)

Unscrambled letters: — — — — — — — — — —

Scripture Pool

MATTHEW 3:2   MATTHEW 6:33   MATTHEW 13:31, 33, 44, 45–47   MATTHEW 18:23
MATTHEW 21:33   MATTHEW 22:2   MATTHEW 25:1   LUKE 17:21   ROMANS 14:17
1 CORINTHIANS 4:20

163

*H*is grace truly is amazing! Complete this grid with the words of one of the church's most famous hymns.

Stanza #1:

_____ _____, how sweet the _____
15 Across   18 Across   6 Down

That _____ a _____ _____ me!
      14 Down   12 Across   67 Down

I _____ was _____ , but now _____
66 Across   13 Across   27 Across

_____ , Was _____ , but _____ I see.
29 Down   21 Across   3 Down

Stanza #2:

_____ grace that taught _____ heart to
37 Across   63 Across

_____ , And grace my _____ _____ ,
59 Down   2 Down   22 Across

How _____ _____ that grace _____
     34 Down   35 Down   39 Across

The _____ I _____ _____ !
    9 Down   45 Across 7 Down

Stanza #3:

_____ many _____ , _____ and _____ ,
49 Down   11 Down   49 Across   38 Down

I _____ _____ _____ ; _____ grace
65 Down   50 Down   56 Down   43 Across

_____ _____ _____ _____ thus
41 Down   21 Down   63 Down   58 Across

_____ , _____ grace will
2 Across   30 Across

_____ me _____ .
23 Down and 67 Across   25 Across and 68 Across

Stanza #4:

The _____ has _____ _____ to _____ ,
     64 Across   51 Across 71 Across   69 Down

His _____ my _____ _____ ; He _____
    48 Down   5 Across   72 Across   61 Across

my _____ and _____ _____ As _____
   44 Across   36 Across 47 Across   62 Down

as life _____ .
        4 Down

Stanza #5:

And when this _____ and _____ shall
              53 Across   32 Down

_____ , And _____ _____ shall _____ ,
45 Down   1 Down   28 Across   33 Down

I shall _____ within the _____ A life of
        40 Down   20 Down

_____ and _____ .
5 Across   19 Across

Stanza #6:

_____ we've been _____ _____ _____
57 Across   8 Down   8 Across 10 Across

_____ , _____ _____ _____ the
70 Across   31 Across 26 Across 42 Down

_____ , We've _____ _____ _____ to
16 Across   60 Across 64 Down 52 Down

_____ _____ _____ Than when _____
24 Down   54 Across 46 Down   73 Across

first _____ .
      17 Down

TO THE CAVE OF ADULLAM

*I*n escaping the jealous wrath of King Saul, David fled to the cave of Adullam. The Bible tells us, "When his brothers and all his father's house heard it, they went down there to him. And everyone who was in distress, everyone who was in debt, and everyone who was discontented gathered to him. So he became captain over them. And there were about four hundred men with him" (1 Samuel 22:1–2).

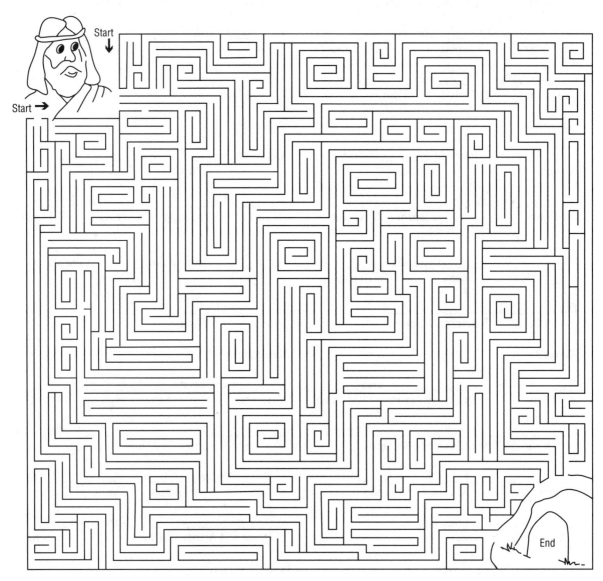

*U*nscramble these words that relate to the intimate, committed, steadfast, guiding, unending relationship the Lord has promised us. Then position the unscrambled words on the grid to reveal God's ultimate promise to us about that relationship.

DEBAI   MIRSNTEEPNO   SYAALW   PNANIOMOC   STTSEAADF
ROTREFMOC   RREEEESNTPV (2 words)   GNILRETSAVE   ROVEREME
LNEETRA   DEINRF   VEROREF   LOSENRUCO   EHEPSRHD   LSPITIRHYO (2 words)
MPENCSASO   OCORETRTP   REVILEDER   HTGENRTS   DNIKSESNGIOLVN (2 words)
TURHT   VELO   ENVI   CEEPA   CMOERVOE   YUNOI (2 words)
DUOLCOLAFIRLP (3 words)   ERFFORIALIPIL (3 words)   GRLYOHANIKHSE (2 words)   IDLEHS

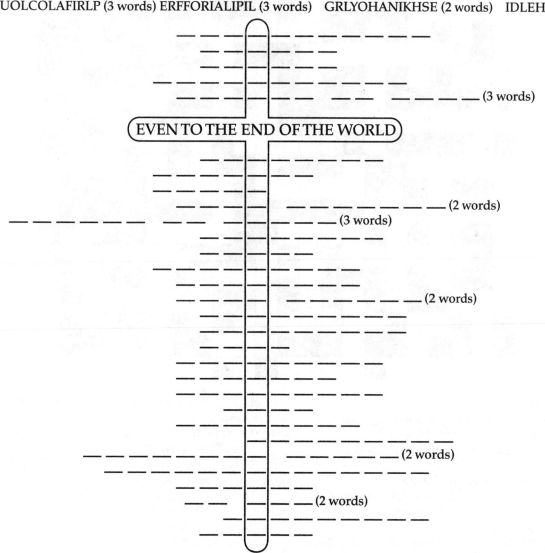

EVEN TO THE END OF THE WORLD

*W*hen Job lost everything he once owned and loved, he hurled bitter complaints and anguished accusations against God—the One he trusted and the One who could have prevented all his misery. But Job eventually came to recognize his shortsighted perspective and repented to the Lord. Job's ultimate comfort? God is sovereign.

Across

1 Job owned three thousand ____ (Job 1:3)

3 Mourning apparel (Job 16:15)

10 "My eye has also grown dim because of ____" (Job 17:7)

12 Pottery fragment (Job 2:8)

13 This adversary accused Job of loving God only because of his material prosperity (Job 1:9)

14 "He hangs the ____ on nothing" (Job 26:7)

17 "____ LORD gave, and ____ LORD has taken away" (Job 1:21)

19 "Till I die I will not put away my ____ from me" (Job 27:5)

21 God commended Job as a "blameless and ____ man" (Job 2:3)

22 "Cause me to understand wherein I have ____ed" (Job 6:24)

24 Job said his grief was heavier than the "sand of the ____ " (Job 6:3)

26 This adversity hit Job from head to foot (Job 2:7)

27 "My justice was like a robe and a ____" (Job 29:14)

30 "In this you are not ____" (Job 33:12)

32 "My ____ is a breath!" (Job 7:7)

35 There were "no women ____ beautiful as the daughters of Job" (Job 42:15)

36 "Who is this who darkens counsel by ____ without knowledge?" (Job 38:2)

38 Job's wife had this suggestion: "____ God and die" (Job 2:9)

41 "Stretch out your ____s toward Him" (Job 11:13)

43 "____ still and consider the wondrous works of God" (Job 37:14)

44 "Though He ____ me, yet will I trust Him" (Job 13:15)

45 "Remember to ____ His work" (Job 36:24)

47 "Have the ____s of death been revealed to you?" God asked Job (Job 38:17)

49 "Naked I came from my mother's ____, and naked shall I return" (Job 1:21)

53 "Therefore I . . . ____ in dust and ashes" (Job 42:6)

55 Job's friend, the Temanite (Job 4:1)

57 "My flesh is caked with ____s" (Job 7:5)

59 "Things ____ wonderful for me, which I did not know" (Job 42:3)

62 "Now . . . I will question you, and you shall ____ Me" (Job 38:3)

63 "____ at peace; Thereby good will come to you" (Job 22:21)

65 God "is excellent in power, in judgment and abundant ____" (Job 37:23)

67 Enclosure (abbr.)

69 "He has made me a ____ of the people" (Job 17:6)

70 What Job did to his robe when he heard about the death of his children (Job 1:20)

71 "I know that my ____ lives" (Job 19:25)

Down

1 "Shall the one who ____ with the Almighty correct Him?" (Job 40:2)

2 "See my ____!" (Job 10:15)

4 Adversity (Job 6:2)

5 "So Job died, old and full ____ days" (Job 42:17)

6 "He does great things ____ finding out" (Job 9:10)

7 "God is ____ than man" (Job 33:12)

8 Satan said God had a ____ around Job, protecting him (Job 1:10)

9 "In all this Job did ____ sin nor charge God with wrong" (Job 1:22)

11 "My righteousness I hold ____" (Job 27:6)

12 "Nor does He regard the rich more than the ____; for they are all the work of His hands" (Job 34:19)

15 "What strength do I have, that I should ____?" (Job 6:11)

16 Job's friends and relatives "came to him and ____ food with him" (Job 42:11)

18 "Where can ____ be found?" (Job 28:12)

20 "They saw that his ____ was very great" (Job 2:13)

23 "I desire to ____ with God" (Job 13:3)

25 The youngest of Job's four friends (Job 32:6)

26 One of Job's friends, a Shuhite (Job 8:1)

28 "You have not spoken of Me what is ____" (Job 42:7)

29 "Behold, God is mighty, but despises ____ one" (Job 36:5)

31 Southwest (abbr.)

33 "My spirit ____ broken, . . . the grave ____ ready for me" (Job 17:1)

34 "To depart from ____ is understanding" (Job 28:28)

37 Job "cursed the ____ of his birth" (Job 3:1)

38 "Miserable ____ers are you all!" (Job 16:2)

39 "Have I ____?" (Job 7:20)

40 Leviathan's "heart is ____ hard ____ stone" (Job 41:24)

42 "My speech settled on them as ____" (Job 29:22)

44 Job "____ his children and grandchildren for four generations" (Job 42:16)

46 "All ____ would perish together" (Job 34:15)

47 Great (abbr.)

48 In spite of his complaints, Job had great "confidence" in God (Job 13:15)

50 "The thing I greatly feared has come upon ____" (Job 3:25)

51 "____ be the name of the LORD" (Job 1:21)

52 "____ were you when I laid the foundations of the earth?" (Job 38:4)

54 God restored to Job "____ as much as he had before" (Job 42:10)

56 One of Job's comforters, a Naamathite (Job 11:1)

58 "What is ____?" (Job 7:17)

60 "If they ____ and serve Him, they shall spend their days in prosperity" (Job 36:11)

61 "I have become like ____ and ashes" (Job 30:19)

64 "Give ____, Job, listen to me" (Job 33:31)

66 "You have heard of the perseverance of Job and seen the ____ intended by the Lord—that the Lord is very compassionate and merciful" (James 5:11)

68 "____ who rebukes God, let him answer it" (Job 40:2)

A word for the mighty, the rich, and the wise.

Clue: **MESSIAH** *is* **RUGGVIM**

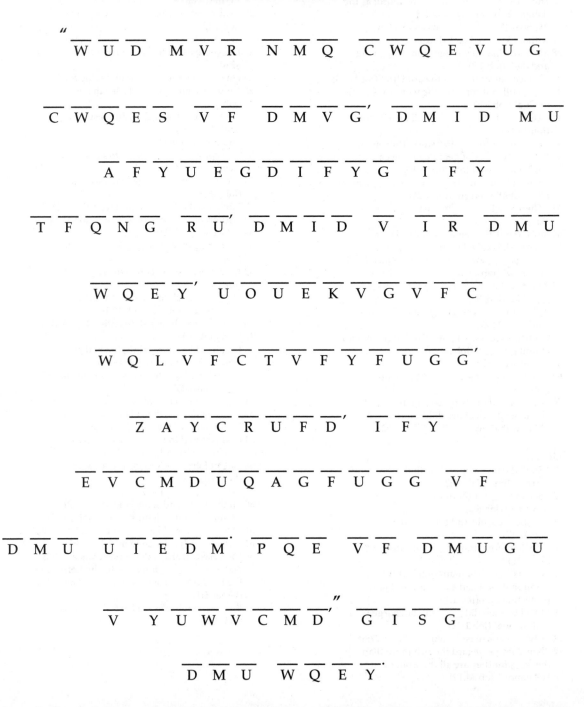

"— — — — — — — — — — — — — — — —
W U D M V R N M Q C W Q E V U G

— — — — — — — — — — ' — — — — — —
C W Q E S V F D M V G ' D M I D M U

— — — — — — — — — — — — —
A F Y U E G D I F Y G I F Y

— — — — — — — ' — — — — — — — — — —
T F Q N G R U ' D M I D V I R D M U

— — — — ' — — — — — — — — — —
W Q E Y ' U O U E K V G V F C

— — — — — — — — — — — — — '
W Q L V F C T V F Y F U G G '

— — — — — — — ' — — —
Z A Y C R U F D ' I F Y

— — — — — — — — — — — — — —
E V C M D U Q A G F U G G V F

— — — — — — — — . — — — — — — — — — —
D M U U I E D M P Q E V F D M U G U

— — — — — — — — " — — — —
V Y U W V C M D ' G I S G

— — — — — — — .
D M U W Q E Y

*S*even of the books in the New Testament were written by the apostle Paul to churches in cities in Europe and Asia Minor. Match the first half of the verse to the correct second half, then unscramble the circled letters in the correctly matched verses to reveal the city in which the church was located. When all the letters are in place, you will find the form in which these books were written.

Column A

1. For we are His workmanship,

2. Be anxious for nothing, but in everything by prayer and supplication, with thanksgiving,

3. Therefore, if anyone is in Christ, he is a new creation;

4. For in Him dwells all the fullness of the Godhead bodily;

5. I have been crucified with Christ; it is no longer I who live, but Christ lives in me;

6. And may the Lord make you increase and abound in love to one another and to all, just as we do to you,

7. For I am not ashamed of the gospel of Christ, for it is the power of God to salvation for everyone who believes, for the Jew first and also for the Greek.

Column B

A. and you are complete in Him, who is the head of all principality and power.

B. so that He may establish your hearts blameless in holiness before our God and Father at the coming of our Lord Jesus Christ with all His saints.

C. created in Christ Jesus for good works, which God prepared beforehand that we should walk in them.

D. let your requests be made known to God.

E. old things have passed away; behold, all things have become new.

F. For in it the righteousness of God is revealed from faith to faith; as it is written, "The just shall live by faith."

G. and the life which I now live in the flesh I live by faith in the Son of God, who loved me and gave Himself for me.

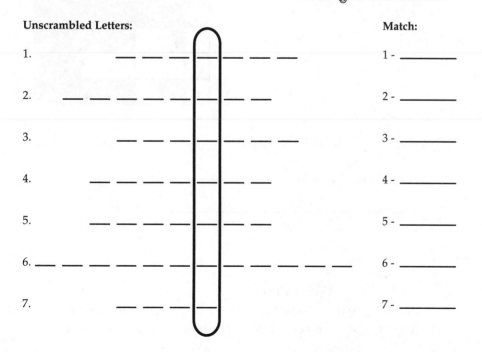

Unscrambled Letters:

1. _ _ _ _ _ _ _

2. _ _ _ _ _ _ _ _

3. _ _ _ _ _ _ _

4. _ _ _ _ _ _ _

5. _ _ _ _ _ _

6. _ _ _ _ _ _ _ _ _ _

7. _ _ _ _ _

Match:

1 - _____

2 - _____

3 - _____

4 - _____

5 - _____

6 - _____

7 - _____

*B*elow is a Word Pool containing two separate sets of words—but the words are all mixed up together. To divide the words into their proper categories, put each word in its correct place on the correct grid. When you unscramble the circled letters you will see how the words are related—and how the sets are opposite!

1.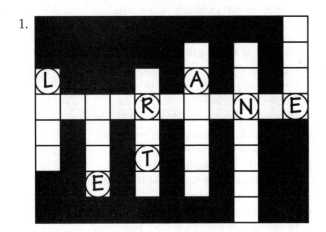

2.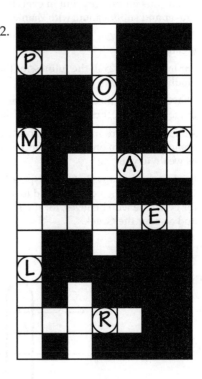

Unscrambled letters:

1. __ __ __ __ __ __ __

2. __ __ __ __ __ __ __ __

Word Pool

LIFE   KNOWLEDGE   TRUTH   WAR   FATHER   LOVE   PAIN   KINGDOM   FAITH

TONGUES   INHERITANCE   MORTALITY   TEARS   HOME   DEATH

The answer to each definition in the first column is contained within one of the names in the second column. The hidden word will be found with its letters in correct order. An example is given for you.

1. __Y__ Large
2. ____ Melody
3. ____ Praise
4. ____ Disturbance
5. ____ Burn
6. ____ Male swan
7. ____ Food shop
8. ____ Bridle
9. ____ Tease
10. ____ Pain
11. ____ Edging
12. ____ Get up
13. ____ Citrus
14. ____ Gratuity
15. ____ Roster
16. ____ Levy
17. ____ Liturgy
18. ____ Survey
19. ____ Stiffen
20. ____ Mountain
21. ____ Top quality
22. ____ Child's toy
23. ____ Insect
24. ____ Transport
25. ____ Hold tightly
26. ____ Eager

A. Issachar
B. Philistines
C. Alphaeus
D. Aristarchus
E. Tabitha
F. Candace
G. Claudius Caesar
H. Artaxerxes
I. Amalekites
J. Potiphar
K. Agrippa
L. Rachel
M. Apollos
N. Nehemiah
O. David
P. Timothy
Q. Iscariot
R. Pharisees
S. Amorites
T. Delilah
U. Agabus
V. Sennacherib
W. Philemon
X. Jacob
➜ Y. Abigail
Z. Zacharias

God has made Himself known to us. Unscramble the letters below and discover some of the ways that God has told us—*and tells us*—about Himself. The circled letters will spell out a word that means what God has made known to us. The second set of scrambled letters makes words that tell us what we are to do with what God has told us. The circled letters spell a word that tells us what we are to *be* with what God has told us.

DROW (1 Samuel 3:21) — — — —

SEUSJ (Galatians 1:12) — — — — —

SHAVENE (Psalm 19:1) — — — — — —

POETSPHR (Amos 3:7) — — — — — — — —

SPOGEL (Romans 1:16–17) — — — — — —

REACTION (Romans 1:19–21) — — — — — — — —

HERAFT (Matthew 11:25; 16:17) — — — — — —

TRIPIS (1 Corinthians 2:10) — — — — — —

KROWS (John 10:25) — — — — —

TWINESEYES (2 Peter 1:16) — — — — — — — — — —

WAKENMONK (Psalm 145:12) — — — — — — — — — (2 words)

MIRACLOP (Isaiah 61:1) — — — — — — — —

LELT (Mark 5:19) — — — —

NEHIS (Philippians 2:15) — — — — —

PORTER (1 Corinthians 14:25) — — — — — —

PAKES (Titus 2:15) — — — — —

SERAPI (Psalm 145:4) — — — — — —

REDLACE (1 Chronicles 16:24) — — — — — — —

FEISTTY (1 Peter 5:12) — — — — — — —

*T*his crossword will sweep out the cobwebs of your mind and refresh your attitude! And when you're finished, there is a special message for you in the circled letters reading diagonally down.

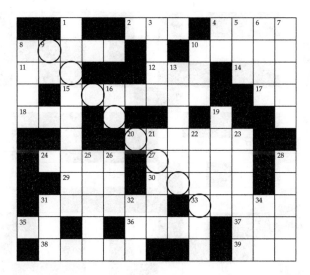

Across

2 Cleopatra's snake
4 Jump
8 Scrub
10 Wash
11 Buddy
12 Name for a lion
14 What #12 Across is
15 Biblical healings often involved this disease
17 "Rise and ____ healed!"
18 Place to take a bath
20 He was made clean in the Jordan River (2 Kings 5:1–14)
24 "You are already clean because of the ____ which I have spoken to you." (John 15:3)
27 Boulder
29 Largest number of lepers that Jesus healed at one time recorded in the Bible (Luke 17:14–17)
30 Red dye
31 Bind up wheat
33 Game with a bull's-eye
35 International press organization (abbr.)
36 ¿Como ____ usted?
37 Hawaiian greeting piece
38 Resource, benefit
39 Affirmative

Down

1 Mid-highway fee collection point (2 words)
3 Farm structure
4 Fa sol ____
5 I.e. and et al's cousin
6 Evil king of Israel; Elijah's foe (1 Kings 16:30)
7 He had a rooftop vision about clean things (Acts 10:9–15)
8 Stain
9 L.A.'s state (abbr.)
10 Young man
13 Manor
16 Philadelphia's home (abbr.)
19 Desert grub for children of Israel
21 Priestly substance of ritual cleansing (Hebrews 9:13–15)
22 Sunday follower
23 Almost
25 Bulrushes
26 Genetic factor
28 Desert watering hole
31 Rest and rejuvenation place
32 Short for retired soldier
34 Place to set your golf ball

This crossword is based on the words of Martin Luther's famous hymn, "A Mighty Fortress." See how much of the puzzle you can complete before consulting the Word Pool.

Word Pool

ABIDETH AGE ALSO AMID ARMED BE BULWARK CRUEL DOOM DOST
EARTH EARTHLY ENDURE EQUAL FAILING FEAR FORTRESS GIFTS GO
GOODS GREAT GRIM HE HIM ILLS IS IT KILL KINDRED KINGDOM LO
LORD MAN MORTAL MUST NAME ON ONE OURS POWER PREVAILING
PRINCE RAGE SAME SEEK STILL STRENGTH STRIVING THO TO TREMBLE
TRIUMPH TRUTH UNDO US WE WIN WOE WORD WORLD

1.

A mighty _____ is our God,
(11 Across)

A _____ never _____;
(42 Down)   (11 Down)

Our Helper He, _____ the flood
(46 Down)

Of mortal _____ _____.
(23 Across) (43 Across)

For _____ our ancient foe
(45 Down)

Doth _____ to work us _____;
(38 Across)   (50 Down)

His craft and _____ are _____,
(52 Across)   (24 Across)

And _____ with _____ hate,
(30 Across)   (44 Across)

On _____ is not His _____.
(3 Down)   (12 Down)

2.

Did we in our own _____ confide,
(13 Across)

Our _____ would be losing,
(34 Across)

Were not the right Man _____ our side,
(10 Down)

The _____ of God's own choosing.
(27 Across)

_____ ask who that may _____?
(18 Down)   (37 Down)

Christ Jesus, _____ _____ _____;
(49 Across) (35 Down) (29 Across)

_____ Sabaoth, His _____,
(21 Across)   (28 Down)

From age to _____ the _____,
(46 Across)   (41 Down)

And He _____ _____ the battle.
(7 Down)   (32 Down)

3.

And _____ this _____, with devils filled,
(5 Down)   (47 Across)

Should threaten to _____ us,
(17 Across)

We will not _____, for God hath willed
(36 Down)

His truth to _____ through us.
(16 Down)

The _____ of Darkness _____,
(43 Down)   (6 Across)

We _____ not for him;
(39 Across)

His _____ _____ can _____,
(1 Across) (4 Down)   (53 Across)

For _____, his _____ is sure;
(40 Across)   (48 Down)

_____ little word shall fell _____.
(20 Across)   (33 Across)

4.

That _____ above all _____ powers,
(47 Down)   (25 Down)

No thanks _____ them, _____;
(15 Down)   (8 Across)

The Spirit and the _____ are _____
(6 Down)   (51 Across)

Thru him who with _____ sideth.
(9 Across)

Let _____ and _____ _____,
(14 Down)   (22 Across) (24 Down)

This _____ life _____;
(31 Down)   (2 Down)

The body they may _____;
(54 Across)

God's _____ abideth still;
(19 Down)

His _____ is forever.
(26 Down)

Use the missing words of Deuteronomy 28:20–30 to complete the grid, and discover an important consequence of behavior.

The LORD will send on you cursing, ____, and ____ in all that you set your hand to do, until you are ____ and until you ____ quickly, because of the wickedness of your doings in which you have forsaken Me. The LORD will make the ____ cling to you until He has consumed you from the land which you are going to possess. The LORD will strike you with ____, with ____,

with ____, with severe burning fever, with the ____, with ____, and with ____; they shall pursue you until you perish. And your heavens which are over your head shall be bronze, and the earth which is under you shall be iron. The LORD will change the rain of your land to powder and ____; from the heaven it shall come down on you until you are destroyed.

The LORD will cause

you to be ____before your enemies; you shall go out one way against them and flee seven ways before them; and you shall become ____ to all the kingdoms of the earth. Your carcasses shall be food for all the birds of the air and the beasts of the earth, and no one shall frighten them away. The LORD will strike you with the ____ of Egypt, with ____, with the ____, and with

the ____, from which you cannot be healed. The LORD will strike you with ____ and ____ and confusion of heart. And you shall grope at noonday, as a blind man gropes in darkness; you shall not prosper in your ways; you shall be only ____ and ____ continually, and no one shall save you.

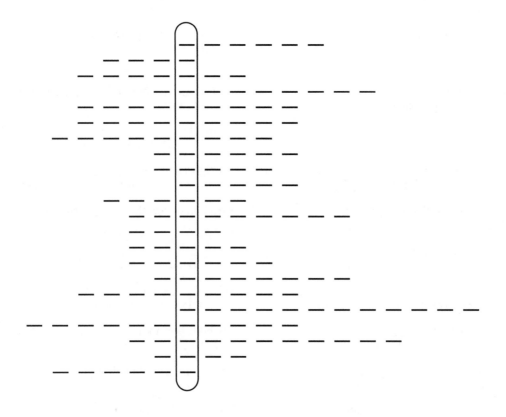

To the Tomb

*H*ave you ever opened a box, hoping to find a special surprise inside—only to discover that the box was empty?

Sometimes empty is good. When we "empty" our lives into God's hands, He can use us to bring others to Him.

When Peter ran to Jesus' tomb on the third day after His crucifixion, finding it empty was wonderful! Jesus had risen from the dead, just as He said He would!

↓ Start

*I*n the letter box below are the words that relate to eight people in the Bible who died and were resurrected and restored to life. See if you can find them in five minutes or less!

```
A  B  C  D  A  U  R  J  A  H  N  A  Z  A  R  D  E  F  O  P  Q
G  H  I  P  S  G  R  A  H  T  I  B  A  T  U  R  S  T  U  V  W
J  K  L  I  H  Z  A  A  H  A  I  B  A  T  S  J  A  I  R  S  N
M  N  O  A  U  T  Z  R  U  H  B  I  S  H  U  A  I  N  S  H  U
O  R  S  T  N  E  J  N  J  P  R  L  U  S  N  T  U  V  E  U  T
T  U  V  S  A  N  A  I  N  E  I  A  S  N  A  Y  C  H  U  S  Z
W  X  Y  H  M  A  I  S  E  R  A  Z  E  R  M  A  R  E  P  H  A
Z  A  B  U  M  L  R  U  S  A  L  J  J  A  Z  T  H  J  E  S  U
C  D  E  T  I  S  U  R  A  Z  A  L  S  I  U  L  A  Z  A  R  U
F  G  H  Y  T  U  S  I  A  J  I  A  N  E  S  N  A  I  T  A  B
I  J  K  C  E  H  S  U  H  C  Y  T  U  E  J  I  T  H  A  D  O
L  M  N  A  L  B  A  T  I  M  M  A  N  S  E  R  C  A  S  E  U
```

Word Pool

SON OF WIDOW IN <u>NAIN</u> TABITHA LAZARUS DAUGHTER OF <u>JAIRUS</u>
SON OF <u>SHUNAMMITE</u> WOMAN EUTYCHUS JESUS
SON OF <u>ZAREPHATH</u> WIDOW

*W*hen it comes to "figurin'"—these words from the Bible are worth rememberin'!

Clue: MESSIAH *is* GYMMCUB

B I H Y M N   Q Y C A B N M   U H X

M W U F Y M   U L Y   N B Y

F I L X M'   U F F   N B Y

Q Y C A B N M   C H   N B Y

V U A   U L Y   B C M   Q I L E.

CORNELIUS'S PLEA

*R*oman soldiers were not given to having visions. But Cornelius, a Gentile and a member of the Italian Regiment, was devout.

In a vision, God told him to send men to Joppa to find Simon Peter, saying, "He will tell you what you must do" (Acts 10:6).

The next day, Peter saw a vision of his own. The message: the gospel is for Jews *and* Gentiles. Therefore, when Cornelius's men arrived, Peter was ready to go with them.

Cornelius's servants must spell Simon Peter's name, in correct letter order. Do not cross back over a path that you have already used.

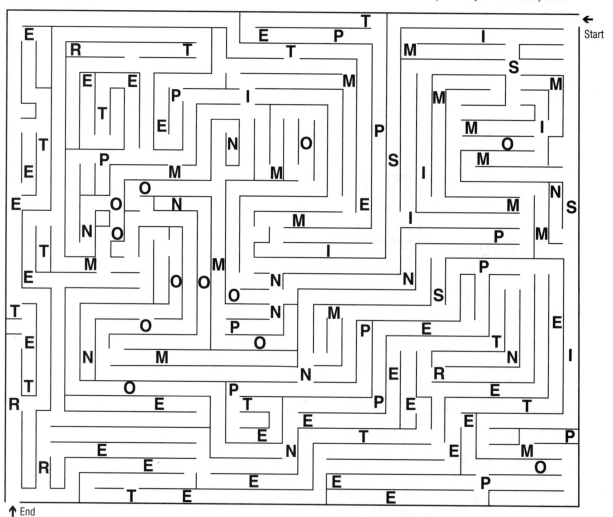

*J*ehoshaphat got the jump on his enemies, thanks to God's intervention. This puzzle about the king is from 2 Chronicles 20.

Across

6 Enemies came up by this "rise" (3 words) (v. 16)
8 Jehoshaphat was king of ____ (v. 35)
9 Jehoshaphat's mother (v. 31)
12 Disaster by "blade" (v. 9)
13 Afterwards, the people gathered in this valley (v. 26)
17 It took ____ days to gather spoils (v. 25)
19 His age when his reign ended (v. 31)
22 They never made it to Tarshish (v. 37)
23 A temple for God (v. 8)

Down

1 Enemies were near the Wilderness of ____ (v. 16)
2 His realm was "peaceful" afterwards (v. 30)
3 Son of Zechariah (v. 14)
4 The people of Judah went into this wilderness (v. 20)
5 Jehoshaphat "lowered" his head (v. 18)
7 Hazazon Tamar, which is ____ ____ (2 words) (v. 2)
10 Praise the "grace" of holiness (v. 21)
11 Ammon and Moab killed inhabitants of ____ ____ (2 words) (v. 23)

12 God will "rescue" (v. 9)
14 Stringed instrument (v. 28)
15 He proclaimed one (v. 3)
16 The Lord set them (sing.) (v. 22)
18 The battle was His (poss.) (v. 15)
20 They returned to Jerusalem with "gladness" (v. 27)
21 His father (v. 32)

*F*ind fifteen things that the Bible describes as hiding out in caves, dens, and lairs.

```
V  A  E  R  G  I  K  O  D  I  S  N  M  M  O  C
I  Y  O  U  N  S  L  A  K  C  A  J  A  P  E  R
E  O  L  G  I  D  E  N  S  M  O  B  N  I  R  G
V  I  P  E  R  S  N  R  E  R  C  D  A  V  R  S
E  N  S  I  M  M  S  E  L  M  S  E  S  E  D  E
R  O  D  G  O  A  R  R  I  E  Y  R  A  C  E  V
Y  R  T  L  C  F  E  Y  O  D  N  T  N  O  M  A
S  E  H  S  Y  L  D  O  M  O  M  L  H  A  M  L
L  A  I  R  S  O  N  U  N  E  G  I  M  G  V  K
A  T  E  I  D  Y  A  L  N  S  V  O  H  T  I  S
V  V  V  L  K  O  M  I  O  E  A  E  I  N  G  M
E  S  E  A  I  U  M  N  J  S  K  L  G  M  E  N
M  B  S  N  G  N  O  S  A  C  S  S  E  M  R  O
I  E  T  S  R  I  C  H  M  E  N  N  R  A  S  M
G  T  L  A  D  T  E  R  E  V  O  S  M  N  V  C
H  Y  V  O  S  M  O  G  S  I  I  O  I  D  A  I
R  I  L  C  H  T  N  T  L  H  L  N  T  X  R  R
M  S  M  R  Q  U  S  H  I  T  G  N  O  B  I  O
J  T  A  C  R  A  J  A  C  K  N  D  C  E  P  R
N  A  S  O  A  R  B  O  E  B  U  E  S  R  N  T
A  I  C  B  M  A  S  A  R  B  O  C  K  A  L  S
L  S  O  K  M  V  I  J  A  G  Y  R  S  Y  O  U
```

Scripture Pool
JOB 37:8   PSALM 10:9; 104:21   ISAIAH 2:18–19; 11:8
JEREMIAH 7:11; 10:22   REVELATION 6:15–17

ALPHA AND OMEGA

Alpha is the first letter of the Greek alphabet, Omega the last letter.

Three times in the book of Revelation, the phrase is used. The first time, in Revelation 1:8, God the Father spoke: "I am the Alpha and the Omega, the Beginning and the End . . . who is and who was and who is to come, the Almighty."

In Revelation 21:6 and 22:13, Jesus was the one speaking: "I am the Alpha and the Omega, the Beginning and the End" and, "I am the Alpha and Omega, the Beginning and the End, the First and the Last."

The threefold use of the phrase underscores its importance.

The phrase points to Christ as being both the source and the sum of everything—the Creator and the Culminator.

Start →

←End

*T*he ark of the covenant had been away from home for too long, so King David decided it was time to bring it back to Jerusalem—which he did—after a couple of interruptions. The answers to this crossword are found in 1 Chronicles 13–16.

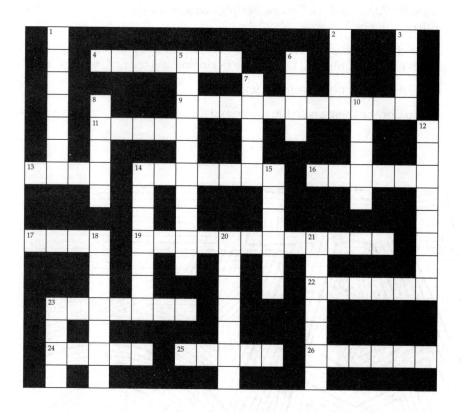

Across

4 Only they could carry the ark (15:2)
9 Where David defeated the Philistines (2 words) (14:10–11)
11 Burnt offerings and ____ offerings (16:2)
13 One of two who drove the cart (13:7)
14 Ask advice (15:13)
16 #14 Down's material (15:19)
17 "Look for" the Lord (16:11)
19 The animals that were sacrificed (3 words) (15:26)
22 The ark's previous location was #18 Down ____ (13:5)
23 Grandeur (16:27)
24 Sacrifices were put on this (16:40)
25 The ark was at the Gittite's house for ____ months (13:13-14)
26 The threshing floor's owner (13:9)

Down

1 One of the ark's doorkeepers (15:23)
2 The other cart driver (13:7)
3 Obed-____ was the Gittite in #25 Across (13:14)
5 David built this home for the ark (16:1)
6 They pulled the cart (13:9)
7 A Levite who helped carry the ark (15:11–12)
8 David wore this linen garment (15:27)
10 One of two priests who helped carry the ark (15:11–12)
12 God dwelt between these two winged creatures on the lid of the ark (13:6)
14 With clashing ____, they made music (13:8)
15 Gratitude (16:8)
18 The ark's previous location ____ #22 Across (13:5)
20 Vocal music makers (15:16)
21 Exult (16:31)
23 David gave all Israelites a loaf of bread, a piece of "flesh," and a raisin cake when the ark returned (16:3)

Decode the message below to find one of the most famous statements from the book of Job.

Clue: MESSIAH *is* ZNVVDOQ

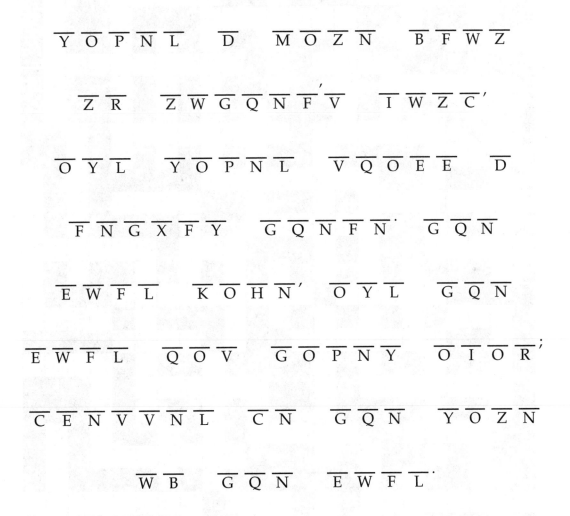

YOPNL D MOZN BFWZ

ZR ZWGQNFV IWZC'

OYL YOPNL VQOEE D

FNGXFY GQNFN GQN

EWFL KOHN' OYL GQN

EWFL QOV GOPNY OIOR;

CENVVNL CN GQN YOZN

WB GQN EWFL.

*A*ll of the clues in the "D-vine," difficult, daring crossword below begin with the letter *D*.

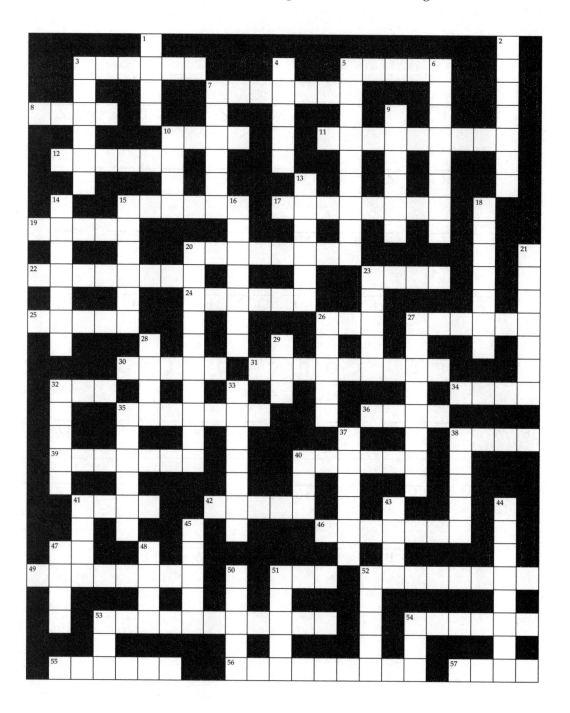

Across

3 Pious

5 Victor over Goliath (1 Samuel 17)

7 Jesus gave His disciples power to heal "all kinds of ____" (Matthew 10:1)

8 Finished

10 Paul said Jesus "will judge the living and the ____" (2 Timothy 4:1)

11 Marked by lies and twisted information

12 The prophet Haggai called the Messiah "the ____ of All Nations" (Haggai 2:7)

15 "The LORD of hosts will ____ them," says Zechariah 9:15

17 Said Paul of Jesus, "Death no longer has ____ over Him" (Romans 6:9)

19 Goddess of Ephesus, whose temple Paul challenged (Acts 19:28–34)

20 Saul met the LORD on the road to this city (Acts 9:1–6)

22 Jesus taught, "A ____ is not above his teacher" (Matthew 10:24)

23 Old English for refuse; anything nauseating or loathsome

24 The king who, against his own personal convictions, had Daniel thrown to the lions (Daniel 6)

25 Demon

26 Jesus accused the money changers of turning the house of prayer into a "____ of thieves" (Matthew 21:13)

27 Paul wrote to Timothy, "Let everyone who names the name of Christ ____ from iniquity" (2 Timothy 2:19)

30 Leah's daughter (Genesis 30:20–21)

31 "Your sons and your ____ shall prophesy" says Joel 2:28

32 Jesus told a parable in which a rich man cried for Lazarus to ____ the tip of his finger in water and touch his parched tongue (Luke 16:24)

34 Goliath called, "I ____ the armies of Israel this day" (1 Samuel 17:10)

35 "____ me speedily" is the psalmist's cry in Psalm 31:2

36 Jesus said, "If anyone desires to come after Me, let him ____ himself, and take up his cross, and follow Me" (Matthew 16:24)

38 Job repented in "____ and ashes" (Job 42:6)

39 Prison; Joseph was called out of this place by Pharaoh (Genesis 41:14)

40 Joseph had a God-given ability to interpret them (Genesis 40–41)

41 Edomite who killed eighty-five priests upon King Saul's order after David's escape (1 Samuel 22:18)

42 Paul commended the Jews in Berea because they "searched the Scriptures ____" (Acts 17:11)

46 The Lord said, "I knew you in the wilderness, in the land of great ____" (Hosea 13:5)

47 Jesus taught, "Observe and ____" (Matthew 23:3)

49 The Lord holds the rulers of the earth who plot against Him "In ____," says Psalm 2:4

51 The Bible says of Noah: "According to all that God commanded him, so he ____" (Genesis 6:22)

52 Paul sent for Timothy, in part, because Titus had departed for ____ (2 Timothy 4:9–10)

53 The ability to correctly see and understand the difference between right and wrong, good and evil

54 Jeweled turban, in Old English

55 "Better is a ____ of herbs where love is, than a fatted calf with hatred" (Proverbs 15:17)

56 "Keep your heart with all ____, for out of it spring the issues of life" (Proverbs 4:23)

57 Fruit of a palm tree in the Middle East

Down

1 After His baptism, Jesus saw "the Spirit of God descending like a ____ and alighting upon Him" (Matthew 3:16)

2 The state of a human being who touches uncleanness (Leviticus 5:3)

3 When the ark of the covenant was brought into Jerusalem, David "____ before the LORD with all his might" (2 Samuel 6:14)

4 He abandoned Paul "having loved this present world" (2 Timothy 4:10)

5 Silversmith who led a revolt against Paul (Acts 19:24–27)

6 The means by which Paul tells Titus to "exhort and convict those who contradict" (Titus 1:9)

7 An "office" in the early church (1 Timothy 3:10)

9 Paul warned the Colossians against those who would "cheat you through philosophy and empty ____" (Colossians 2:8)

10 Jesus healed a man with this condition by putting His fingers in his ears (Mark 7:32–35)

13 Also called Tabitha, Peter raised her from the dead (Acts 9:36–41)

14 Jesus taught, "Every city or house ____ against itself will not stand" (Matthew 12:25)

15 He was thrown into a den of lions (Daniel 6:16)

16 A woman believer in Athens (Acts 17:34)

18 She helped Barak lead the Israelites into battle against Sisera (Judges 4:4–16)

20 Ceremony of commitment to the Lord (Nehemiah 12:27)

21 Divinely ordained future; role in the kingdom of God

23 Modern for "thou shalt not" (2 words)

26 Philistine god, whose image fell in presence of the ark (1 Samuel 5:1–5)

27 He who hates his brother "is in ____," according to 1 John 2:9

28 To eat together

29 "The evening and the morning were the first ____" (Genesis 1:5)

32 "Make known His ____ among the peoples!" declares Psalm 105:1

33 Samson's downfall (Judges 16:4–21)

35 Ehud's weapon, used to kill Eglon (Judges 3:16)

37 A waterless place

38 Jesus taught, "If you have faith and do not ____" you will receive whatever things you ask in prayer (Matthew 21:21–22)

40 Elijah and Elisha crossed the Jordan on ____ ground (2 Kings 2:8)

41 Rhoda forgot to open it in her excitement at hearing Peter's voice (Acts 12:13–16)

43 Plain on which golden image of Nebuchadnezzar was set up (Daniel 3:1)

44 Peter admonished, "Be ____ to be found by Him in peace, without spot and blameless" (2 Peter 3:14)

45 "Let them praise His name with the ____," says Psalm 149:3

47 The psalmist's soul panted for God like the "____ pants for the water brooks" (Psalm 42:1)

48 Gives up life

50 Supped and eaten

51 To reside

52 One of Noah's great-great-grandsons (Genesis 10:1.6–7)

53 Bilhah's son, one of the twelve tribes of Israel (Genesis 35:25)

54 "Blessed are the dead who ____ in the Lord" (Revelation 14:13)

The number seven in the Bible is the number of completion and perfection. In the letter box below are hidden seventeen words from the book of Revelation that are associated with the number seven. After you have circled all the hidden words, read the remaining words to find the promise found in Revelation 3:5–6.

H	E	W	H	O	O	V	E	R	C	O	S	M	E	S	S
H	A	S	E	Y	E	L	L	B	E	S	C	L	L	O	T
H	E	R	D	I	N	W	H	I	N	T	E	A	A	G	A
R	M	E	E	S	E	H	C	R	U	H	C	M	N	E	T
S	A	D	N	D	I	W	O	I	L	L	N	P	O	T	S
B	L	N	O	S	T	H	O	U	T	H	I	S	S	N	A
T	R	U	M	P	E	T	S	M	E	F	M	T	R	O	M
T	H	H	E	A	B	U	O	O	K	E	O	A	F	L	I
F	E	T	D	B	U	T	G	I	D	W	I	N	L	L	C
O	N	S	F	E	S	S	K	A	S	H	I	D	S	N	A
M	E	P	B	T	L	E	I	F	L	S	S	S	O	R	E
M	Y	I	A	F	E	D	N	A	T	P	H	L	E	R	A
N	D	R	B	E	G	F	G	O	R	M	E	H	W	I	S
A	S	I	N	G	N	E	S	N	I	A	T	N	U	O	M
L	S	T	H	E	A	W	H	O	H	L	A	S	A	N	B
E	A	S	R	L	E	T	H	I	M	H	E	A	R	W	H
A	T	T	H	E	S	P	I	R	I	T	S	A	Y	S	.

Word Pool

ANGELS BOWLS CHURCHES DIADEMS EYES HEADS HORNS KINGS
LAMPS LAMPSTANDS MOUNTAINS PLAGUES SEALS SPIRITS STARS
THUNDERS TRUMPETS

To the Cathedral

We were created to have a personal relationship with God and to worship Him. Private Bible study and prayer are essential to our fellowship with God, but we also need to meet with other believers on a regular basis.

Hebrew 10:24–25 says, "And let us consider one another in order to stir up love and good works, not forsaking the assembling of ourselves together."

One voice can praise God, but how beautiful is the harmony of sopranos, altos, tenors, and basses.

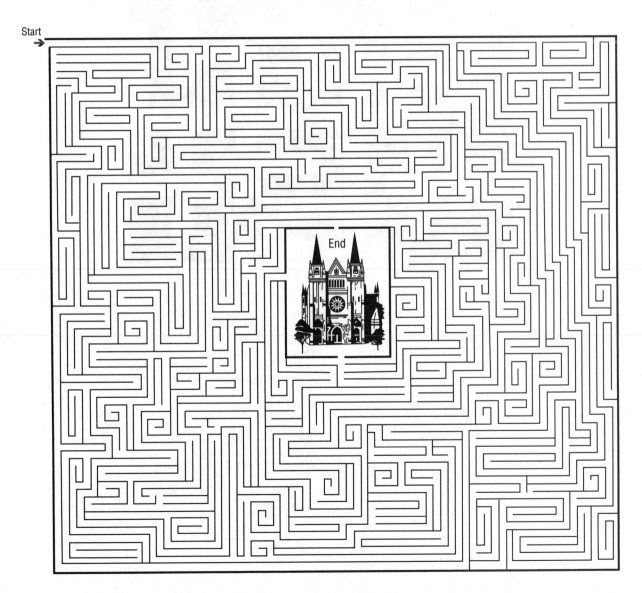

*W*hatever form suffering takes in our lives, it's comforting to know that Jesus was no stranger to it, either. And because He endured to the end, so can we.

Across

3 Forbearance (James 5:10)
5 Deserving (Acts 5:41)
7 Postscript (abbr.)
8 Ill (James 5:14)
10 Some Galileans' blood was "mixed" with their sacrifices by Pilate (Luke 13:1)
11 Like
12 This church will suffer ten days of tribulation (Revelation 2:8, 10)
13 Woman with a flow of ____ (Mark 5:25–26)
17 Inactive (Proverbs 19:15)
18 Compliance (Hebrews 5:8)
19 For nothing, or in ____ (Galatians 3:4)
20 Take down a notch (Deuteronomy 8:2)
22 Intimidate (1 Peter 2:23)
25 Christ suffered for us in the "body" (1 Peter 4:1–2)
26 His sickness was for God's glory (John 11:2–4)
27 Anguish (Revelation 21:4)

28 Paul's ____ in the side (2 Corinthians 12:7–10)
29 Upbraid (1 Timothy 4:10)

Down

1 Take up your ____, and follow Him (Matthew 16:24–25)
2 After testing, we become pure ____ (Job 23:10)
4 Strife (Philippians 1:30)
6 Lured (Hebrews 2:18)
7 Jesus ate this last meal with His disciples (Luke 22:15)
8 The Philistines took his sight (Judges 16:20–21)
9 We suffer for the "realm" of God (2 Thessalonians 1:5)
14 Anxiety (Romans 8:35)
15 Be plentiful (2 Corinthians 1:5)
16 "The ____ of His sufferings" (Philippians 3:10)
21 The just suffered for the ____ (1 Peter 3:18)
23 Tribulations (1 Peter 1:6)
24 "Is anyone . . . suffering? Let him ____" (James 5:13)
26 Paul gladly suffered the "forfeiture" of all things for Jesus' sake (Philippians 3:8)

Complete the message below to discover what is said in the wake of the opening of the sixth seal, and its resulting great earthquake, in the book of Revelation.

Clue: MESSIAH *is* AIUUEMF

The kings of the earth, the great men, the rich men, the commanders, the mighty men, every slave and every free man, hid themselves in the caves and in the rocks of the mountains, and said to the mountains and rocks,

"F̲ A̲ L̲ L̲   O̲ N̲   U̲ S̲   A̲ N̲ D̲
  H M B B   Y Z   S U   M Z J

H̲ I̲ D̲ E̲   U̲ S̲   F̲ R̲ O̲ M̲   T̲ H̲ E̲
  F E J I   S U   H V Y A   T F I

F̲ A̲ C̲ E̲   O̲ F̲   H̲ I̲ M̲   W̲ H̲ O̲
  H M K I   Y H   F E A   Q F Y

S̲ I̲ T̲ S̲   O̲ N̲   T̲ H̲ E̲   T̲ H̲ R̲ O̲ N̲ E̲
  U E T U   Y Z   T F I   T F V Y Z I

A̲ N̲ D̲   F̲ R̲ O̲ M̲   T̲ H̲ E̲   W̲ R̲ A̲ T̲ H̲
  M Z J   H V Y A   T F I   Q V M T F

O̲ F̲   T̲ H̲ E̲   L̲ A̲ M̲ B̲!   F̲ O̲ R̲
  Y H   T F I   B M A L   H Y V

T̲ H̲ E̲   G̲ R̲ E̲ A̲ T̲   D̲ A̲ Y̲   O̲ F̲
  T F I   G V I M T   J M O   Y H

H̲ I̲ S̲   W̲ R̲ A̲ T̲ H̲   H̲ A̲ S̲   C̲ O̲ M̲ E̲'
  F E U   Q V M T F   F M U   K Y A I

A̲ N̲ D̲   W̲ H̲ O̲   I̲ S̲   A̲ B̲ L̲ E̲   T̲ O̲
  M Z J   Q F Y   E U   M L B I   T Y

S̲ T̲ A̲ N̲ D̲?"
  U T M Z J

One of the most beloved and frequently memorized psalms is Psalm 23. See how many of the words you can supply for the grid below without looking up this passage in the Bible.

The LORD is my shepherd; I shall not want. He (3) me to (25) (19) in (6) (12); He leads me beside the (20) (29). He (9) my soul; He (7) me in the (1) of (2) for (16) (23) sake.

Yea, (22) I (4) through the (30) of the (5) of (17), I will fear no (24); for You are (8) me; Your (27) and Your (28), they (10) me.

You (15) a (32) before me in the presence of my (14); You (26) my head with oil; My cup (18) over. (21) (31) and (11) shall follow me all the days of my life; and I will dwell in the (13) of the LORD forever.

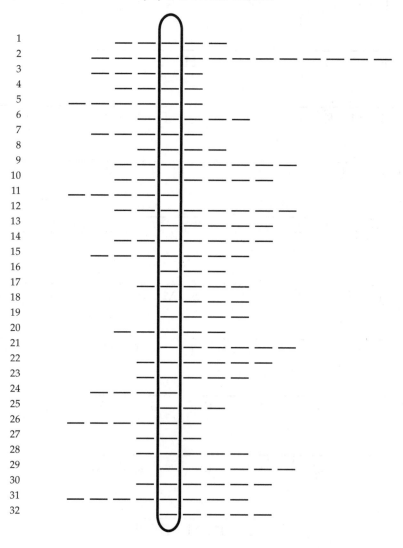

RACING THE STORM

Elijah knew the power of God. So he wasn't surprised when God sent fire from heaven to consume a burnt sacrifice that had been soaked with water (1 Kings 18:30–38).

In the third year of a drought, he knew he could tell King Ahab that the rain was about to come (1 Kings 18:41).

And when the rain came, do you think Elijah was surprised that God helped him outrun the downpour—and Ahab's chariot—to the entrance of Jezreel?

Start

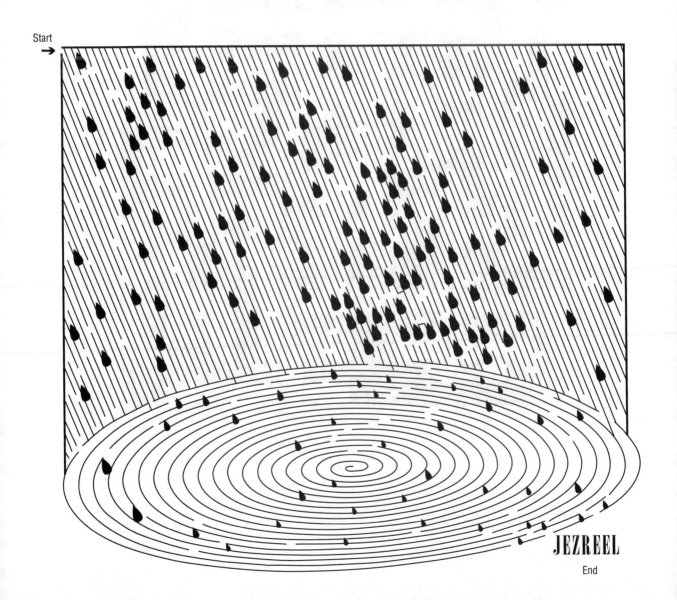

JEZREEL

End

*M*any Bible scholors believe that Colossians 1:15–20 is a hymn of the early church. Complete the words to this passage to complete the crossword. We've provided a Word Pool to help you.

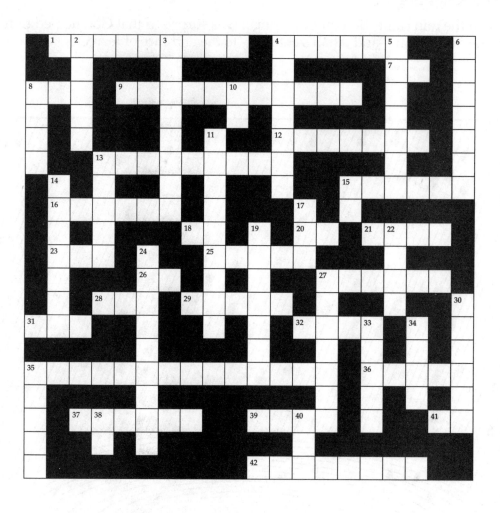

He is the _____ of the _____ _____, the _____ _____ all _____. For
(13 Down)   (13 Across)(17 Down)   (11 Down)(22 Down)   (3 Down)

_____ _____ all _____ _____ created that _____ in heaven and that are on _____,
(15 Down)(28 Across) (37 Across) (34 Down)   (31 Across)   (2 Down)

_____ and invisible, whether _____ or _____ or _____ _____ _____. All things were
(6 Down)   (12 Across) (24 Down) (35 Across) (41 Across) (27 Across)

_____ through Him and _____ Him. And _____ is _____ all things, and _____ Him all
(4 Down)   (8 Across)   (38 Down)   (15 Across)   (7 Across)

things _____. And He_____ the _____ of the _____, the _____, who is the beginning,
(19 Down)   (10 Down)   (32 Across)   (21 Across)   (4 Across)

the firstborn _____ the _____, that in _____ things He may have the _____. For _____
(8 Down)   (39 Across)   (40 Down)   (9 Across)   (18 Across)

_____ the _____ that in Him all _____ _____ should _____, and by Him to _____
(27 Down)   (30 Down)   (23 Across) (42 Across)   (33 Down)   (1 Across)

all thing to _____, by Him, _____ things _____ _____ or things in _____ , having made
(5 Down)   (14 Down)   (20 Across) (36 Across)   (16 Across)

_____ through the _____ _____ His _____ .
(35 Down)   (25 Across) (26 Across)   (29 Across)

Word Pool

ALL   ARE   BEFORE   BLOOD   BODY   BY   CHURCH   CONSIST   CREATED
CREATION   CROSS   DEAD   DOMINIONS   DWELL   EARTH   EARTH
FATHER   FIRSTBORN   FOR   FROM   FULLNESS   GOD   HE   HEAD
HEAVEN   HIM   HIMSELF   IMAGE   IN   INVISIBLE   IS   IT   OF   ON   OR
OVER   PEACE   PLEASED   POWERS   PREEMINENCE   PRINCIPALITIES
RECONCILE   THE   THINGS   THRONES   VISIBLE   WERE   WHETHER

(Duplicate words are intentional.)

Complete the titles of these eleven famous Christmas songs to discover one of the most famous descriptions of Christmas Eve.

1 "Good _____ Men, Rejoice"

2 "O Come, All Ye _____"

3 "Joy to the _____"

4 "Hark! The Herald _____ Sing"

5 "O _____ _____" (2 words)

6 "We _____ King of Orient Are"

7 "It Came Upon a _____ Clear"

8 "The _____ Drummer Boy"

9 "Away in a _____"

10 "O Little Town of _____"

11 "The _____ Noel"

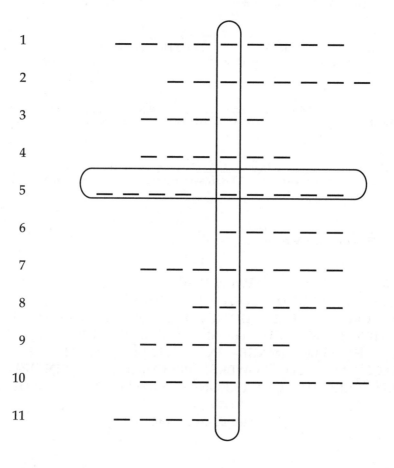

1

2

3

4

5

6

7

8

9

10

11

Find fifteen words in the letter box below that relate to "heavenly beings." See how many you can find before consulting the Word Pool below.

```
M   A   N   G   A   R   R   C   H   A   E   M   E   S   S   E   N   W   O   R
N   I   T   H   R   E   N   G   E   L   T   N   C   I   M   G   N   I   W   S
I   G   N   T   F   O   A   H   M   I   D   W   O   R   S   H   I   P   O   H
W   M   S   I   N   E   A   C   R   I   G   I   H   R   L   E   A   H   M   I
H   I   C   D   S   M   N   I   A   L   H   N   A   L   H   U   C   I   C   P
P   U   B   I   N   T   G   C   H   A   E   P   E   E   F   T   I   E   R   T
L   A   I   N   I   A   E   L   E   I   R   B   A   G   T   S   H   I   D   I
E   R   M   G   S   M   L   R   G   M   O   V   T   R   H   H   R   P   I   M
G   E   S   S   T   L   B   A   I   B   E   S   O   H   E   E   A   O   E   N
N   H   A   E   R   E   R   C   O   N   R   E   S   Y   L   S   V   S   W   G
A   C   R   I   N   I   H   L   L   C   G   A   P   H   N   E   S   M   M   S
H   S   E   S   G   A   N   Y   E   H   L   S   H   I   M   E   R   I   H   C
C   T   R   V   E   E   H   V   N   M   E   G   P   T   N   E   B   P   H   M
R   N   A   L   V   O   A   Y   L   C   I   N   R   I   S   U   I   E   N   I
A   T   E   H   S   E   H   G   A   B   R   I   H   C   R   B   R   I   M   N
M   H   A   T   O   H   O   R   H   T   E   W   E   E   O   I   T   S   I   G
E   O   I   R   W   R   S   N   E   L   N   O   H   A   B   R   T   E   R   S
S   P   H   S   E   M   F   I   C   U   E   C   N   I   R   P   A   S   V   E
S   E   N   G   R   E   G   N   E   S   S   E   M   H   T   S   T   N   S   R
```

Word Pool

SERAPHIM   HEAVENLY HOST   LUCIFER   MICHAEL   CHERUBIM   PRINCE
ARCHANGEL   GABRIEL   WINGS   TIDINGS   MINISTERING SPIRITS   ANGEL
THRONE   MESSENGER   WORSHIP

Complete the words to Isaiah 45:18–25—an "autobiography of the Almighty"—to work this crossword.

For thus says the LORD, Who _____ the _____, Who _____ _____, Who _____ the earth
(14 Across)   (46 Across)   (37 Across) (35 Across)   (2 Down)

and made it, Who has_____ it, Who did not _____ it in vain, Who formed it to be_____ :
(11 Down)   (55 Across)   (28 Across)

"_____ _____(2 words) the LORD, and there is no other. I have not spoken in _____, in a _____
(36 Across)   (9 Down)   (50 Across)

place of the earth; I did not _____ to the _____of Jacob, '_____ _____ in vain'; I, the LORD,
(38 Down)   (9 Across)   (45 Down) (12 Across)

speak righteousness, I declare things that are _____.
(3 Down)

"_____ yourselves and come; draw_____ _____, you who have _____ from the nations. They
(20 Across)   (53 Down) (32 Across)   (44 Down)

_____ no knowledge, _____ _____ the _____ of their carved _____, and _____ to a
(33 Down)   (22 Down) (27 Down)   (26 Down)   (10 Across)   (34 Across)

god that cannot _____.Tell and _____ forth your _____; yes, let them take _____ together.
(16 Down)   (24 Across)   (13 Across)   (23 Across)

Who has _____this from _____ _____ (2 words)? Who has _____ it from that time? Have not I,
(18 Down)   (40 Across)   (49 Across)

the LORD? And there is _____ _____God _____ Me, a _____ God and a _____; there is
(19 Across) (52 Down)   (29 Down)   (21 Across)   (6 Across)

_____besides Me.
(5 Across)

"Look to Me, and _____ saved, all _____ _____ of the _____! For I am God, and there is no
(8 Down)   (48 Across) (59 Across)   (56 Across)

other. I have sworn by _____; the _____ has _____out of My mouth in _____ , and shall not
(42 Down)   (58 Across)   (4 Across)   (7 Down)

_____, that to Me every _____ shall _____, every _____ shall _____ _____ (2 words)
(43 Down)   (1 Down)   (25 Across)   (15 Down)   (49 Down)

oath. He shall say, 'Surely in the _____ I have righteousness and _____. To Him _____
(31 Down)   (39 Down)   (17 Across)

shall_____, and all shall be _____ who are _____ against Him. In the LORD _____ the _____
(13 Down)   (41 Across)   (28 Down)   (30 Across)   (47 Across)

of _____ _____ be justified, and shall _____.'"
(57 Across) (54 Across)   (51 Down)

*F*ind the common "thread" that binds these two hearts together "as one in Christian love."

Solve the message below to discover four major commands given by Jesus, each with a promise.

Clue: MESSIAH *is* SBVVRMQ

D X A P B   T U W'   M T A   Y U X

V Q M F F   T U W   N B   D X A P B A.

O U T A B S T   T U W'   M T A   Y U X

V Q M F F   T U W   N B   O U T A B S T B A.

C U I P R J B'   M T A   Y U X   K R F F

N B   C U I P R J B T.   P R J B'   M T A

R W   K R F F   N B   P R J B T   W U   Y U X:

P U U A   S B M V X I B'   G I B V V B A

A U K T'   V Q M E B T   W U P B W Q B I'

M T A   I X T T R T P   U J B I   K R F F

N B   G X W   R T W U   Y U X I   N U V U S.

"Through the LORD's mercies we are not consumed, because His compassions fail not. They are new every morning" (Lamentations 3:22–23). Great is His faithfulness . . . and His mercy.

Across

4 Paul calls showing mercy a "present" (Romans 12:6–8)

6 Would Joseph show mercy and release this brother? (Genesis 42:24; 43:14)

7 The blind man wouldn't be "silent"—he asked Jesus for mercy (Luke 18:39)

9 "Sow . . . righteousness, 'gather up' in mercy," said Hosea (Hosea 10:12)

10 The mercies given this favorite king were Israel's for the asking (Isaiah 55:3)

12 We obtain mercy at the "seat" of grace (Hebrews 4:16)

13 As the "ordained" of God, put on tender mercies (Colossians 3:12)

15 David knew God's mercies exceeded those of this "person" (2 Samuel 24:14)

16 He and Jeduthun were chosen to thank the Lord for His enduring mercy (1 Chronicles 16:41)

17 God withheld mercy from Jerusalem and Judah for _____ years in Zechariah's time (Zechariah 1:12)

19 Jesus was made like us so He could be merciful and "devoted" High Priest (Hebrews 2:17)

23 The weightier matters of the law, Jesus said, are _____, mercy, and faith (Matthew 23:23)

24 God sends storms for correction, for the "earth," or for mercy (Job 37:13)

26 God wouldn't take His mercy from Solomon as He took it from this king (2 Samuel 7:15)

27 His descendants don't beg bread; He is merciful and "loans" (Psalm 37:25–26)

28 The mercy seat was made of this pure element (Exodus 25:17)

29 Not she, but_____

30 These "lookouts" from the house of Joseph showed mercy to a man of Bethel, but not to the rest of the city (Judges 1:22–24)

31 God extended mercy to Ezra before this king of #22 Down (Ezra 7:21–28)

32 Ben-Hadad hoped this king of Israel was as merciful as advertised (1 Kings 20:13, 31–32)

33 Their mercy saved Lot's life (Genesis 19:15–19)

Down

1 Show no mercy to these Canaanite peoples or to the other six nations, God told Israel (Deuteronomy 7:1–2)

2 Remember Your "gentle" mercies and lovingkindness, David said (Psalm 25:6)

3 "Dear ones," said Jude, look for the mercy of our Lord (Jude 20–21)

5 Mary said, "His mercy is on those who 'stand in awe of' Him" (Luke 1:50)

8 God is kind and merciful to the "ungrateful"(Luke 6:35)

9 Her appearance at the well proved God's mercy to Abraham (Genesis 24:15–27)

11 "Mercy and truth be with you," David told _____ the Gittite, urging him to go home (2 Samuel 15:19–20)

14 God shows mercy to how many who love Him and keep His commandments? (Exodus 20:6)

15 First-person singular possessive

18 God can use "containers" of mercy to show the riches of His glory (Romans 9:23)

20 By the mercies of God, present these as a living sacrifice (Romans 12:1)

21 God will arise and have mercy on this "city," whose name means "fortification" (Psalm 102:13)

22 Thanks to mercy in the eyes of the kings of this nation, Ezra and the people could rebuild the temple (Ezra 9:9)

23 God's mercy gave him favor in the prison keeper's sight (Genesis 39:21)

25 Backsliding Israel could return and enjoy God's mercy and avoid the fall of His "wrath" (Jeremiah 3:12)

29 Be merciful, Lord, "restore" my soul, for I've sinned, said David (Psalm 41:4)

*A*ll the clues from the number puzzles below are from New Testament verses telling about the spread of the gospel and the growth of Christianity. Complete the math problems to find the numbers of the chapter and verse in the book of Revelation where John tells us how many people he saw praising God before the Lamb's throne in heaven. Then complete the following puzzle to find out what these people were saying.

I.

The number of people on the ship that wrecked on the isle of Malta (Acts 27:37)   = ____

Minus . . .
The number of stripes Paul received each time he was beaten (2 Corinthians 11:24)   — ____

Divided by . . .
The number times Paul was shipwrecked (2 Corinthians 11:25)   ÷ ____

Multiplied by . . .
The number of times Paul was beaten by Jewish persecutors (2 Corinthians 11:24)   × ____

Plus . . .
The number of disciples in Jerusalem (Acts 1:15)   + ____

Minus . . .
The approximate number of persons who saw Jesus after the resurrection (1 Corinthians 15:6)   — ____

Minus . . .
The number of years Aeneas was paralyzed before he was healed (Acts 9:33)   — ____

Equals . . .
The chapter number in the book of Revelation where John saw the saints praising God in heaven   = ____

II.

The number of men who believed when Peter preached in Jerusalem (Acts 2:41)   = ____

Plus . . .
The number of persons who followed the false leader Theudas (Acts 5:36)   + ____

Divided by . . .
More than this number of conspirators sought to take Paul's life (Acts 23:12–13)   ÷ ____

Multiplied by . . .
The number of Sabbaths Paul taught in the synagogue in Thessalonica (Acts 17:1–2)   × ____

Plus . . .
The number of horsemen accompanying Paul to Caesarea to appear before Governor Felix (Acts 23:23)   + ____

Divided by . . .
The number of days it took for Paul to sail from Philippi to Troas (Acts 20:6)   ÷ ____

Minus . . .
The number of years Paul stayed in Ephesus preaching the gospel (Acts 19:10)   — ____

Divided by . . .
The number of deacons appointed to distribute provisions to the Greek widows in Jerusalem (Acts 6:3)   ÷ ____

Equals . . .
The verse number in the book of Revelation where John saw the saints praising God in heaven   = ____

Answer: Revelation ____:____

*D*ecode this message to discover one of the most wonderful passages about redemption in the Bible.

Clue: MESSIAH *is* TPWWRND

R   YRFF   QRKP   ZUX   N

GPY   DPNIJ   NGB   HXJ   N

GPY   WHRIRJ   YRJDRG

ZUX ;   R   YRFF   JNSP   JDP

DPNIJ   UC   WJUGP   UXJ

UC   ZUXI   CFPWD   NGB

QRKP   ZUX   N   DPNIJ   UC

CFPWD.   R   YRFF   HXJ   TZ

WHRIRJ   YRJDRG   ZUX

NGB   ONXWP   ZUX   JU

YNFS   RG   TZ   WJNJXJPW '

NGB   ZUX   YRFF   SPPH

TZ   EXBQTPGJW   NGB   BU

JDPT.

*F*irst Chronicles 29:10–15 is a great praise song by King David. Fill in the blanks from this scripture and you'll have all the words you need to complete the crossword grid! (A Word Pool is supplied to help you.)

200

_____ _____ You, _____ _____ _____
(28 Down) (47 Down)   (64 Down) (62 Across) (7 Across)

_____ , our _____ , _____ and _____ .
(10 Down)   (2 Across) (67 Across)   (68 Across)

_____ , O LORD, is _____ _____ , the _____
(22 Across)   (15 Across) (43 Across)   (17 Across)

and the _____ , the _____ and the _____ ;
        (20 Across)   (5 Down)   (25 Down)

for all that is in _____ and in _____ _____
                   (26 Across)   (33 Down) (24 Across)

Yours; _____ is the _____ , O _____ , and
       (18 Across)   (44 Across)   (35 Across)

You are _____ as _____ _____ all.
        (31 Across)   (42 Down) (63 Down)

_____ _____ and _____ come _____
(40 Across) (11 Across)   (53 Down)   (27 Across)

You, and You _____ _____ _____ (2 words).
             (4 Down)   (59 Across)

_____ _____ hand is _____ and _____ ;
(24 Down) (70 Across)   (57 Down)   (29 Down)

_____ Your _____ it is to _____ _____
(36 Across)   (38 Down)   (45 Down) (19 Down)

and to _____ _____ to all.
       (37 Across) (41 Across)

Now therefore, our God, _____ thank You and
                        (56 Across)

_____ Your _____ name.
(30 Down)   (1 Down)

But _____ _____ I, _____ who _____
    (52 Across) (60 Down) (58 Across)   (66 Across)

_____ people, that we _____ _____ _____
(25 Across)   (46 Down) (6 Down) (55 Down)

to _____ _____ _____ _____ this?
   (50 Down) (49 Down) (34 Down) (48 Across)

_____ _____ things _____ from You,
(27 Down) (9 Across)   (51 Across)

and _____ Your _____ we _____ given You.
    (65 Down)   (21 Down)   (61 Down

For we _____ _____ and _____ _____
       (14 Across) (3 Down)   (13 Across) (69 Across)

You, as _____ all _____ _____ ; our _____
        (56 Down)   (23 Down) (8 Down)   (54 Across)

_____ _____ are _____ a _____ , and
(16 Across)(39 Across)   (32 Down) (49 Across)

without _____ .
        (12 Down)

Word Pool

ABLE ALIENS ALL AM AND ARE ARE ARE AS AS BE BEFORE
BLESSED BOTH COME DAYS EARTH EARTH EVER EXALTED FATHER
FATHERS FOR FOREVER FROM FROM GIVE GLORIOUS GLORY
GOD GREAT GREATNESS HAND HAVE HEAD HEAVEN
HONOR HOPE IN IN IS ISRAEL KINGDOM LORD LORD MAJESTY
MAKE MIGHT MY OF OFFER ON OUR OVER OVER ALL OWN
PILGRIMS POWER POWER PRAISE REIGN RICHES SHADOW SHOULD
SO STRENGTH THE VICTORY WE WERE WHO WILLINGLY YOUR
YOURS YOURS

(Duplicate words are intentional.)

In Revelation (see puzzle 68), John recorded his vision of heaven in which he saw the redeemed "of all nations, tribes, peoples, and tongues, standing before the throne and before the Lamb, clothed with white robes, with palm branches in their hands, and crying out with a loud voice." Fit each block of squares correctly into the blank grid to reveal the message of praise to God.

*F*or centuries, Christians have used bells as a part of ceremonies and holidays and to call believers to church services. Find your way through this maze of bells.

Start

↖ End

The book of James asks lots of questions! Complete the questions below, and then use the words to fill in the crossword.

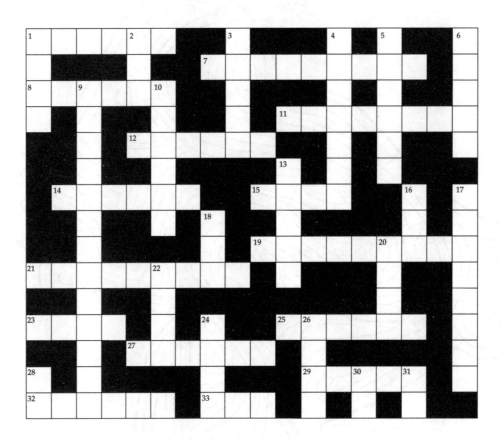

Word Pool

BODY BRETHREN CHEERFUL COURTS DEAD ENMITY FAITH FIGHTS FIGS
GRAPEVINE HE IF IS JUDGE JUSTIFIED LIFE MAN NOBLE NOT OFFERED
OLIVES PEACE PROFIT SCRIPTURE SICK SISTER SON SPIRIT SPRING TREE
UNDERSTANDING VAIN YEARNS YOU

1. Does a _____ send forth fresh water
   (1 Across)
   and bitter from the same opening? (3:11)

2. Can a fig _____, my brethren,
   (20 Down)
   bear_____, or a _____ bear
   (25 Across)   (21 Across)
   _____? (3:12)
   (24 Down)

3. Who is wise and _____ among you? (3:13)
   (9 Down)

4. Where do wars and _____ come from
   (32 Across)
   among you? (4:1)

5. Who are you to _____ another? (4:12)
   (3 Down)

6. What is your _____ ? (4:14)
   (26 Down)

7. _____ anyone among you
   (30 Down)
   suffering? (5:13)

8. Is anyone _____ ? (5:13)
   (11 Across)

9. Is anyone among you _____ ? (5:14)
   (1 Down)

10. Do not the rich oppress you and drag you

    into the _____ ? (2:6)
    (8 Across)

11. Do they not blaspheme that _____ name
    (6 Down)
    by which you are called? (2:7)

12. What does it _____, my _____, if
    (14 Across)   (17 Down)
    someone says _____ has faith but does
    (31 Down)
    not have works? (2:14)

13. _____ a brother or _____ is naked
    (28 Down)   (12 Across)
    and destitute of daily food, and one of you

    says to them,"Depart in _____ , be
    (13 Down)
    warmed and filled," but you do not give

    them the things which are needed for the

    _____ , what does it profit? (2:15–16)
    (23 Across)

14. Do you _____ know that friendship
    (2 Down)
    with the world is _____ with God? (4:4)
    (27 Across)

15. Do _____ think that the _____
    (16 Down)   (19 Across)
    says in _____,"The _____ who
    (22 Down)   (10 Down)
    dwells in us _____ jealously"? (4:5)
    (5 Down)

16. But do you want to know, O foolish

    _____, that faith without works is
    (18 Down)
    _____? Was not Abraham our father
    (15 Across)
    _____ by works when he _____
    (7 Across)   (4 Down)
    Isaac his _____on the altar? Do you see
    (33 Across)
    that faith was working together with his

    works, and by works _____ was made
    (29 Across)
    perfect? (2:20–22)

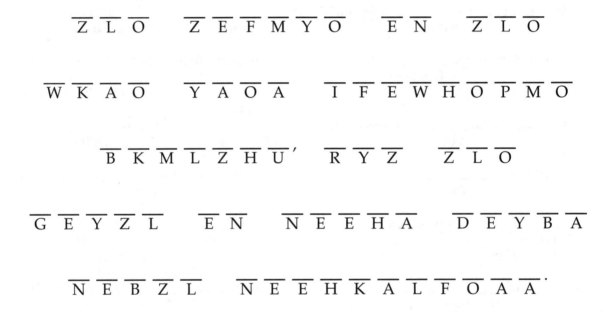

204

*D*ecode the following message to discover a Bible truth about the power of our words.

Clue: MESSIAH *is* GOAAKSL

Z L O   Z E F M Y O   E N   Z L O

W K A O   Y A O A   I F E W H O P M O

B K M L Z H U'   R Y Z   Z L O

G E Y Z L   E N   N E E H A   D E Y B A

N E B Z L   N E E H K A L F O A A.

String together the letters below to reveal a Bible verse about the watchfulness of our heavenly Father.

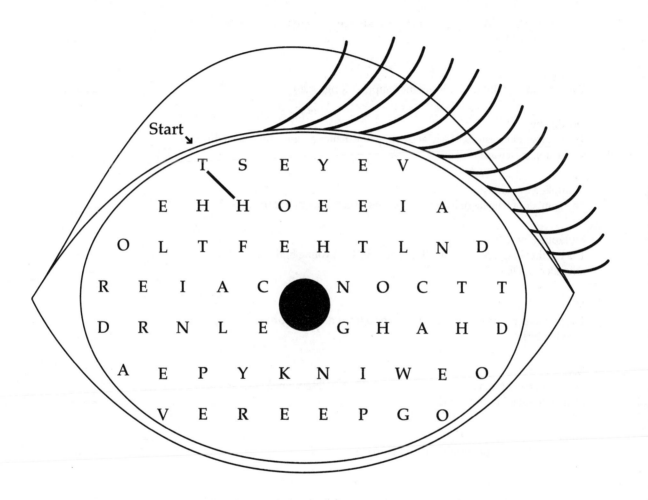

When Jesus turned the water into wine He made enough so the wedding host wouldn't run out again. Complete the puzzle below to find out how much water miraculously became wine.

The number of baths of oil given to the woodsmen who cut timber for the temple (2 Chronicles 2:10)

$=$ _____

Minus . . .
The capacity in baths of the Sea of the temple (1 Kings 7:26)

$-$ _____

Divided by . . .
The number of measures of wheat owed by the debtor after his bill was reduced by the unjust steward (Luke 16:7)

$\div$ _____

Multiplied by . . .
The number of homers of barley Hosea paid to get Gomer back (Hosea 3:2)

$\times$ _____

Multiplied by . . .
The fraction of an ephah of fine flour offered with a young bull as a sacriftce (Numbers 15:9)

$\times$ _____

Minus . . .
The fraction of a hin of wine that was to be offered daily as a drink offering (Exodus 29:40)

$-$ _____

Divided by . . .
The least amount of homers of quail gathered in the desert when God sent flocks of quail to eat (Numbers 11:32)

$\div$ _____

Minus . . .
The omer is _____ of an ephah (Exodus 16:36)

$-$ _____

Plus . . .
The number of omers of manna gathered for each person on the sixth day of the week (Exodus 16:22)

$+$ _____

Divided by . . .
The number of seahs of barley sold for a shekel during the famine in Samaria (2 Kings 7:1)

$\div$ _____

Equals . . .
The number of waterpots filled with water that Jesus turned into wine (John 2:6)

$=$ _____

What kind of wisdom do we need in this life? The kind that leads us to build our lives upon the Rock.

Across

2 "Joyful" is he who finds wisdom (Proverbs 3:13)
6 Jesus increased in wisdom and _____ (Luke 2:52)
8 Wisdom is better than these red jewels (Proverbs 8:11)
11 The mouth of the "godly" speaks wisdom (Proverbs 10:31)
13 "To _____ or not . . . "
14 Wisdom from above is "undefiled" (James 3:17)
15 He rewarded Joseph's wisdom (Genesis 41:39–40)
16 The beginning of wisdom (4 words) (Proverbs 9:10)
18 Not off, but _____
20 He learned the wisdom of the Egyptians (Acts 7:22)
23 Who put wisdom in the "brain"? (Job 38:36)
24 Wisdom is the "primary" thing (Proverbs 4:7)
25 A wise man fears "wickedness" (Proverbs 14:16)
26 A wise man shouldn't "delight" in his wisdom (Jeremiah 9:23)
27 Wisdom and "strength" are God's (Daniel 2:20)

Down

1 Wisdom is better than weapons of "combat" (Ecclesiastes 9:18)
3 The wisdom of wise men shall "crumble" (Isaiah 29:14)
4 Wise-hearted women spun "thread" of goats' hair (Exodus 35:26)
5 Paul: A "man who owed" to the wise and unwise (Romans 1:14)
7 Huram from _____ had wisdom in bronze work (1 Kings 7:13–14)
9 God's testimony makes the "ingenuous" wise (Psalm 19:7)
10 "Divide the living child in two!" he said (1 Kings 3:15, 25)
12 By wisdom, God made the "skies" (Psalm 136:5)
13 This wise son of Uri did artwork (Exodus 31:2–4)
14 Put faith in God's "force," not human wisdom (1 Corinthians 2:5)
16 God uses the _____ to shame the wise (1 Corinthians 1:27)
17 The depth of the "wealth" of God's wisdom (Romans 11:33)
19 The thoughts of the wise are "useless" (1 Corinthians 3:20)
21 Wisdom makes the face "glow" (Ecclesiastes 8:1)
22 Don't be unwise; understand God's "intention" (Ephesians 5:17)
23 The three wise men

One of the items in each set below doesn't belong to the set. Cross out the one that doesn't belong and identify the reason why.

1.   Moses, Elijah, Jesus, John the Baptist

2.   Coin, Mustard seed, Son, Sheep

3.   Burning bush, Shadrach, Tares, Faith

4.   Rahab, Gomer, Mary Magdalene, Zacchaeus

5.   Upper Room, Heart, Tabernacle, Zion

6.   Sarah, Jochebed, Hannah, Elizabeth

7.   Hebrews, Romans, Galatians, Philemon

8.   Levi, Issachar, Dan, Joel

9.   Jehoshaphat, Jehoiakim, Josiah, Jotham

10.   Matthew, Mark, Luke, John

11.   Faith, Joy, Hope, Love

12.   Athens, Corinth, Galatia, Thessalonica

13.   Apostles, Scribes, Prophets, Teachers

14.   Zacharias, Philip, Titus, Herod

15.   Gentleness, Freedom, Self-control, Peace

16.   Ram's horn, Manna, Aaron's rod that budded, Stone tablets

17.   Urim and thummin, Rainbow, Fleece, Pillar of cloud

18.   James, John the Baptist, Stephen, Timothy

19.   Cattle, Fish, Man, Serpent

20.   Lamp, Fire, Chariot, Sword

LETTER TO ROME

*W*hen Paul wrote his letter to the church at Rome, there was no postal service to deliver it for him. It had to be hand-carried.

Since the Jews were plotting against Paul, he had to make a detour on his way to Rome. He asked Phoebe, a friend and a "servant of the church" in Cenchrea (near Corinth), to take the letter to the Roman believers.

Phoebe must visit twelve of Paul's friends before she delivers his letter to Rome. Do not cross back over a path that you have already used.

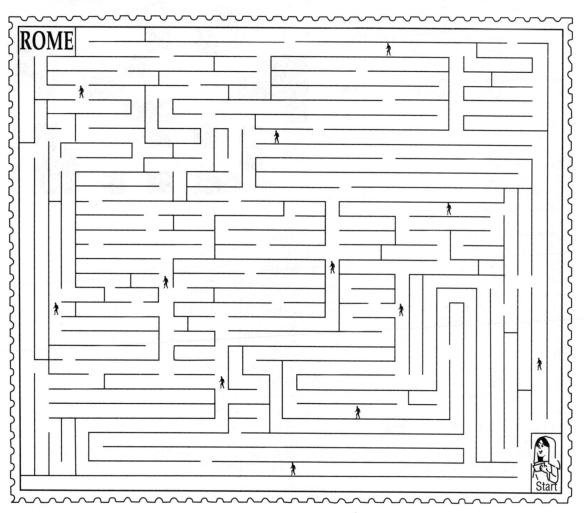

*M*any of the answers come from the life of Samuel and those associated with him. When you complete the crossword, assemble and rearrange the circled letters to reveal a hidden message about Samuel.

Across

1 Samuel anointed Saul, who was the ____ ____ of Israel (2 words)
7 God to Moses: "Tell them I ____ has sent you" (Exodus 3:14)
9 Exclamation
10 Lassie's breed
12 Victory
15 ____ wife turned out to be pretty salty, (poss.)
16 Samuel's mom (1 Samuel 1:20)
17 Do re ____
18 Initials on the side of a ship
20 Priest, young Samuel's boss (1 Samuel 1:25)
21 Tear
22 Diminish
25 Lease
27 Market
28 Barley and oats
31 David's instrument
32 Felonious fire
34 Officer in training
35 David's father (1 Samuel 17:17)
37 1992 riot scene (abbr.)
38 Water transportation
39 Either's partner
40 What Saul was looking for when he met Samuel (1 Samuel 9:3)
41 Having it in a city resulted in a plague of tumors (1 Samuel 5:6–12)

Down

1 Elkanah's relationship to Samuel (1 Samuel 1:19–20)
2 ____ cats and dogs
3 Avoid
4 David's daughter, pursued by Amnon (2 Samuel 13:1)
5 Duke University state (abbr.)
6 He fell for David (1 Samuel 21:9)

7 Hgt. for an airplane
8 Reason for a trip
11 ____ and behold!
13 Abnormal breathing noise
14 Goliath was one
19 Direction from Chicago to Miami
23 Feather or constrictor
24 Capture
26 Pro ball player's cause for a move
29 Plural of am
30 Negatory, good buddy
33 Mails
34 Singer Vicki ____
35 Grief's opposite
36 Where the star was
37 Mauna ____
38 Where Samuel was when God spoke to him as a child (1 Samuel 3:3–4)

Hidden message:

— — — — — — —

*J*eremiah 51:19–20 presents a description of the Lord of hosts as "my battle-ax and weapons of war." In the box of letters below, find seventeen things that will be destroyed or broken in pieces by the Lord of hosts. (See Jeremiah 51:20–23.) (Note: Two of the items have more than one word.)

F	A	R	M	F	L	C	O	S	R	E	L	U	R
D	R	E	H	P	E	H	S	C	K	G	O	V	E
P	E	N	S	F	M	A	S	N	O	S	E	H	R
I	H	A	H	O	I	R	E	D	I	R	H	S	N
E	S	T	E	R	E	I	A	T	I	O	P	K	O
K	N	I	P	N	V	O	N	N	R	N	H	O	R
P	I	O	H	O	R	T	G	S	K	R	N	Y	S
T	O	N	G	S	O	M	E	C	I	E	E	A	M
A	N	S	G	F	W	I	F	O	D	V	R	D	Y
F	O	E	M	D	A	N	L	I	S	O	F	O	O
Y	L	R	L	R	O	A	A	N	O	G	K	L	U
I	N	O	M	A	I	M	T	M	I	E	D	O	N
K	G	T	C	V	D	E	S	A	O	O	G	C	G
E	D	O	I	K	N	K	N	F	M	W	N	I	K
V	N	A	M	G	N	U	O	Y	S	H	E	P	H
G	O	I	T	A	N	X	F	L	W	Y	N	E	E
O	F	A	R	M	E	R	N	O	A	O	I	D	R
R	O	N	R	N	V	E	A	M	M	K	A	M	D

*H*is people might stray, but God always has a plan for bringing them back into the fold. This puzzle is taken from Jeremiah 31 and concerns Israel's restoration.

Across

3 Crying (v. 9)
7 God "bought back" Jacob (v. 11)
10 The seed of Israel could "end" (v. 36)
11 God's "night lights" (3 words) (v. 35)
16 Surveyor's line will go over this hill (v. 39)
17 God's "agreement" with Israel (v. 31)
19 The fathers ate ____ grapes (v. 29)
21 The "remaining part" of Israel (v. 7)
22 Watchmen will cry on Mount ____ (v. 6)

Down

1 Valley and fields won't be "tossed" down again (v. 40)
2 God will forget their "wrongdoing" (v. 34)
4 Their soul will have abundance (v. 14)
5 Grain (v. 12)

6 God put his "statutes" (pl.) in their minds (v. 33)
8 They survived the "saber" (v. 2)
9 God will sow the houses of Israel and Judah with the seed of ____ ____ ____ (3 words) (v. 27)
10 Scolded (v. 18)
12 Set up "markers" (v. 21)
13 "A voice was heard in ____" (v. 15)
14 Imprisonment (v. 23)
15 She cries for her children (v. 15)
18 After #8 Down, they found this in the wilderness (v. 2)
20 They'll plant these (sing.) on mountains (v. 5)
21 Room (abbr.)

KEYS TO THE KINGDOM

*J*esus asked His disciples, "Who do men say that I, the Son of Man, am?" and then again, "Who do you say that I am?" (Matthew 16:13, 15). Peter replied to the question, "You are the Christ, the Son of the living God" (v. 16). Jesus then said to Peter, "Blessed are you, Simon Bar-Jonah, for flesh and blood has not revealed this to you, but My Father who is in heaven. And I also say to you that you are Peter, and on this rock I will build My church, and the gates of Hades shall not prevail against it. And I will give you the keys of the kingdom of heaven, and whatever you bind on earth will be bound in heaven, and whatever you loose on earth will be loosed in heaven" (v. 17–19).

St. Peter's Cross usually depicts these keys of the kingdom with an inverted cross—the shape of the cross on which Peter was martyred. One key is usually shown in silver, the other in gold.

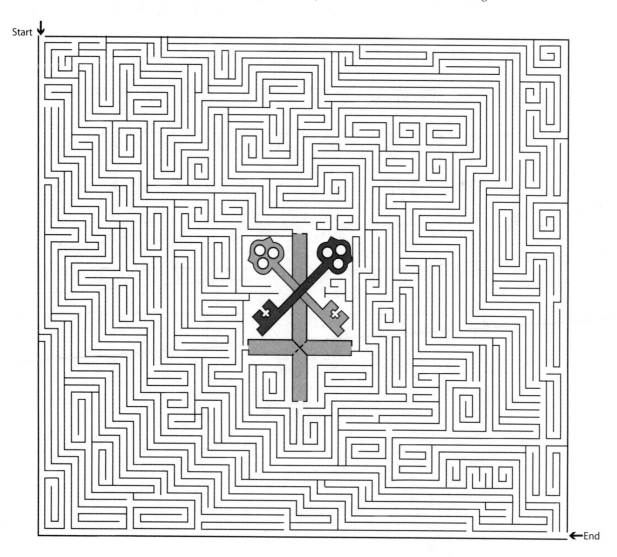

214

Solve the puzzle below to find one of the passages in the Psalms that speaks of the Messiah.

Clue: MESSIAH *is* GKDDIMQ

I   BISS   UVMIDK   AFC'

PFV   AFC   QMXK   MTDBKVKO

GK'   MTO   QMXK   NKLFGK

GA   DMSXMWIFT   WQK

DWFTK   BQILQ   WQK

NCISOKVD   VKRKLWKO

QMD   NKLFGK   WQK   LQIKP

LFVTKVDWFTK   WQID   BMD

WQK   SFVOD   OFITJ'   IW

ID   GMVXKSFCD   IT   FCV

KAKD.

Puzzle Answers

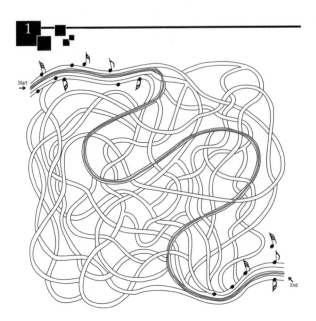

1

2

You are worthy, O Lord to receive glory and honor and power; for You created all things, and by Your will they exist and were created.
(Revelation 4:11)

3

1. John
2. Absalom
3. Esau
4. Moses
5. Benjamin
6. Seth
7. Chilion

8. Lazarus
9. Dinah
10. Hophni
11. Rufus
12. Gershon
13. Joab
14. Abinadab

Household of God

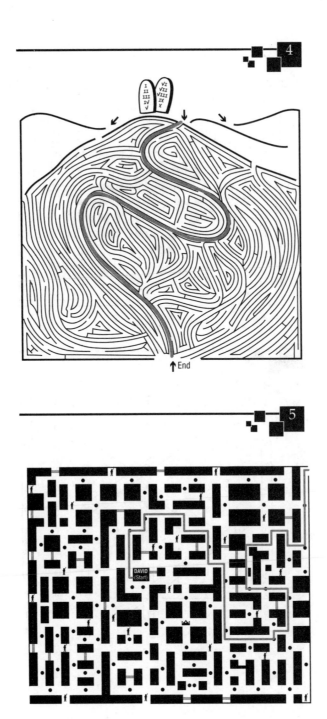

4

End

5

DAVID
(Start)

Puzzle Answers

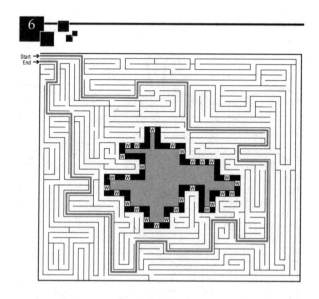

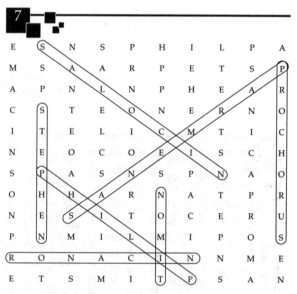

The first seven deacons are listed in Acts 6:5.

8

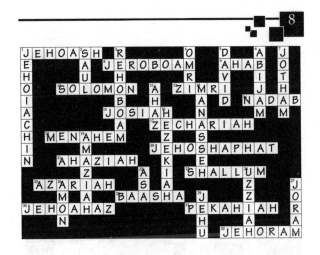

9

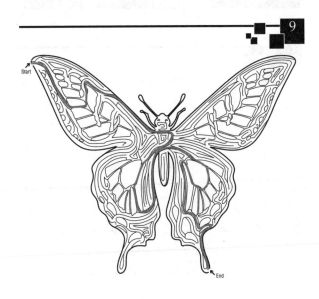

10

$$39 + 5 + 12 - 21 - 17 + 5 + 4 = 27$$

11

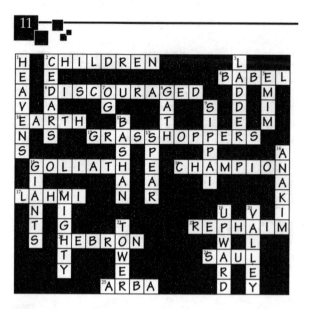

12

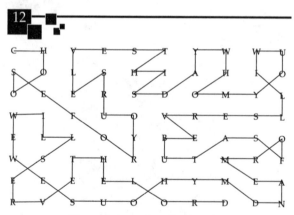

Choose for yourselves this day whom you will serve…. But as for me and my house, we will serve the LORD. (Joshua 24:15)

13

The seven churches from Revelation are Pergamos, Sardis, Ephesus, Laodicea, Thyatira, Philadelphia, and Smyrna.

1-E, 2-C, 3-G, 4-F, 5-A, 6-D, 7-B

14

15

Blessed are the poor in spirit, for theirs is the kingdom of heaven. (Matthew 5:3)

16

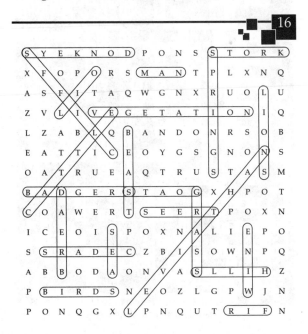

PUZZLE ANSWERS

17

$$60 \times 5 + 40 \div 2 + 30 \div 20 + 5 + 20 \div 5 = 7$$

18

19

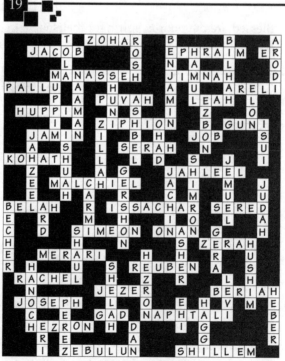

Israel's sons and daughters

Blessed are those who mourn, for they shall be comforted. (Matthew 5:4)

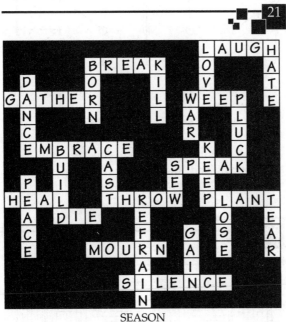

SEASON
PURPOSE

PUZZLE ANSWERS

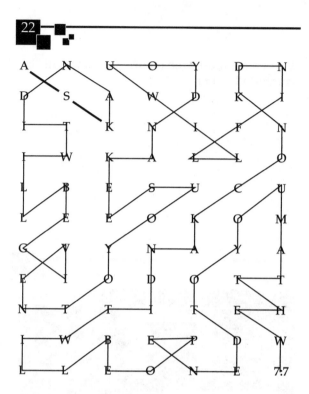

Ask, and it will be given to you; seek, and you will find; knock, and it will be opened to you. (Matthew 7:7)

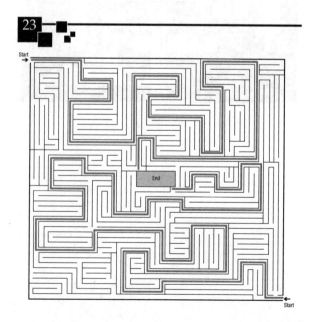

24

INVI**TE**
HUSBAND
WIF**E**
HONORA**B**LE
BRIDE
K**I**SS
WED**D**ING
F**E**AST
L**O**VE
G**I**FT
CHUR**CH**
BETROT**H**ED
BRIDEG**R**OOM
SANCT**I**FIED
GUE**S**TS
GARMEN**T**S

Come to the wedding. (Matthew 22:4)

25

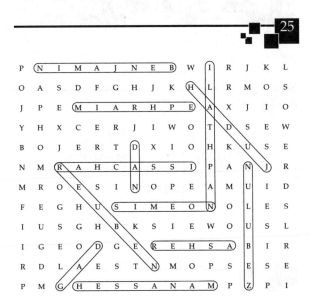

PUZZLE ANSWERS

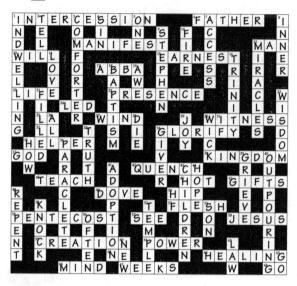

Crossword answers (grid 26):
INTERCESSION · FATHER · MANIFEST · EARNEST · ABBA · PRESENCE · WIND · WITNESS · GLORIFY · HELPER · GOD · KINGDOM · QUENCH · TEACH · HOT · GIFTS · DOVE · HIP · FLESH · PENTECOST · SEE · JESUS · CREATION · POWER · HEALING · MIND · WEEKS · GO

GABRIEL   ARCHANGEL
CHERUBIM   LUCIFER
HEAVENLY HOST   SERAPHIM
MICHAEL

MESSENGER

Confess your trespasses to one another, and pray for one another that you may be healed. The effective, fervent prayer of a righteous man avails much. (James 5:16, NKJ)

29

Bonus: MOTHER-IN-LAW

30

$8 \times 11 + 30 + 2 \div 4 + 40 - 10 + 21 - 52 + 2 - 6 + 10 + 5 = 40$

31

BATTLE   LAMPS
MIDIANITES   PITCHERS
GAP   FLEECES
SHOUT

GIDEON

PUZZLE ANSWERS

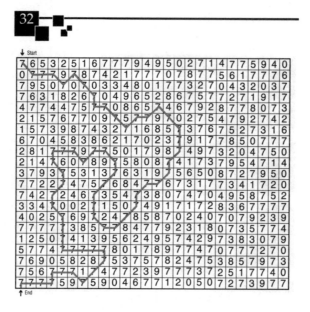

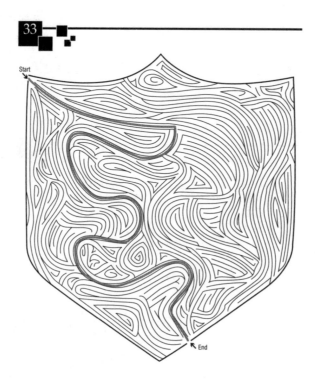

34

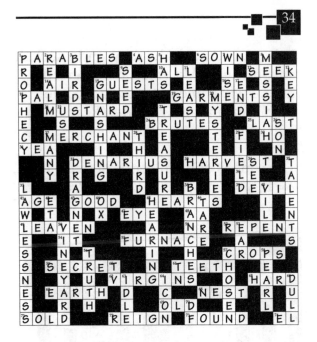

35

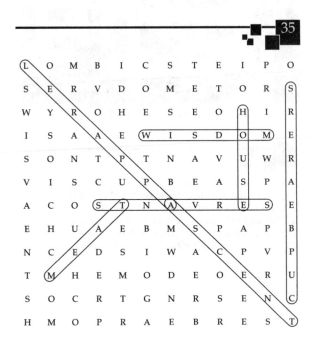

PUZZLE ANSWERS

36

Behold, I stand at the door and knock. If anyone hears My voice and opens the door, I will come in to him and dine with him, and he with Me. (Revelation 3:20, NKJ)

The code is done in series of fives: 1 = A, 2 = B, 3 = C, 4 = D, 5 = E, 1 = F, 2 = G, etc.

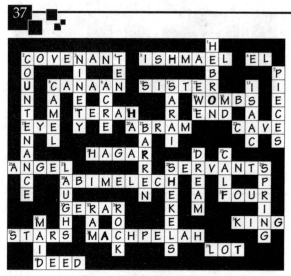

Bonus: THROUGH FAITH

Go therefore and make disciples of all nations, baptizing them in the name of the Father and of the Son and of the Holy Spirit, teaching them to observe all things that I have commanded you; and lo, I am with you always, even to the end of the age. (Matthew 28:19-20, NKJ)

39

40

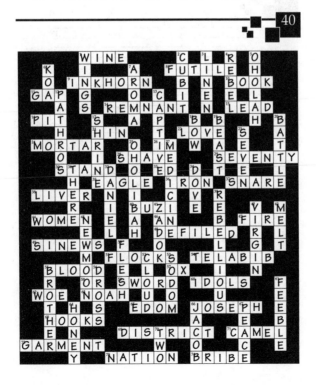

PUZZLE ANSWERS

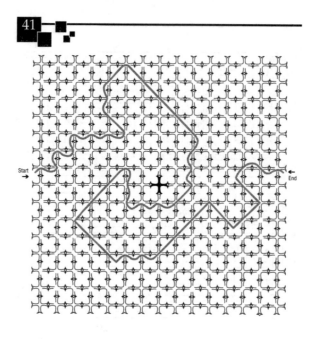

41

Start
→

End
←

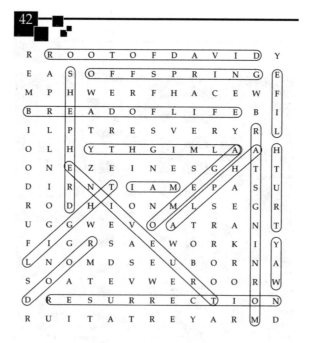

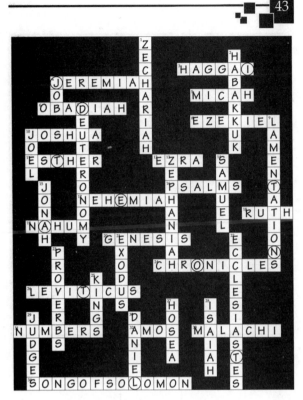

Unscrambled letters: JOT AND TITTLE

Unscrambled words: hand weapon, staff, vessels, ark, cross, idols, doors, cart, fire, floors, block, yokes, poles, boats, bars, canopy, bows, cherubim, manger, carved image, temple, gods, arrows, platform, table, siegeworks, musical instruments, walls, altar, offering, tabernacle, molded image, ships, boards, threshing implements, gopher, palanquin, pillars

Unscramble verse: And now abide faith, hope, love, these three; but the greatest of these is love. (1 Corinthians 13:13, NKJ)

PUZZLE ANSWERS

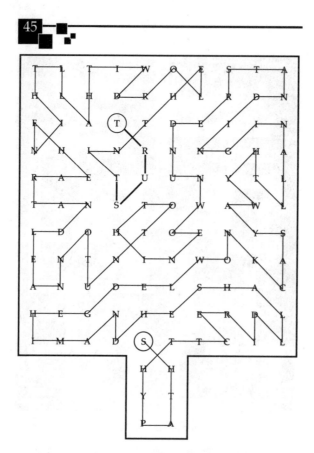

TRUST IN THE LORD WITH ALL THINE HEART;
AND LEAN NOT UNTO THINE OWN UNDER-
STANDING. IN ALL THY WAYS ACKNOWLEDGE
HIM, AND HE SHALL DIRECT THY PATHS.
(Proverbs 3:5-6)

46

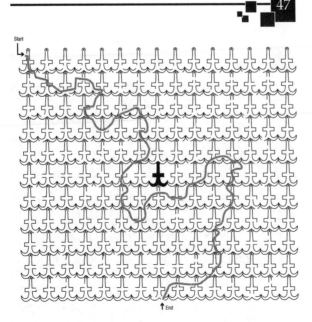

47

Puzzle Answers

48

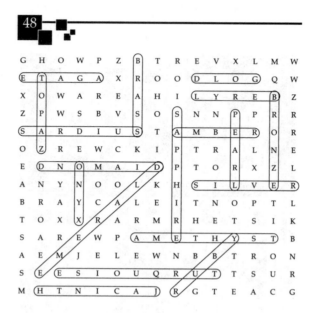

49

$$7 + 7 \times 10 \times 3 \div 6 + 14 \div 2 + 7 +$$
$$15 - 1 \div 7 - 2 = 7$$

50

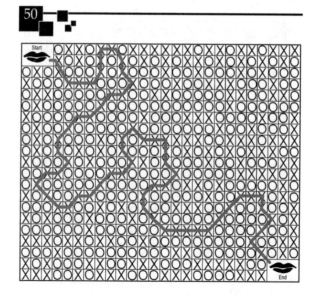

51

ABIRAM AND DATHAN
ACHAN
HEROD AGRIPPA I
AHAZ
JEROBOAM I
ABIHU AND NADAB
AMNON
ATHALIAH

DOEG THE EDOMITE
PASHHUR
SANBALLAT
REHOBOAM
TERTULLUS
ZEDEKIAH
ELYMAS

TRIBULATION

52

For God so loved the world, that he gave his only begotten Son, that whosoever believeth in him should not perish, but have everlasting life. (John 3:16)

53

Unscrambled letters: FORGIVENESS

PUZZLE ANSWERS

54

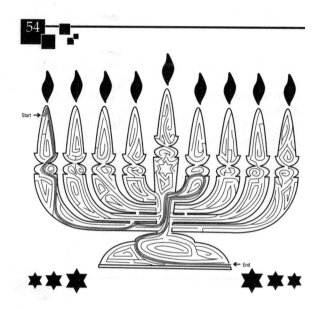

Start →

← End

55

TRUST
WORS**H**IP
STR**E**NGTH
GL**O**RY
DOMI**N**ION
LIFE
ENERG**Y**
KNO**W**LEDGE
KINGDOM
AN**S**WERS
REWARD
ALLE**G**IANCE
HONOR
OBE**D**IENCE
DEV**O**TION
FUT**UR**E
P**R**AISE
RE**S**OURCES
M**A**JESTY
LO**V**E
CHO**IC**E
P**O**WER
C**R**OWN

56

57

PHILISTINES   AHAB   JEZEBEL
GIDEON   AMALEKITES   JORAM
AHINOAM   ELIJAH   JEHU
ISH-BOSHETH   NABOTH   MIDIANITES

              JEZREEL

PUZZLE ANSWERS

58

Start ↓

↑ End

59

And they were all filled with the Holy Spirit and began to speak with other tongues, as the Spirit gave them utterance. (Acts 2:4, NKJ)

60

FREE	ACCUSED
SPIRIT	OLD MAN
GLORY	CARNAL
HEIRS	BONDAGE
LIBERTY	FLESH
LIFE	ENMITY
OBEDIENCE	SIN
REQUIREMENT	LAW
SONS AND DAUGHTERS	DEATH
ADOPTION	GUILT
PEACE	CORRUPTION
JESUS CHRIST	SELF-SEEKING
JUSTIFIED	
	CONDEMNATION
RIGHTEOUSNESS	

61

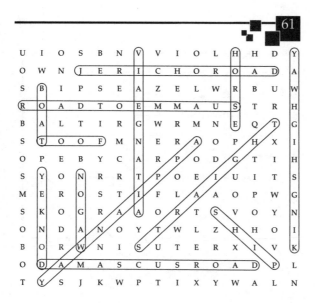

62

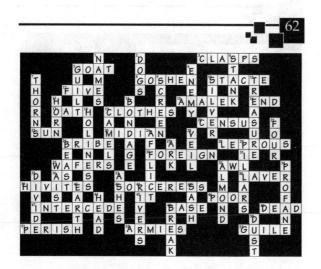

63

The code: Take the alphabet and number from front (A) to back (Z) to middle (M, N) and repeat until all letters have a number A=1, Z=2, M=3, N=4, B=5, Y=6, L=7, O=8, C=9, X=10, K=11, P=12, and so on.

Do not be wise in your own eyes; fear the LORD and depart from evil. (Proverbs 3:7, NKJ)

PUZZLE ANSWERS

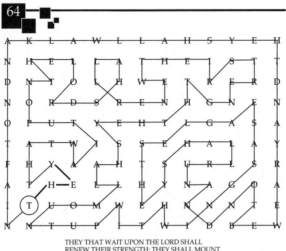

THEY THAT WAIT UPON THE LORD SHALL
RENEW THEIR STRENGTH; THEY SHALL MOUNT
UP WITH WINGS AS EAGLES; THEY SHALL RUN,
AND NOT BE WEARY; AND THEY SHALL WALK
AND NOT FAINT. (Isaiah 40:31)

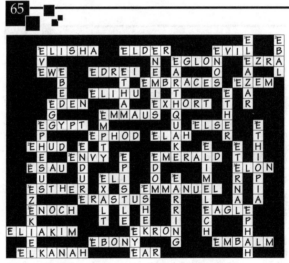

For My yoke is easy and My burden is light.
(Matthew 11:30, NKJ)

66

$$365 + 182 \times 2 - 600 + 969 - 75 +$$
$$130 \div 3 + 162 + 105 + 70 - 20 +$$
$$130 - 30 + 65 + 12 = 1000$$

67

ETHBAAL   ELIJAH
PROPHETS   DOGS
QUEEN   JEZREEL
SIDONIAN   VINEYARD
NABOTH   JEHU
EUNUCHS   AHAB

JEZEBEL

68

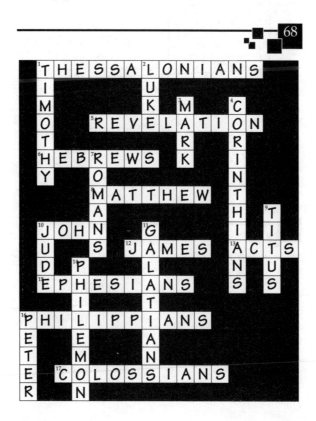

69

The code: The vowels — a, e, i, o, u — are numbers 1,
2, 3, 4, 5. The rest of the alphabet is then numbered,
beginning with 6. B=6, C=7, D=8, F=9, etc.

For unto us a Child is born, unto us a Son is given;
and the government will be upon His shoulder. And
His name will be called wonderful, Counselor,
Mighty God, everlasting Father, Prince of Peace.

PUZZLE ANSWERS

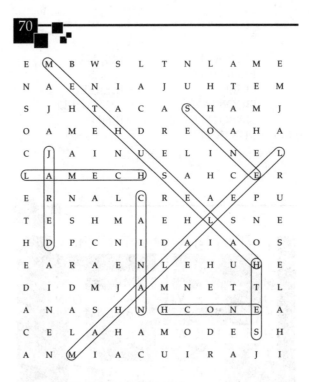

MOSES   ABEL
LABAN   JACOB
MESHA   LORD
DAVID   JOSEPH
JAZIZ   ABRAHAM

     SHEPHERD

For I consider that the sufferings of this present time are not worthy to be compared with the glory which shall be revealed. (Romans 8:18, NKJ)

PUZZLE ANSWERS

74

1. Do not enter the path of the wicked, and do not walk in the way of evil. (Proverbs 4:14, NKJ)

2. Honor the LORD with your possessions, and with the firstfruits of all your increase. (Proverbs 3:9, NKJ)

3. Evil pursues sinners, but to the righteous good shall be repaid. (Proverbs 13:21, NKJ)

4. A wise son makes a glad father, but a foolish son is the grief of his mother. (Proverbs 10:1, NKJ)

5. Hatred stirs up strife, but love covers all sins. (Proverbs 10:12, NKJ)

Unscrambled letters: Apples of gold

75

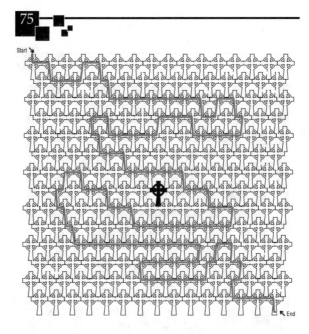

SO**RROWS**
CU**T OFF**
STR**IPES**
SMI**TTEN**
NO B**E**AUTY
DE**S**PISED
BRUI**S**ED
STR**I**CKEN
ARM
CHASTISEMENT
R**OO**T
WO**U**NDED
TENDE**R**PLANT
REJE**C**TED
SHEEP
GRIEF
AFFL**IC**TED
OPPRE**S**SED
INIQUI**T**Y

PUZZLE ANSWERS

The 13 words are the 12 disciples — plus the disciple who later replaced Judas: Philip, Simon, James, Thaddaeus, Judas, Thomas, John, James, Peter, Andrew, Matthew, Bartholomew, and Matthias.

Unscrambled letters: Praise His Name!

80

Pass through each item of offering before bringing it to Moses.
Do not cross back over a path that you have already used.

◆ = Offering

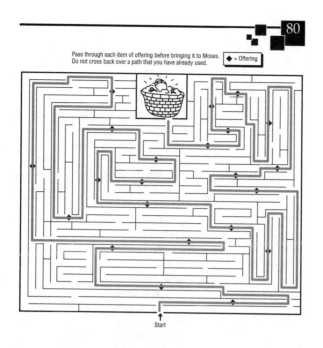

Start

81

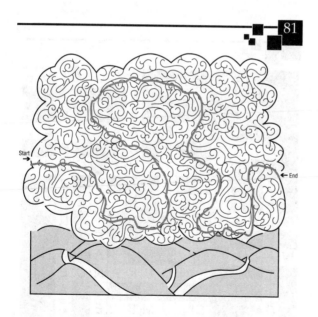

Start

End

PUZZLE ANSWERS

WATER
CLOTHING
FAITH
DELIVERANCE
KNOWLEDGE
SHELTER
FORGIVENESS
INSIGHT
VICTORY
WISDOM
FRIENDSHIP
GUIDANCE
HEALING
STRENGTH
FOOD
SUPPLY
REWARDS
SALVATION
INSPIRATION
PRESENCE
PROTECTION

84

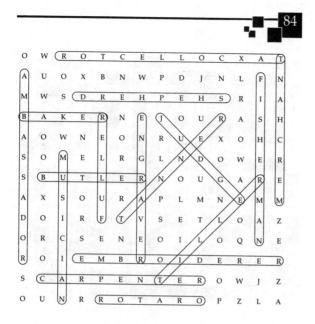

```
O   W  R  O  T  C  E  L  L  O  C  X  A  T
A   U  O  X  B  N  W  P  D  J  N  L  F  N
M   W  S  D  R  E  H  P  E  H  S  R  I  A
B   A  K  E  R  N  E  J  O  U  R  A  S  H
A   O  W  N  E  O  N  R  U  E  X  O  H  C
S   O  M  E  L  R  G  L  N  D  O  W  E  R
S   B  U  T  L  E  R  N  O  U  G  A  R  E
A   X  S  O  U  R  A  P  L  M  N  E  M  M
D   O  I  R  F  T  V  S  E  T  L  O  A  Z
O   R  C  S  E  N  E  O  I  L  O  Q  N  E
R   O  I  E  M  B  R  O  I  D  E  R  E  R
S   C  A  R  P  E  N  T  E  R  O  W  J  Z
O   U  N  R  R  O  T  A  R  O  P  Z  L  A
```

85

SANCTUARY
YA**H**WEH
CHILDR**E**N OF ISRAEL
AR**K** OF THE COVENANT
RAD**I**ANCE
TABER**N**ACLE
PILL**A**R OF CLOUD
HOLY PLACE
PRESENCE OF **G**OD
DWE**L**LING
M**O**UNT SINAI
PILLA**R** OF FIRE
M**Y** PEOPLE

SHEKINAH GLORY

Where God dwells now:
IN YOU

Puzzle Answers

88

But we all, with unveiled face,
beholding as in a mirror the glory of the
Lord, are being transformed into the
same image from glory to glory.
(2 Corinthians 3:18)

89

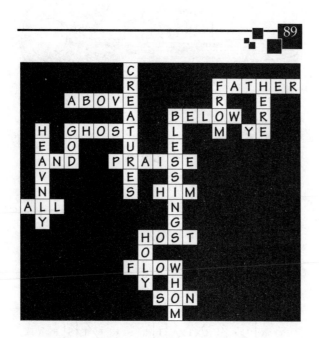

Puzzle Answers

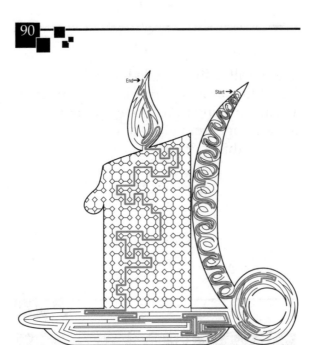

L B A N O S O J U R V D C A A I A N P
E U T E G Y A I T N I S N A A I T I T
G J O W I L F C I D O S A L V I D I S
Y A H M A N D S H E S A E G Y M P T A
P S E S M A A C A D A B A L A A M I U
J F P J T H R U R A S E B N H N A A C
O I H O O B A E N B G L A A I O A N B
N W E S U N H H A Y H E P D L A L S A
A H C E R P A T P D E H C A A H C B A
D O A P E H C T A I R S C B T S P A L
A A I H R T I N H V D L I U I W E A J
V M S U L A S O D A S A R D D I S C O
M A A D N U A J C D N B A A M F O I N
A N B A E L A H P E S V N O J E J S A
N O E V I A C S A J I O N A T H A R W
O A S A A C B A A C I W N A M H T U I
H R U T D A V I J O S E A E B A F G C
R L A B S I C A A C E B L G Y P N I A

92

1 — C, Romans 6:17
2 — G, 1 Peter 1:22
3 — E, Romans 5:19
4 — B, Deuteronomy 13:4
5 — F, l Samuel 15:22
6 — A, John 14:23
7 — D, Jeremiah 7:23

93

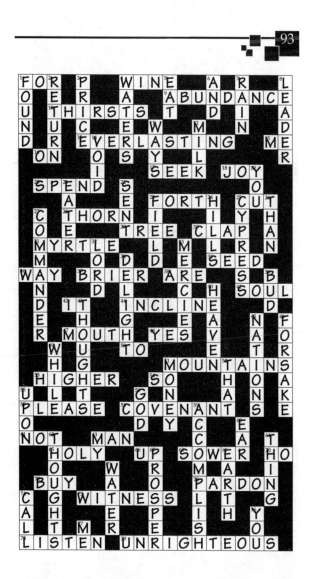

PUZZLE ANSWERS

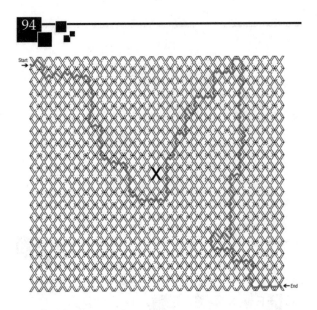

VINE
FR**U**IT
TE**N**D
KE**E**PERS
SPICE**D** WINE
BRANCHES
OWN**E**R
CLU**S**TERS
BLO**S**SOMS
PRUN**E**
G**R**APES

VINEDRESSER

96

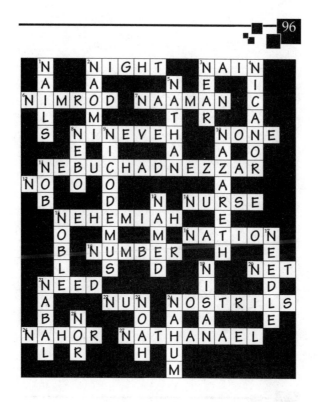

97

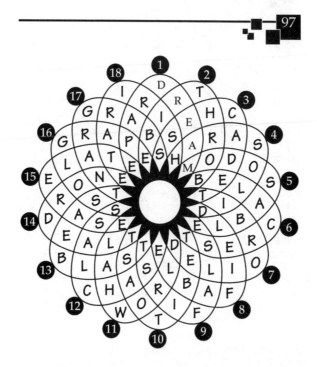

PUZZLE ANSWERS

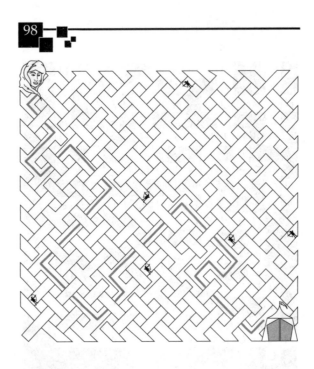

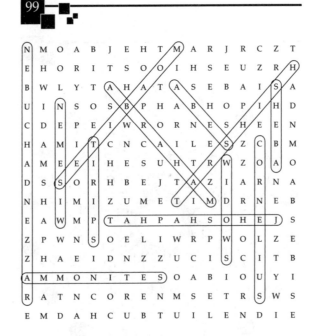

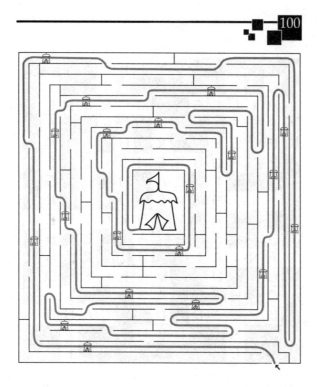

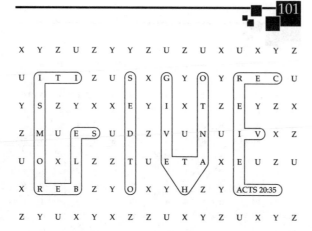

Eliminate all of the letters U, X, Y, and Z. Draw a line around the letters remaining, including the Bible reference. You will have the word *GIVE*. Within the lines of the word *GIVE* you will find this message from Acts 20:35: "It is more blessed to give than to receive"

(The letters of the verse are in the order they would be in if you were writing the word *GIVE*.)

PUZZLE ANSWERS

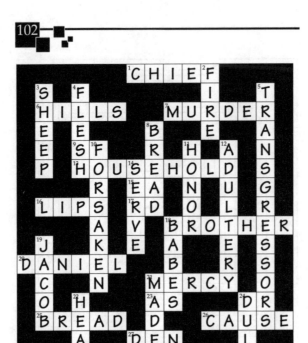

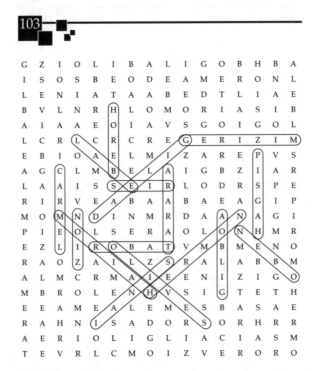

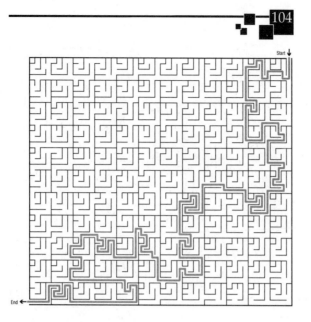

104

Start ↓

End ←

105

My little children, these things I write to you, so that you may not sin. And if anyone sins, we have an Advocate with the Father, Jesus Christ the righteous. And He Himself is the propitiation for our sins, and not for ours only but also for the whole world. (1 John 2:1–2)

PUZZLE ANSWERS

He who does not love Me does not keep
My words; and the word which you
hear is not Mine but the Father's who
sent Me. (John 14:24)

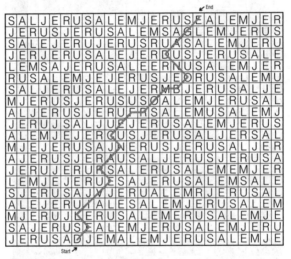

Let not your heart be troubled; you
believe in God, believe also in Me.
(John 14:1)

BAT**H**SHEBA
R**A**CHEL
ZI**P**PORAH
ZIL**P**AH
MAR**Y**
BASE**M**ATH
JOCHEBED
RU**T**H
LEA**H**
EVE
HAGA**R**
SARAH
A**D**AH
H**A**NNAH
MAR**Y**

HAPPY MOTHER'S DAY

Bonus: HEAVEN

Puzzle Answers

Start →

← End

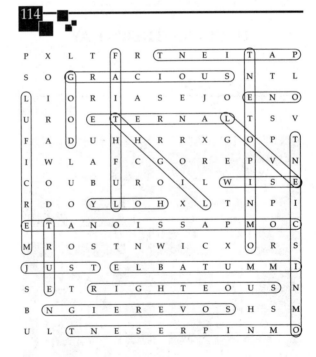

Bonus: SEVENTH DAY

SIL**A**S
MARK
TIM**O**THY
TYRA**N**NUS
A**G**ABUS
EU**T**YCHUS
TY**CH**ICUS
AEN**E**AS
LUK**E**
G**A**IUS
DAMA**R**IS
LYDIA
MAR**Y**
PRIS**C**ILLA
TROP**H**IMUS
E**R**ASTUS
AQU**I**LA
ARI**S**TARCHUS
TABI**T**HA
S**I**LVANUS
SOP**A**TER
COR**N**ELIUS
ONE**S**IMUS

AMONG THE EARLY CHRISTIANS

PUZZLE ANSWERS

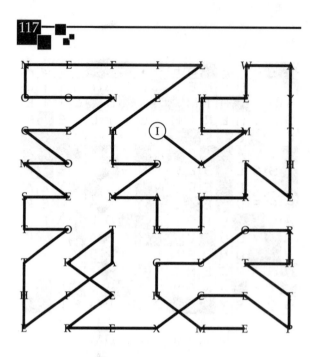

I am the way, the truth, and the life. No one comes to the Father except through Me. (John 14:6)

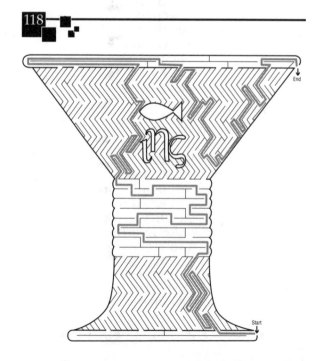

119

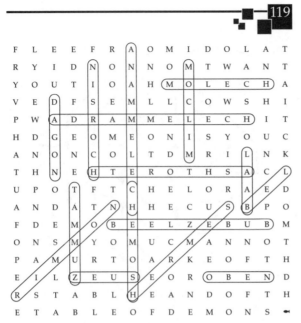

```
F L E E F R A O M I D O L A T
R Y I D N O N N O M T W A N T
Y O U T I O A H M O L E C H A
V E D F S E M L L C O W S H I
P W A D R A M M E L E C H I T
H D G E O M E O N I S Y O U C
A N O N C O L T D M R I L N K
T H N E H T E R O T H S A C L
U P O T F T C H E L O R A E D
A N D A T N H H E C U S B P O
F D E M O B E E L Z E B U B M
O N S M Y O M U C M A N N O T
P A M U R T O A R K E O F T H
E I L Z E U S E O R O B E N D
R S T A B L H E A N D O F T H
E T A B L E O F D E M O N S
```

Flee from idolatry… I do not want you
to have fellowship with demons. You
cannot drink the cup of the Lord and the
cup of demons; you cannot partake of
the Lord's table and of the table of
demons. (1 Corinthians 10:14b, 20b–21)

120

```
S A M A R I A   F   A N D   O
H     S   R   S H U N A M M I T E
D E A T H   A R E A     A     L
  E   B E S T   T     M     T
  P L A S T E R S   S T A F F H
A B E     I   I   C H A N E L R
R I V E R J O R D A N   N O S E
  E     O     P   C U T E
  E L I J A H   C H O K E R
  D   E   N   A X     S   O
G E H A Z I   W A T E R   H Y M N
O R E   E   B E N   N A T U R A L
  R   B A R L E Y   G   T I N Y
T   N   E   A     R E D C A T
W H I R L W I N D     H   L
O   A   D O T H A N     M E N
```

Bonus: ELIJAH

PUZZLE ANSWERS

He who does not love does not know
God, for God is love. (1 John 4:8)

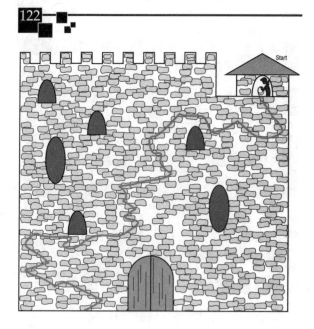

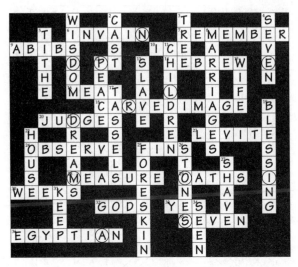

Bonus: PROMISED LAND

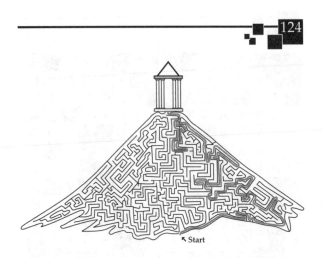

↖ Start

PUZZLE ANSWERS

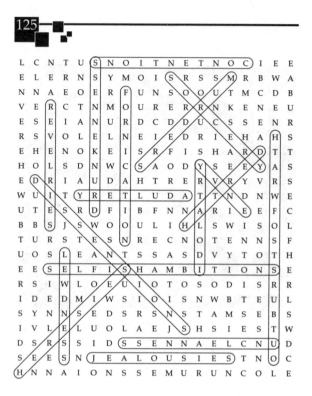

125

```
L C N T U S N O I T N E T N O C I E E
E L E R N S Y M O I S R S S M R B W A
N N A E O E R F U N S O O U T M C D B
V E R C T N M O U R E R R N K E N E U
E S E I A N U R D C D D U C S S E N R
R S V O L E L N E I E D R I E H A H S
E H E N O K E I S R F I S H A R D T T
H O L S D N W C S A O D Y S E E Y A S
E D R I A U D A H T R E R V R Y V R S
W U I T Y R E T L U D A T T N D N W E
U T E S R D F I B F N N A R I E E F C
B B S J S W O O U L I H L S W I S O L
T U R S T E S N R E C N O T E N N S F
U O S L E A N T S S A S D V Y T O T H
E E S E L F I S H A M B I T I O N S E
R S I W L O E U I O T O S O D I S R R
I D E D M I W S I O I S N W B T E U L
S Y N N S E D S R S N S T A M S E B S
I V L E L U O L A E J S H S I E S T W
D S R S S I D S S E N N A E L C N U D
S E E S N J E A L O U S I E S T N O C
H N N A I O N S S E M U R U N C O L E
```

126

```
 A P O   O F F   C S L     S
   E X A M P L E   C H O O S E
   T A   R E A D   S H E L T I E
 S E R V A N T   T H E R E   L M
 H A T E D   H E R O D   S O S
 O C H R E   C U R D S   A   R
 W H E Y   P R O T E A   L E I
   N   L   N H   R   V   G
 O   P   A E R O   S   S M A S H
 P R O C L A I M   A   M O T E T
 E   T O A S T I N G   A S I A
 N   G R E E C E   A L S O
 S P A S M   S T E A L   N O R
```

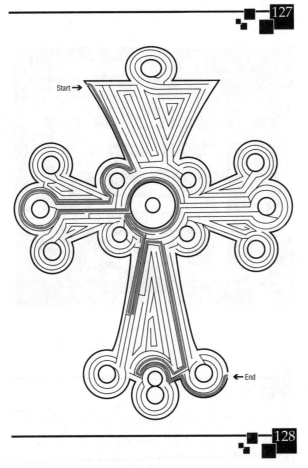

Start →

← End

NOT **P**ARADE ITSELF
ABID**E**
ENDU**R**ES
NOT PU**F**FED UP
NOT **E**NVY
NOT REJOI**C**E IN INIQUITY
GREA**T**EST
BE**L**IEVES
THINKS N**O** EVIL
NOT PRO**V**OKED
THERE IS NO F**E**AR IN LOVE. BUT…
BE**C**AME A MAN
NOT BEH**A**VE RUDELY
NOT **S**EEK ITS OWN
FACE **T**O FACE
I**S** KIND
H**O**PES
S**U**FFERS
TRUTH
NEVER **F**AILS
P**E**RFECT
AS I **A**LSO AM KNOWN
BEA**R**S

There is no fear in love; but perfect love
casts out fear. (1 John 4:18)

PUZZLE ANSWERS

129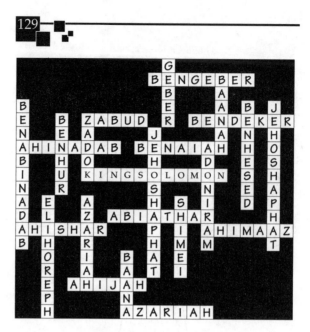

130

Come to Me, all you who labor and are heavy laden, and I will give you rest. Take My yoke upon you and learn from Me, for I am gentle and lowly in heart, and you will find rest for your souls. For My yoke is easy and My burden is light. (Matthew 11:28–30)

JUST ONE
WOND**E**RFUL
SERVANT
OUR RIGHTEO**U**SNESS
COUN**S**ELOR
KING OF **T**HE JEWS
C**H**RIST
VIN**E**
ALPHA AND O**M**EGA
PRINCE OF P**E**ACE
MAN OF **S**ORROWS
DAY**S**PRING
MED**I**ATOR
BRIGHT **A**ND MORNING STAR
SHEP**H**ERD

JESUS THE MESSIAH

PUZZLE ANSWERS

133

Blood   Pestilence   Locusts
Frogs   Boils   Darkness
Lice   Hail   Death
Flies

Unscrambled letters: HARDENED HEART

134

$$30,000 \times 0.25 \div 480 \times 4 \times 60 \div 3 \times 20$$
$$- 3,300 \div 20 \times 2 - 2,000 + 40 \div 30 = 7$$

135

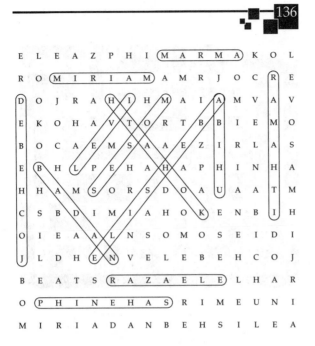

Levi—great-grandfather; Kohath—grandfather;
Amram—father; Jochebed—mother;
Moses—brother; Miriam—sister; Elisheba—wife;
Nadab, Abihu, Eleazar, Ithamar—sons;
Phinehas—grandson

PUZZLE ANSWERS

The crossword answers include:

ELIJAH, AH, D, P, N, TRUTH, JEHOSHAPHAT, D, LIFE, T, WATER, AMORITES, W, BOISTEROUS, WISDOM, REBUKE, MULTIPLIED, ESAU, WINDANDSEA, CAESAR, FOREVER, SYNAGOGUE, RACHEL

JACOB   ELIJAH
NOAH   children of REUBEN and GAD
ABRAHAM   LEVITES
MOSES

Unscrambled letters: ALTAR

In every place where I record My name I will come to you, and I will bless you. (Exodus 20:24)

141

142

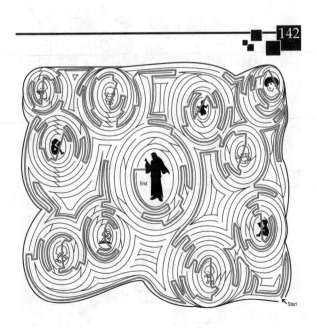

PUZZLE ANSWERS

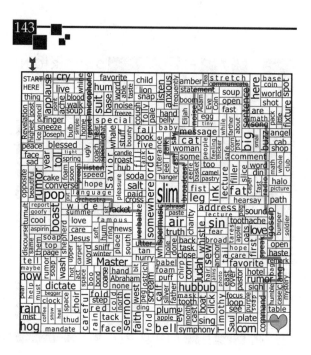

143

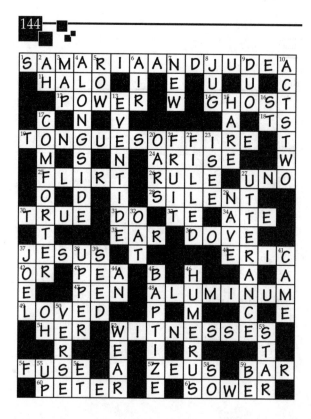

144

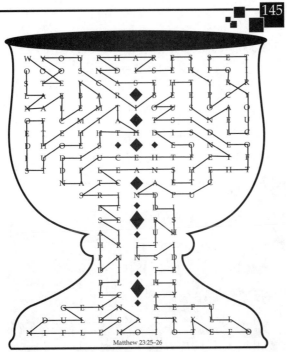

Matthew 23:25–26

Woe to you, scribes and Pharisees, hypocrites! For you cleanse the outside of the cup and dish, but inside they are full of extortion and self-indulgence. Blind Pharisee, first cleanse the inside of the cup and dish, that the outside of them may be clean also. (Matthew 23:25–26)

Rejoice always, pray without ceasing, in everything give thanks; for this is the will of God in Christ Jesus for you. (1 Thessalonians 5:16–18)

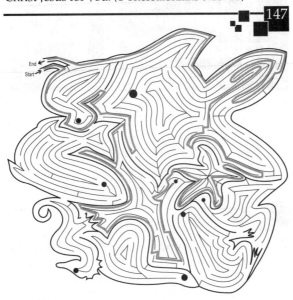

Puzzle Answers

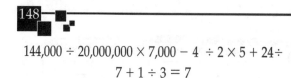

$$144{,}000 \div 20{,}000{,}000 \times 7{,}000 - 4 \div 2 \times 5 + 24 \div$$
$$7 + 1 \div 3 = 7$$

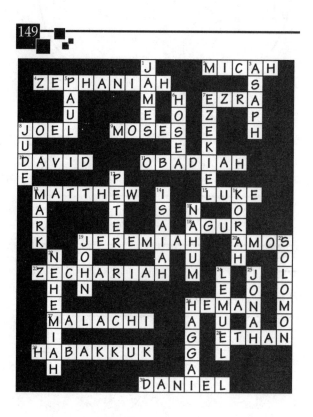

Be strong and of good courage; do not be afraid, nor be dismayed, for the Lord your God is with you wherever you go. (Joshua 1:9)

151

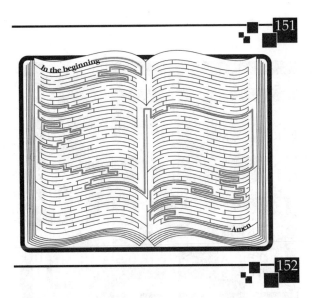

152

WHITE	BLUE	GOLDEN
BLACK	PALE	YELLOW
GREEN	RED	BROWN
CRIMSON	SCARLET	GRAY
PURPLE		

Unscrambled letters: TUNIC
STONES
EAGLE

153

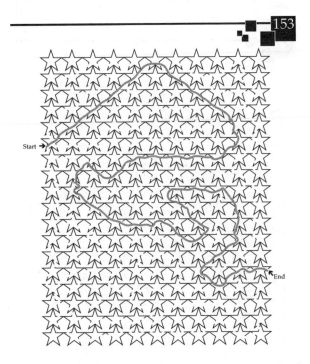

PUZZLE ANSWERS

154

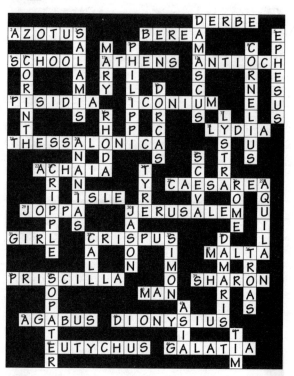

155

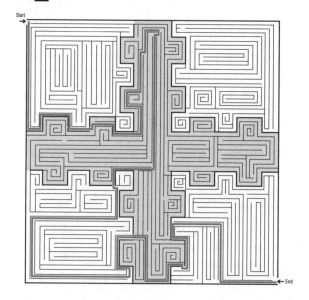

Start

End

PUZZLE ANSWERS

156

Let not your heart be troubled; you believe in God, believe also in Me. (John 14:1)

157

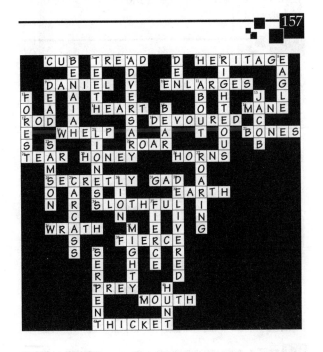

158

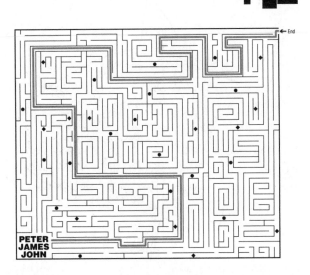

PUZZLE ANSWERS

159

These things I have written to you who believe in the name of the Son of God, that you may know that you have eternal life, and that you may continue to believe in the name of the Son of God. (1 John 5:13)

160

161

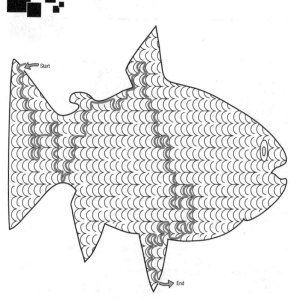

162

CERTAIN **K**ING
WITH**I**N YOU
HID**D**EN TREASURE
DRA**G**NET
LAND**O**WNER
J**O**Y
MUSTARD SEED

PEARL **O**F GREAT PRICE
MARRIAGE **F**EAST

RIG**H**TEOUSNESS
REP**E**NT
PE**A**CE
LEA**V**EN
POW**E**R
TE**N** VIRGINS

Unscrambled letters: SEEK FIRST

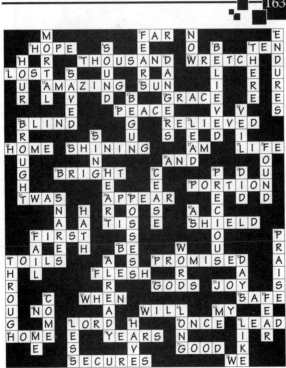

163

Amazing grace, how sweet the sound
That saved a wretch like me!
I once was lost, but now am found,
Was blind, but now I see.

"Twas grace that taught my heart to fear,
And grace my fears relieved;
How precious did that grace appear
The hour I first believed!

Through many dangers, toils, and snares,
I have already come;
"Tis grace hath brought me safe thus far,
And grace will lead me home.

The Lord had promised good to me,
His word my hope secures;
He will my shield and portion be
As long as life endures.

And when this flesh and heart shall fail,
And mortal life shall cease,
I shall possess within the veil
A life of joy and peace.

When we 've been there ten thousand years,
Bright shining as the sun,
We've no less days to sing God's praise
Than when we first begun.

PUZZLE ANSWERS

164

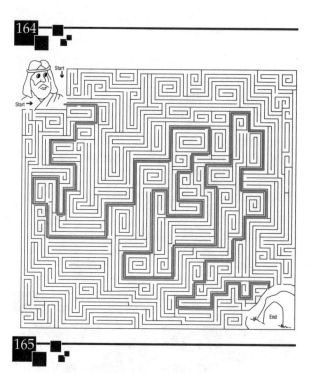

Start ↓

Start →

End

165

Unscrambled words:
ABIDE OMNIPRESENT ALWAYS COMPAINION
STEADFAST COMFORTER EVER PRESENT EVERLASTING
EVERMORE ETERNAL FREIND FOREVER COUNSELOR
SHEPHERD HOLY SPIRIT ENCOMPASS PROTECTOR
DELIVERER STRENGTH LOVINGKINDNESS
TRUTH LOVE VINE PEACE OVERCOME
IN YOU PILLAR OF CLOUD PILLAR OF FIRE
SHEKINAH GLORY SHIELD

OMNIPRESENT
ALWAYS
SHIELD
EVERLASTING
PILLAR OF FIRE
EVEN TO THE END OF THE WORLD
EVERMORE
FOREVER
ABIDE
EVER PRESENT
PILLAR OF CLOUD
SHEPHERD
PEACE
DELIVERER
STRENGTH
HOLY SPIRIT
PROTECTOR
COUNSELOR
VINE
ENCOMPASS
ETERNAL
COMFORTER
LOVE
OVERCOME
STEADFAST
SHEKINAH GLORY
LOVINGKINDNESS
FRIEND
IN YOU
COMPANION
TRUTH

I WILL NEVER LEAVE YOU NOR FORSAKE YOU

166

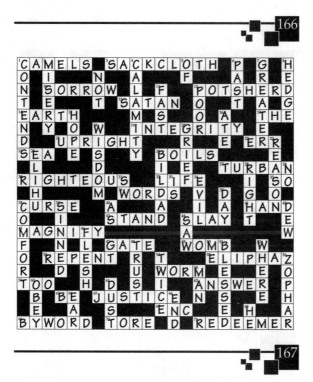

167

"Let him who glories glory in this, that he understands and knows Me, that I am the LORD, exercising lovingkindness, judgment, and righteousness in the earth. For in these I delight," says the LORD" (Jeremiah 9:24)

168

Match 1-C (Ephesians 2:10), 2-D (Philippians 4:6), 3-E (2 Corinthians 5:17), 4-A (Colossians 2:9–10), 5-G (Galatians 2:20), 6-B (1 Thessalonians 3:12-13), 7-F (Romans 1:16–17)

EPHESUS
PHILIPPI
CORINTH
COLOSSE
GALATIA
THESSALONICA
ROME
EPISTLE

PUZZLE ANSWERS

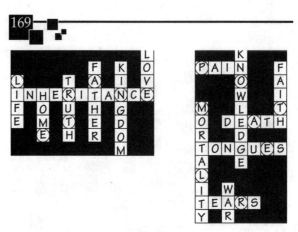

169

Unscrambled letters:
1. ETERNAL
2. TEMPORAL

All the items in the first grid are eternal;
the items in the second grid are temporal.

170

1. Y. Abigail
2. Z. Zacharias
3. G. Claudius Caesar
4. Q. Iscariot
5. A. Issachar
6. X. Jacob
7. T. Delilah
8. E. Tabitha
9. V. Sennacherib
10. L. Rachel
11. N. Nehemiah
12. R. Pharisees
13. W. Philemon
14. J. Potiphar
15. B. Philistines
16. H. Artaxerxes
17. S. Amorites
18. M. Apollos
19. D. Aristarchus
20. C. Alphaeus
21. F. Candace
22. I. Amalekites
23. P. Timothy
24. U. Agabus
25. K. Agrippa
26. O. David

WORD
JESUS
HEAVENS
PROPHETS
GOSPEL
CREATION
FATHER
SPIRIT
WORKS
EYEWITNESS

REVELATION

MAKE KNOWN
PROCLAIM
TELL
SHINE
REPORT
SPEAK
PRAISE
DECLARE
TESTIFY

WITNESSES

172

T ASP LEAP
SCOUR I BATHE
PAL LEO CAT
O LEPROSY BE
TUB A T M R
O NAAMAN
WORD STONE O
TEN HENNA A
SHEAVE DARTS
AP D ESTA LEI
ASSET Y YES

173

RAGE W T GRIM M
L ABIDETH I US
S R O F O S
FORTRESS STRENGTH
A H Q T S O
I T UNDO T ONE
LORD A O KINDRED
I I ILLS U S
N U T GREAT K
G MAN O A HE I
P ARMED R W N
HIM O STRIVING
F E R B H S N D
SEEK TREMBLE LO
A S A Y B M
PREVAILING CRUEL
R M L S
I AGE WORLD W IT
N M W O O A I
C I OURS POWER L
ENDURE D M KILL

TUMORS
ITC**H**
MADN**E**SS
S**C**ORCHING
CONF**U**SION
DEST**R**OYED
OPPRE**S**SED
P**E**RISH
B**O**ILS
FEVER
MIL**D**EW
BL**I**NDNESS
DU**S**T
SW**O**RD
RE**B**UKE
D**E**FEATED
PLUN**D**ERED
INFLAMMATION
TROUBL**E**SOME
CO**N**SUMPTION
S**C**AB
PLAGU**E**

THE CURSE OF DISOBEDIENCE

PUZZLE ANSWERS

176

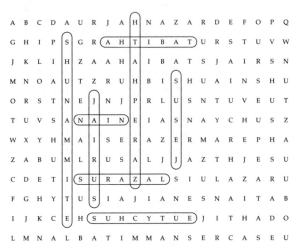

```
A B C D A U R J A H N A Z A R D E F O P Q
G H I P S G R A H T I B A T U R S T U V W
J K L I H Z A A H A I B A T S J A I R S N
M N O A U T Z R U H B I S H U A I N S H U
O R S T N E J N J P R L U S N T U V E U T
T U V S A N A I N E I A S N A Y C H U S Z
W X Y H M A I S E R A Z E R M A R E P H A
Z A B U M L R U S A L J J A Z T H J E S U
C D E T I S U R A Z A L S I U L A Z A R U
F G H Y T U S I A J I A N E S N A I T A B
I J K C E H S U H C Y T U E J I T H A D O
L M N A L B A T I M M A N S E R C A S E U
```

177

Honest weights and scales are the LORD's;
all the weights in the bag are His work.
(Proverbs 16:11)

178

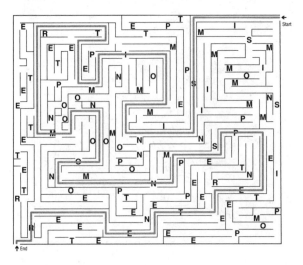

179

180

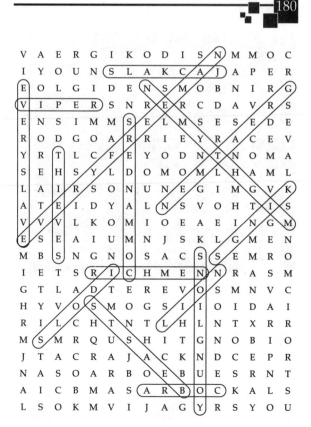

PUZZLE ANSWERS

181

Start →

End ←

182

183

Naked I came from my mother's womb,
and naked shall I return there. The LORD
gave, and the LORD has taken away;
blessed be the name of the LORD. (Job 1:21)

184

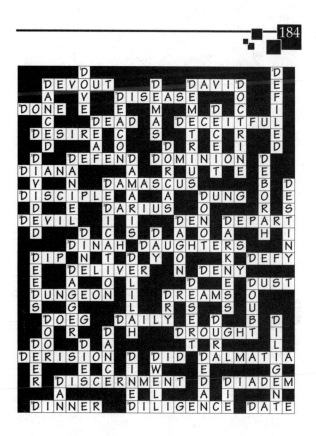

Puzzle Answers

185

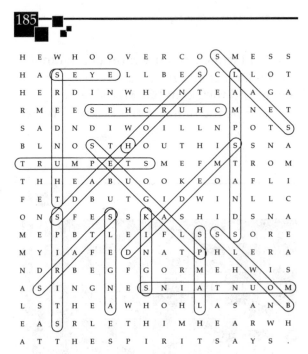

Hidden verses: He who overcomes shall be clothed in white garments, and I will not blot out his name from the Book of Life; but I will confess his name before My Father and before His angels. He who has an ear, let him hear what the Spirit says. (Revelation 3:5–6)

186

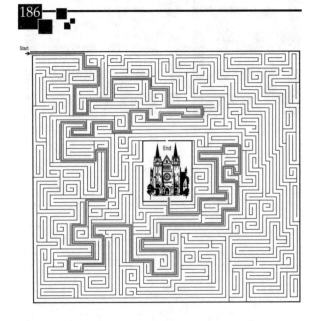

187

188

Fall on us and hide us from the face of
Him who sits on the throne and from
the wrath of the Lamb! For the great day
of His wrath has come, and who is able
to stand? (Revelation 6:16–17)

Puzzle Answers

189

PATHS
RIGHTEOUSNESS
MAKES
WALK
SHADOW
GREEN
LEADS
WITH
RESTORES
COMFORT
MERCY
PASTURES
HOUSE
ENEMIES
PREPARE
HIS
DEATH
RUNS
DOWN
STILL
SURELY
THOUGH
NAMES
EVIL
LIE
ANOINT
ROD
STAFF
WATERS
VALLEY
GOODNESS
TABLE

THE LORD IS MY SHEPHERD, I SHALL NOT WANT

190

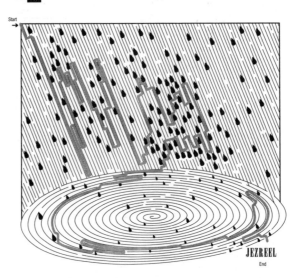

CHRI**S**TIAN
FA**I**THFUL
WOR**L**D
ANG**E**LS
HOLY **N**IGHT
THREE
MID**N**IGHT
LITTLE
MAN**G**ER
BET**H**LEHEM
FIRS**T**

SILENT NIGHT, HOLY NIGHT

PUZZLE ANSWERS

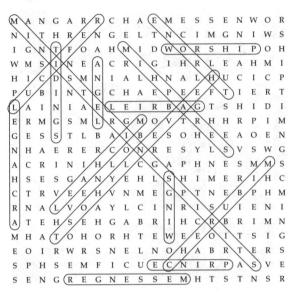

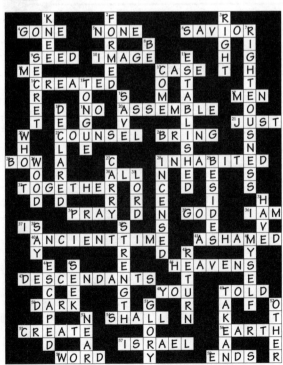

196

Judge not, and you shall not be judged. Condemn not, and you shall not be condemned. Forgive, and you will be forgiven. Give, and it will be given to you: good measure, pressed down, shaken together, and running over will be put into your bosom. (Luke 6:37–38*a*)

PUZZLE ANSWERS

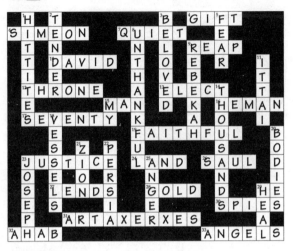

I. $276 - 39 \div 3 \times 5 + 120 - 500 - 8 = 7$

II. $3{,}000 + 400 \div 40 \times 3 + 70 \div 5 - 2 \div 7 = 9$

A great multitude which no one could number. (Revelation 7:9)

199

I will give you a new heart and put a new spirit within you; I will take the heart of stone out of your flesh and give you a heart of flesh. I will put My Spirit within you and cause you to walk in My statutes, and you will keep My judgments and do them. (Ezekiel 36:26–27)

200

201

Salvation belongs to our God who
sits on the throne, and to the Lamb!
(Revelation 7:10)

PUZZLE ANSWERS

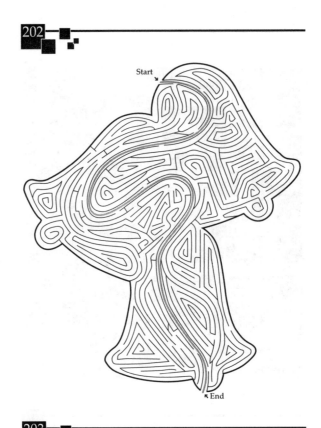

Start

End

204

The tongue of the wise uses knowledge rightly, but the mouth of fools pours forth foolishness. (Proverbs 15:2)

205

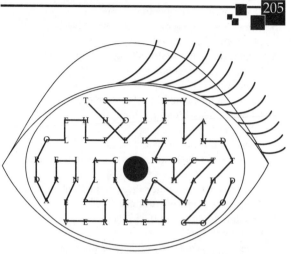

The eyes of the LORD are in every place, keeping watch on the evil and the good. (Proverbs 15:3)

206

$20,000 - 2,000 \div 80 \times 1.5 \times .3 - .25 \div 10 - .1 + 2 \div 2 = 6$

207

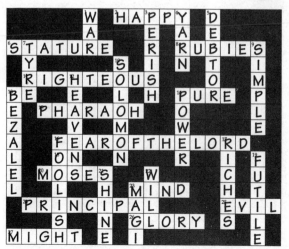

Puzzle Answers

208

1. John the Baptist was not on the Mount of Transfiguration
2. Mustard seed was not lost and then found
3. Tares were burned up in the fire, the others were not consumed
4. Gomer was an unrepentant sinner
5. Upper Room is not described in the Bible as a place where God dwells
6. Jochebed was not a barren woman before God blessed her with children
7. Hebrews was not written by Paul
8. Joel is not the name of a tribe of Israel
9. Jehoiakim was not a good king
10. John is not a synoptic gospel
11. Joy is not one of the three virtues
12. Athens is not the location of a church that received a letter from Paul
13. Scribes is not one of the offices in the church
14. Titus was not visited by angels
15. Freedom is not one of the fruits of the Spirit in Galations 5:22–23
16. Ram's horn is not one of the items in the ark of the covenant
17. Rainbow was not a means of divine guidance in the Bible
18. Timothy was not put to death for his faith
19. Fish were not created on the sixth day
20. Chariot is not a term used to describe the Bible

209

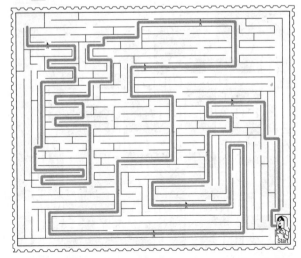

210

Hidden message: PROPHET

211

F A R M F L C O S R E L U R
D R E H P E H S C K G O V E
P E N S F M A S N O S E H R
I H A H O I R E D I R H S N
E S T E R E I A T I O P K O
K N I P N V O N N R N H O R
P I O H O R T G S K R N Y S
T O N G S O M E C I E E A M
A N S G F W I F O D V R D Y
F O E M D A N L I S O F O O
Y L R L R O A A N O G K L U
I N O M A I M T M I E D O N
K G T C V D E S A O O G C G
E D O I K N K N F M W N I K
V N A M G N U O Y S H E P H
G O I T A N X F L W Y N E E
O F A R M E R N O A O I D R
R O N R N V E A M M K A M D

Puzzle Answers

212

213

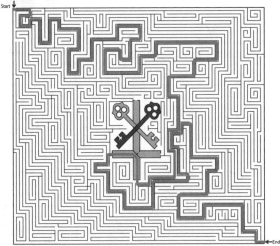

214

I will praise You, for You have answered me, and have become my salvation. The stone which the builders rejected has become the chief cornerstone. This was the LORD's doing; it is marvelous in our eyes. (Psalm 118:21–23)

TELL ME A STORY

TRUE OR FALSE 1

1. Jesus did not explain the Parable of the Sower.

_____

2. When Jesus spoke in parables, he spoke things that were kept secret from the foundation of the world.

_____

3. Jesus explained the Parable of the Wheat and Tares to all the people who heard the parable.

_____

4. In the Parable of the Hidden Treasure, the man sold all he had to buy a field.

_____

5. In the Parable of the Pearl of Great Price, the man sold all he had to buy a pearl.

_____

6. Jesus delivered the Parable of the Dog and the Lamb.

_____

7. In the Parable of the Dragnet, God Himself will separate the wicked from the just.

____

8. In telling the Parable of the Dragnet, Jesus asked the disciples if they understood "all these things."

____

9. According to the Gospel of Matthew, when Jesus finished telling the Parables of the Sower, Wheat and Tares, Mustard Seed, and Dragnet, he left for his home, Nazareth.

____

10. The point of the Parable of the Lost Sheep is the God cares about every one of his children.

____

MULTIPLE CHOICE 1

1. In the Parable of the Lost Sheep, Jesus says that one should not despise children because:
A. their angels always see the face of God
B. they possess the spirit that we should aim for
C. they're just so cute
D. their actions reflect the teachings of their parents

2. How many sheep did the shepherd have?
A. 1000
B. 100
C. 50
D. none, he lost them

3. The Parable of the Unforgiving Servant was told in response to the question:
A. "Here I am."
B. "Who will be the greatest in the kingdom of Heaven?"
C. "Who will sit at the right hand of Jesus in Heaven?"
D. "How often shall my brother sin against me, and I forgive him?"

4. The Parable of the Unforgiving Servant ends with the servant:
A. forgiven
B. married
C. in jail and tortured
D. dead

5. It is harder for a rich man to enter heaven than:
A. to find a needle in a haystack
B. a camel to go through the eye of a needle
C. a needle to go through the eye of a camel
D. a sheep to find its way back to the fold

6. In the Parable of the Workers in the Vineyard, the agreed wage was:
A. a denarius a day
B. ten denarii a day
C. ten denarii a week
D. four sheep and one chicken per day

7. Jesus ends the Parable of the Workers in the Vineyard by saying:
   A. All that are called are chosen.
   B. Honor your mother and father
   C. Many are called but few are chosen.
   D. The owner may choose those that it pleases him to choose.

8. The workers complained about
   A. the heat
   B. the people the owner chose
   C. the neighboring field
   D. the amount of pay

SHORT ANSWER 1

1. Why did Jesus curse the fig tree?

_____

_____

2. What did Jesus say the disciples could do if they had faith?

_____

_____

3. In the Parable of the Two Sons, Jesus said that who believed before the priests and the elders believed?

_____

_____

4. In the Parable of the Wicked Vinedressers, the vinedressers killed whom?

_____

_____

5. Who thought this parable was about themselves?

_____

_____

6. What was their reaction to this parable?

_____

_____

7. In the Parable of the Wedding Feast, who hosts the wedding?

_____

_____

8. What is the king's reaction to his servants' deaths?

_____

_____

UNSCRAMBLE 1 *(parables)*

1. Wesor

    _____

2. Tusmard Dese

    _____

3. Tols Eshpe

    _____

4. Siwe dan Ofosilh Givirns

    _____

5. Dogo Masriatna

    _____

6. Lots Nico

    _____

7. Chir Lofo

    _____

8. Lantets

    _____

9. Degiwdn Eafst

    _____

10. Remnuifcul Verastn

    _____

MATCHING 1

1. Lamp Under a basket

2. The Marriage

3. Patched Garment

4. Leaven

5. Pearl of Great Price

6. Wedding Garment

7. Wise and Foolish Virgins

8. Lost Coin

9. Persistent Widow

10. Children in the Marketplace

A. Chief priests and Pharisees

B. Pharisees and Scribes

C. Pharisees and Disciples of John

D. Multitudes concerning John the Baptist

E. Disciples on the Mount of Olives

F. Disciples

G. Multitude on the Seashore

MULTIPLE CHOICE 2

1. Jesus did not speak to the people without what, according to Mark 4:34?
   A. moral lessons
   B. parables
   C. John the Baptist's followers
   D. his disciples listening and learning

2. Jesus, in speaking to the disciples about salt, said everyone will be seasoned with:
   A. trials
   B. bitumen
   C. fire
   D. salt

3. When people brought their little children to see Jesus, the disciples:
   A. rebuked them
   B. welcomed them
   C. taught them
   D. babysat them

4. Who gave more to the church than all the rich who had contributed to the treasury?
   A. the Pharisees
   B. Zacchaeus
   C. David
   D. the widow with two mites

5. The fig tree's leaves will wither away unlike:
   A. the stones of Petra
   B. the Word of God
   C. the Temple of God
   D. the heavens and the earth

6. What topic was Jesus discussing with the teachers in the temple as a child when his parents found him there?
   A. we don't know
   B. interpretations of the Torah
   C. whether or not women could divorce their husbands
   D. the laws regarding the Jewish diet

7. The story in which the wise man built his house upon the rock is a lesson about:
   A. carpentry
   B. faith
   C. hypocrisy
   D. predestination

8. In the Parable of the Sower, the seed that was sown by the wayside:
   A. was choked by rocks
   B. was eaten by cows
   C. grew into a cedar forest
   D. was trampled and eaten by birds

SHORT ANSWER 2

1. When Jesus explained the Parable of the Sower, what happened to those whose seed was sown onto the rocks?

_____

2. Those whose seed fell on the good ground do what?

_____

3. What is the point of the Parable of the Revealed Light?

_____

4. The Parable of the Good Samaritan only appears in which gospel?

_____

5. Who tested Jesus, that he told the Parable of the Good Samaritan?

_____

6. What did the Samaritan do for the wounded man?

_____

7. Why did Jesus tell the Parable of the Rich Fool?

_____

8. What happened to the Rich Fool when he had an overabundance of crops that he desired to keep for the years to come?

_____

ANSWERS

TRUE OR FALSE 1

1. False
2. True
3. False
4. True
5. True
6. False
7. False
8. True
9. True
10. True

MULTIPLE CHOICE 1

1. A
2. B
3. D
4. C
5. B
6. A
7. C
8. D

SHORT ANSWER 1

1. because nothing grew on it but leaves
2. move a mountain into the sea
3. tax collectors and harlots
4. servants and the owner's son
5. chief priests and Pharisees
6. wanted to lay hands on him but feared the people
7. the King, for his son
8. sent out armies and burned the cities, then invited strangers

UNSCRAMBLE 1

1. Sower
2. Mustard Seed
3. Lost Sheep
4. Wise and Foolish Virgins
5. Good Samaritan
6. Lost Coin
7. Rich Fool
8. Talents
9. Wedding Feast

10. Unmerciful Servant

MATCHING 1

1. F
2. C
3. C
4. G
5. F
6. A
7. E
8. B
9. F
10. D

MULTIPLE CHOICE 2

1. B
2. C
3. A
4. D
5. B
6. A
7. C
8. D

SHORT ANSWER 2

1. have no root and in time of temptation fall away
2. keep it and bear fruit with patience
3. to whoever has, more will be given; whoever does not have, even what he seems to have will be taken away
4. Luke
5. a lawyer
6. bandaged his wounds, poured oil and wine on him, had him taken care of at an inn
7. a man in the crowd demanded that Jesus tell his brother to divide an inheritance between the two
8. he died

TEACHINGS AND ILLUSTRATIONS OF CHRIST

WHAT JUST HAPPENED?

MULTIPLE CHOICE 1

1. Which of the following occurred as a result of Adam and Eve's sin?
   A. They experienced knowledge of evil.
   B. They experienced shame and guilt.
   C. They feared God's presence.
   D. all of the above

2. What happened immediately after Adam and Eve made clothes for themselves?
   A. They went out of the garden.
   B. They heard God walking in the garden.
   C. They ate the fruit.
   D. They hid in the trees.

3. God sent The Flood to cover the earth because:
   A. The wickedness of man was great in the earth, and all his thoughts were evil.
   B. The people of Ur hated God.
   C. The people of the earth laughed in the face of his warnings.
   D. Abel sinned

4. How long did The Flood cover the earth?
   A. 2 years
   B. 4 days
   C. 5 months
   D. 40 days

SHORT ANSWER 1

1. The tower of Babel was built to do what?

_____

2. How did God punish the men who built the tower?

_____

3. What event sparked God's destruction of Sodom?

_____

4. Who pulled Lot out of the city of Sodom?

_____

MATCHING 1

1. Abraham

2. Samson

3. Ruth

4. David

5. Lot

6. Nehemiah

7. Hosea

8. Rahab

9. Esther

A. escaped burning city with wife and daughters

B. hid spies in her home

C. rebuilt a city wall

D. was asked to sacrifice his son

E. met her husband while working in the fields

F. won a beauty pagent

G. destroyed a house full of Philistines

H. married a prostitute

I. murdered a soldier

SHORT ANSWER 2

1. Rahab lived in:

_____

_____

2. Ehud killed this king:

_____

_____

3. This King had Uriah killed:

_____

_____

4. This city was raided by Israel:

_____

_____

5. Ruth's first mother-in-law was:

_____

_____

6. The Philistines stole this important item from the Israelites:

_____

7. This man ran from God to Tarshish:

_____

_____

8. Lot's wife turned into:

_____

_____

PUT THE FOLLOWING IN ORDER 1

Plagues

1. Flies

2. Livestock died

3. Darkness over the land

4. Water turned to blood

5. Hail storm

6. Frogs

7. Locusts

8. Boils

9. Death of the first born

10. Lice

_____

_____

_____

_____

_____

_____

_____

_____

_____

Ten Commandments

1. Remember the Sabbath Day and keep it holy

2. Do not commit adultery

3. Have no other gods before Me

4. Do not covet

5. Honor your father and mother

6. Have no graven images

7. Do not murder

8. Do not lie

9. Do not take God's name in vain

10. Do not steal

_____

_____

_____

_____

_____

_____

_____

_____

_____

TRUE OR FALSE 1

1. Passover commemorates Israel's deliverance from Egypt and is a reminder that Christ spared the first born.

_____

2. The Feast of Unleavened Bread is symbolized by communion in modern days.

_____

3. The Day of Firstfruits dedicated the firstfruits of the wheat harvest.

_____

4. The Feast of Pentecost, Harvest, and Weeks is symbolized by the outpouring of the Holy Spirit.

_____

5. The Day of Trumpets commemorates Israel's defeat of Jericho.

_____

6. The Day of Atonement is fulfilled in Christ's crucifixion.

_____

7. The Feast of Tabernacles commemorates God's deliverance.

_____

8. The Feast of Purim was held to recognize the goodness God bestowed on his people because of their sacrifices.

_____

MULTIPLE CHOICE 2

1. Moses did what to part the Red Sea?
   A. commanded the waters to part
   B. hit it with a rod
   C. sang
   D. lifted up rod and stretched out hand

2. How many people exited Egypt with Moses?
   A. six hundred men with their families
   B. six thousand men with their families
   C. six hundred thousand men with their families
   D. none

3. Where was the Promised Land?
   A. the mountains of the Amorites all the way to the land of the Canaanites and Lebanon as far as the river Euphrates
   B. the mountains of the Amorites all the way to the land of the Canaanites but not beyond, for that is the land of the pagan peoples
   C. the Arabian Peninsula
   D. all the land of the Canaanites, and no more

4. What flowed in the Promised Land?
   A. milk
   B. honey
   C. wine
   D. manna

5. Which of the spies who entered Canaan thought the Israelites should enter?
   A. Moses and Aaron
   B. Joshua and Caleb
   C. Miriam and Levi
   D. Reuben and Igal

6. Why did the Israelites go to war with the Benjaminites?
   A. Saul was a Benjaminite
   B. They pillaged the Israelite's land
   C. A Levite's concubine was raped
   D. They stole the ark of the covenant

7. What was Samson's riddle about?
   A. a lion
   B. a bear
   C. the Greeks
   D. a Philistine

8. Which of the following were Delilah's attempts to weaken Samson?
   A. bound him with fresh bowstrings
   B. tied him with weathered ropes
   C. wove five locks of his hair
   D. kept him from sleeping for several days

TRUE OR FALSE 2

1. David put only one stone in his bag when he prepared to fight Goliath.

_____

2. Saul gave his daughter Michal to another man while she was still married to David.

_____

3. A medium brought Samuel back from the dead to speak to Saul.

_____

4. David built a temple.

_____

5. Assyria captured the northern kingdom of Israel.

_____

6. Both Elijah and Elisha raised boys from the dead.

_____

7. The first thing the Israelites built when returning from captivity in Babylon was a new temple.

_____

8. Israel wanted a king so that they could be like other nations and fight.

_____

9. Solomon had a hard time getting dates.

_____

10. Jonah stayed in the fish for forty days and nights.

_____

MULTIPLE CHOICE 3

1. The wise men saw the star how many times?
  A. one
  B. two
  C. zero
  D. four

2. How did Joseph know that God did not want him to take Jesus back to Judea when the family returned from Egypt?
  A. dream
  B. Mary knew
  C. one of the wise men told him
  D. finger writing on the wall

3. Who saw the Holy Spirit descend on Jesus like a dove?
  A. Jesus
  B. all who had eyes to see
  C. Jesus and John the Baptist
  D. temple priests

4. The centurion said to Jesus:
  A. "Only speak a word, and my servant will be healed."
  B. "Please, come and heal my servant."
  C. "You are the beloved son."
  D. "Your will be done."

5. What name completes this prophecy: "Out of ___ I called my Son."
  A. Mary
  B. Bethlehem
  C. Africa
  D. Egypt

6. What was Jesus doing when the tempest arose around the boat?
   A. preaching
   B. eating
   C. sleeping
   D. fishing

7. What interrupted Jesus on his way to heal Jairus's daughter?
   A. a hemorrhaging woman
   B. a demon-possessed man
   C. the High Priest
   D. a centurion

8. Whose Son did the two blind men who were following Jesus say that He was?
   A. God's
   B. David's
   C. Joseph's
   D. Saul's

UNSCRAMBLE 1

1. Gansirfatruniot   _____

2. Recrusretnoi   _____

3. Lumacteima Peretonic   _____

4. Ficurxnioci   _____

5. Salt Puresp   _____

6. Tesoctnep   _____

7. Siarminoys Njoruyes   _____

8. Lapu febreo het Hendrsani   _____

9. Dingdwe Puesrp fo het Ambl   _____

Answers

MULTIPLE CHOICE 1

1. D
2. B
3. A
4. D

SHORT ANSWER 1

1. to make a name for themselves
2. confused their language
3. the men of the city desired to rape the angels staying in Lot's home
4. the angels pulled Lot, his wife and two daughters out

MATCHING 1

1. D
2. G
3. E
4. I
5. A
6. C
7. H
8. B
9. F

FILL IN THE BLANKS 1

1. Jericho
2. Eglon
3. David
4. Bezek
5. Naomi
6. Ark
7. Jonah
8. Salt

PUT THE FOLLOWING IN ORDER 1

Plagues
4, 6, 10, 1, 2, 8, 5, 7, 3, 9

10 Commandments
3, 6, 9, 1, 5, 7, 2, 10, 8, 4

TRUE OR FALSE 1

1. True
2. False
3. False
4. True
5. False
6. True
7. True
8. False

MULTIPLE CHOICE 2

1. D
2. C
3. A
4. A, B
5. B
6. C
7. A
8. A

TRUE OR FALSE 2

1. False
2. True
3. True
4. False
5. True
6. True
7. False
8. True
9. False
10. False

MULTIPLE CHOICE 3

1. B
2. A
3. C
4. A
5. D
6. C
7. A
8. B

UNSCRAMBLE 1

1. Transfiguration
2. Resurrection
3. Immaculate Reception
4. Crucifixion
5. Last Supper
6. Pentecost
7. Missionary Journeys
8. Paul before the Sanhedrin
9. Wedding Supper of the Lamb

WHEN?

MULTIPLE CHOICE 1

1. Which Sumerian city, ruled by King Meskalamdug and Queen Shub-ad, first emerged around 2700 B.C.?
   A. Chaldee
   B. Suppiluliuma
   C. Ur
   D. Damascus

2. The first true pyramid was built in:
   A. 2613 B.C.
   B. 1613 B.C.
   C. 613 B.C.
   D. 6000 B.C.

3. Assyrian archivists recorded what event in 763 B.C. which was also recorded in Amos 8:9?
   A. the eclipse of the moon
   B. the emperor's death
   C. a flood
   D. the eclipse of the sun

4. David's reign as King was in the same century as:
   A. plague kills 50,000 in Israel
   B. Josiah cleansed the temple
   C. first map of the world created
   D. first stamped coins appear in Lydia

MATCHING 1

1. Abraham arrives in Canaan

2. Absalom's Rebellion

3. Beer is invented by Egyptians

4. Virgil writes the Aeneid

5. Moses builds the Ark of the Covenant

6. Solomon worships Ashtaroth

7. Amalekites attack Israel

8. The term *agnostic* is coined

9. The Aeropagus is founded

A. 984 B.C.

B. A.D. 1876

C. 2153 B.C.

D. 404 B.C.

E. 1491 B.C.

F. 24 B.C.

G. 1507 B.C.

H. 1024–1023 B.C.

I. 1491 B.C.

PUT THE FOLLOWING IN ORDER
(from oldest to most recent) 1

1. King David's reign ends

2. First Olympic Competition

3. Events in the Acts of the Apostles take place

4. Bananas and tea appear in India

5. Ammonites attack Israel

6. Jerusalem destroyed by Sennacherib's army 7. Muhammed announces himself the "Messenger of God" and founds Islam

8. Prophets Amos and Hosea are active

9. Baal is worshipped by King Ahab

10. Jesus Christ is born

_____

_____

_____

_____

_____

_____

_____

_____

_____

TRUE OR FALSE 1

1. The period of the Judges lasted from 1375 to 1050 B.C.

_____

2. Ehud was a judge for only 3 years.

_____

3. Esther ruled as a queen in the fifth century B.C.

_____

4. The temple was destroyed in Jerusalem around 608 B.C.

_____

5. Around 1444 B.C. the Tabernacle was built by divinely appointed artisans.

_____

6. The Romans destroyed Herod's Temple shortly before Christ's death.

_____

7. Paul was converted almost a decade after Christ's death.

_____

8. Paul's first missionary journey was almost ten to fifteen years after his conversion.

_____

9. Paul was in his fifties when he went on his missionary journeys and was almost in his eighties when he died.

_____

MULTIPLE CHOICE 2

1. Elijah and Elisha lived when in relation to King David:
   A. 100 years before him
   B. 100 years after him 274
   C. at the same time as him
   D. 200 years before him

2. Around 773 B.C. Micah and Isaiah warned Israel that this nation would be an instrument of God's displeasure against them:
   A. Babylon
   B. Rhythm Nation
   C. Egypt
   D. Assyria

3. The most common animal sacrifice among Indian kingdoms around 600 B.C. was:
   A. horse
   B. dove
   C. fish
   D. lamb

4. The Book of Daniel, written ca. 165 B.C., tells of events that happened during his Babylonian captivity:
   A. 100 years earlier
   B. 1,000 years earlier
   C. 50 years later
   D. 400 years earlier

5. First and Second Chronicles were completed about the same time as what major event?
   A. Muhammed's vision
   B. Buddha's vision
   C. John's baptism
   D. The formation of India as a nation

6. Ezra, who led Jews back to Jerusalem in 458 B.C., had what job title?
   A. Babylonian magician
   B. Babylonian priest and scribe
   C. Israelite prophet and leader
   D. Israelite priest

7. Who destroyed the Jewish temple on the Nile River in 410 B.C.?
   A. Israelite loyalists
   B. Cushites
   C. Assyrian rebels
   D. Egyptian priests

8. Simon Maccabaeus, hero of the apocryphal book bearing his name, established his Hasmonaean dynasty when?
   A. 142–135 B.C.
   B. 521–490 B.C.
   C. 8/7 Central
   D. A.D. 200–300

PUT THE FOLLOWING IN ORDER
(from longest life to shortest life) 2

1. Noah

2. Adam

3. Abraham

4. Isaac

5. Enoch

6. Seth

7. Joseph

8. Methuselah

9. Lamech

10. Jacob

_____

_____

_____

_____

_____

_____

_____

_____

_____

TRUE OR FALSE 2

1. The Jews, under leadership of Simeon Bar-Kokhba, launched an attack against the Romans which they won in 135 B.C.

———

2. St. Denis converted Paris to Christianity in A.D. 500

———

3. In A.D. 325, a major council was held by the Emperor Constantine to discuss the canon.

———

4. The word *God* does not appear in the book of Esther.

———

5. St. Patrick of Ireland chronologically comes before the Emperor Justinian.

———

6. St. Columba reportedly saw the Loch Ness Monster about the same time as Buddhism became the state religion of Japan.

———

7. Buddhism was declared the state religion of China in A.D. 300, almost 1,000 years after it was introduced (and the same year that St. Jerome began his work on the Vulgate Bible).

———

MULTIPLE CHOICE (on 20th-century dates) 3

1. In 1908, Pope Pius X declared what about the United States of America?
A. It was a center of religious revival.
B. U.S. Citizens could be canonized.
C. It was no longer a missionary area.
D. The Vatican was establishing a consulate in Iowa.

2. Billy Graham, born in North Carolina in 1918, was born the same year as:
A. James Dean and Greta Garbo
B. Elvis
C. Ella Fitzgerald and Nelson Mandela
D. Margaret Thatcher and Bob Dylan

3. In 1922 the U.S. Episcopal Church deleted what word from the traditional marriage vows:
A. submit
B. honor
C. love
D. obey

4. In what year did Mother Teresa begin her ministry in Calcutta:
A. 1948
B. 1909
C. 1960
D. 1808

5. Leaders of the World Christian Church celebrated what in Moscow in 1988?
A. the end of communist control
B. 1,000 years of Christianity in Russia
C. the entrance of Christianity to Russia
D. required church attendance

6. What was the center of attention at a controversial auction on June 26, 1984?
A. a piece of Noah's ark
B. a scrap torn from the Shroud of Turin
C. a map to the lost ark of the covenant
D. 32 Hebrew manuscripts

7. In October 1979, Pope John Paul II made the first papal visit to what country:
   A. Afghanistan
   B. Ireland
   C. Italy
   D. Russia

8. November 26, 1976 marked what change in Italy?
   A. The Vatican became the capital..
   B. A new pope was installed.
   C. Catholicism was no longer the state religion.
   D. Structural additions were made to the Vatican.

ANSWERS

MULTIPLE CHOICE 1

1. C
2. A
3. D
4. C

MATCHING 1

1. C
2. H
3. D
4. F
5. I
6. A
7. E
8. B
9. G

PUT THE FOLLOWING IN ORDER 1

1. Bananas and tea appear in India 2000 B.C.
2. Ammorites attack Israel 1143 B.C.
3. King David's reign ends 961 B. C.
4. Baal is worshipped by King Ahab 918 B.C.
5. First Olympic Competition 776 B.C.
6. Prophets Amos and Hosea are 765–735 active B.C.
7. Jerusalem is destroyed by Sennacherib's army 700 B.C.
8. Jesus Christ is born 4 B.C.
9. Events in the Acts of the Apostles take place 63 A.D.
10. Muhammed announces himself the "Messenger of God" and founds Islam 610 A.D.

TRUE OR FALSE 1

1. True
2. False
3. True
4. True
5. True
6. True
7. False
8. False
9. True
10. False

MULTIPLE CHOICE 2

1. B
2. D
3. A
4. D
5. B
6. B
7. D
8. A

PUT THE FOLLOWING IN ORDER 1

1. Methuselah 969 years
2. Noah 950 years
3. Adam 930 years
4. Seth 912 years
5. Lamech 777 years
6. Enoch 365 years
7. Isaac 180 years
8. Abraham 175 years
9. Jacob 147 years
10. Joseph 110 years

TRUE OR FALSE 2

1. True
2. True
3. True
4. False
5. False
6. True
7. True
8. True
9. True
10. False

MULTIPLE CHOICE 3

1. C
2. C
3. D
4. A
5. B
6. D
7. B
8. C

WHERE IN THE WORLD?

MULTIPLE CHOICE 1

1. Where did the ark rest after the flood?
   A. Mt. Ararat
   B. Mt. Olives
   C. Mt. Horeb
   D. Mt. Gerazim

2. What name did Jacob give the place where he dreamed about a ladder reaching to heaven?
   A. Luz
   B. Bethel
   C. Salem
   D. Gerar

3. Moses fled to where after he killed the Egyptian?
   A. Canaan
   B. Edom
   C. Midian
   D. Assyria

MATCHING 1

Place	Event
Place	**Event**
1. Ur	*A.* Job's homeland
2. Sodom and Gomorrah	*B.* 10 Commandments given
3. Jericho	*C.* God destroyed them
4. Moab	*D.* Abram's early life
5. Uz	*E.* Rahab lives and helps spies
6. Shushan	*F.* Saul's disobedient sacrifice
7. Gilgal	*G.* Tower of Babel
8. Mt. Sinai	*H.* Esther becomes Queen
9. Shinar	*I.* Moses died

PUT THE FOLLOWING IN ORDER
(where they lived, from birth to death) 1

Abraham:

1. Ur

2. Mamre

3. Mt. Moriah

4. Shechem

5. Haran

6. Bethel

_____

_____

_____

_____

_____

_____

Jacob:

1. Bethel

2. Penuel

3. Haran

4. Mamre

5. Beersheba

6. Egypt

_____

_____

_____

_____

_____

_____

UNSCRAMBLE 1

1. Deen

2. Oirjech

3. Doosm

4. Ru

5. Resial

6. Ybonlab

7. Zaratneh

8. More

9. Nitorch

TRUE OR FALSE 1

1. Jesus came from Nazareth to the Jordan to be baptized by John the Baptist.

_____

2. Jesus was tempted on the Mount of Olives.

_____

3. Simon and James had were from Bethsaida but had houses in Capernaum.

_____

4. John the Baptist's family lived in the hill country of Judah.

_____

5. Nazareth was known as "The city of David."

_____

6. Capernaum was the home base of Jesus' travels during his ministry.

_____

7. Jesus cleansed the temple during Passover in Bethlehem.

_____

8. Jesus was in Galilee, near the sea, when the Jews took up stones to kill him for blasphemy.

_____

9. The Jews led Jesus from Caiaphas to the Praetorium, but would not go inside so that they would not be defiled.

_____

10. The apostles were in Jerusalem when Jesus told them to wait for the Promise of the Father.

_____

MULTIPLE CHOICE 2

1. Before his ascension, Jesus told the disciples to be witnesses to:
   A. Jerusalem
   B. Judea and Samaria
   C. the ends of the earth
   D. all of the above

2. Where did the disciples gather to wait for the gift of the Holy Spirit?
   A. the temple
   B. an upper room
   C. Mt. Olivet
   D. Caesarea

3. What is the name of the porch on the temple?
   A. the outer court
   B. Solomon's porch
   C. Herod's wing
   D. David's porch

4. The road from Jerusalem to Gaza travels through which kind of terrain?
   A. desert
   B. countryside
   C. mountains
   D. flatlands

MATCHING 2

Place	Event
1. Damascus	*A.* Disciples first called Christians
2. Corinth	*B.* Name means "little fountains"
3. Antioch	*C.* Phoebe delivers Paul's letter to this church
4. Galatia	*D.* Believer's turn to a different gospel
5. Ephesus	*E.* Converts include pagans, God-fearing Greeks, and Jews
6. Philippi	*F.* Paul preaches first sermon
7. Thessalonica	*G.* Philemon's hometown
8. Colosse	*H.* Center for pagan worship and magical arts
9. Rome	*I.* John writes Revelation here
10. Patmos	*J.* Chloe's church is here

PUT THE FOLLOWING IN ORDER
(Paul's first missionary journey from start to finish) 2

1. Antioch

2. Pisidian Antioch

3. Derbe

4. Seleucia

5. Paphos

6. Perga

7. Attalia

8. Iconium

9. Lystra

10. Salamis

(some will be used twice)

_____

_____

_____

_____

_____

_____

_____

_____

_____

_____

_____

_____

_____

_____

_____

_____

MULTIPLE CHOICE 3

1. Which of the following were churches addressed in Revelation?
   A. Pergamos
   B. Thyatira
   C. Sardis
   D. Londinium
   E. Philadelphia
   F. All of the above

2. In the throne room of Heaven there are which of the following:
   A. a rainbow
   B. an emerald throne
   C. twenty-four thrones
   D. lightning and thunder
   E. lamps of fire
   F. a sea of glass, like crystal

3. Where were the four angels standing when they opened the scrolls?
   A. the throne room
   B. the four corners of the earth
   C. before David
   D. in the four churches

4. Where does the River of Life proceed from?
   A. the new Euphrates
   B. the tree of life
   C. God's throne
   D. the Lamb of God

ANSWERS

MULTIPLE CHOICE 1

1. A
2. B
3. C

MATCHING 1

1. D
2. C
3. E
4. I
5. A
6. H
7. F
8. B
9. G

PUT THE FOLLOWING IN ORDER 1

Abraham:
1. Ur
2. Haran
3. Shechem
4. Bethel
5. Mt. Moriah
6. Mamre

Jacob:
1. Beersheba
2. Bethel
3. Haran
4. Penuel
5. Egypt
6. Mamre

UNSCRAMBLE 1

1. Eden
2. Jericho
3. Sodom
4. Ur
5. Israel
6. Babylon
7. Nazareth
8. Rome
9. Corinth

TRUE OR FALSE 1

1. True
2. False
3. False
4. True
5. False
6. True
7. False
8. False
9. True
10. True

MULTIPLE CHOICE 2

1. D
2. B
3. B
4. A

MATCHING 2

1. F
2. J
3. A
4. D
5. H
6. B
7. E
8. G
9. C
10. I

PUT THE FOLLOWING IN ORDER 2

1. Antioch (In Syria) Acts 13
2. Seleucia (In Syria) Acts 13
3. Salamis (In Cyprus) Acts 13
4. Paphos (In Cyprus) Acts 13
5. Perga (Mediterranean Coast) Acts 13
6. Pisidian Antioch (In Phrygia) Acts 13
7. Iconium (In Lycaonia) Acts 14
8. Lystra (In Lycaonia) Acts 14
9. Derbe (In Lycaonia) Acts 14
10. Back to Lystra
11. Back to Iconium
12. Back to Pisidian Antioch
13. Back to Perga
14. To Attalia
15. Back to Seleucia
16. Back to Antioch

MULTIPLE CHOICE 3

1. A, B, C, E
2. A, B, C, D, E, F
3. B
4. C

WOMEN'S ISSUES

MULTIPLE CHOICE 1

1. According to the Genesis Story, Eve's function was:
   A. Adam's helper
   B. to collect fruit
   C. to watch over the animals
   D. gardener

2. More space is devoted to this woman than any other in the Bible:
   A. Eve
   B. Sarah
   C. Esther
   D. Tamar

3. Who is the only wife named among the "heroes of the faith"?
   A. Sarah
   B. Ruth
   C. Jezebel
   D. Esther

4. Hagar was the mother of:
   A. Mephibosheth
   B. Jacob
   C. Joab
   D. Ishmael

TRUE OR FALSE 1

1. Lot's wife's name is never mentioned.

_____

2. Rebekah was Jacob's bride.

_____

3. Rebekah's choice to marry and leave home was her own.

_____

4. Rachel gave birth to Jacob's favorite son.

_____

5. Leah had "delicate" or "weak" eyes.

_____

6. Dinah was one of Jacob's two daughters.

_____

7. Tamar disguised herself as a fortune-teller in order to trick her father-in-law into sleeping with her.

_____

8. Moses sent his wife Zipporah back to live at her father's house.

_____

9. Moses married an Ethopian woman.

_____

10. Miriam was struck with leprosy after criticizing Moses' choice of a wife.

_____

UNSCRAMBLE 1

1. Pozrahip   _____

2. Calhre   _____

3. Hrut dna Animo   _____

4. Yarm Degnlamea   _____

5. Braah   _____

6. Thebaabsh   _____

7. Rasha   _____

8. Ramy dan Thamra   _____

9. Lebezje   _____

10. Kerbeah   _____

MATCHING 1

1. Mahlah, Noah, Hoglah, Milcah, and Tirzah

    A. father offered her as a wife to whoever could defeat Kirjath Sepher

2. Rahab

    B. name means "bee"

3. Achsah

    C. cut Samson's hair

4. Deborah

    D. Boaz was one of her offspring

5. Jael

    E. warned by an angel that she would have a child

6. Samson's mother

    F. her son stole 1000 pieces of silver from her

7. Delilah

    G. free to choose husbands and inherit land

8. Micah's mother

    H. raped as retribution for the Levite's concubine's death

9. Daughters of Benjaminites

    I. killed Sisera

10. Orpah

    J. Naomi's other daughter-in-law

MULTIPLE CHOICE 2

1. Ruth's name means:
   A. sight, friendship
   B. honor, loyalty
   C. God's child
   D. my father's joy

2. Hannah was accused of what when she prayed for a child:
   A. witchcraft
   B. theft
   C. drunkenness
   D. laziness

3. Michal was what relation to Saul?
   A. wife
   B. daughter
   C. sister
   D. none

4. What happened to Michal when she made fun of King David's dancing?
   A. lost her voice
   B. dropped dead
   C. lost her vision
   D. lost her ability to have children

5. Abigail, the wife of Nabal, was described as being:
   A. beautiful
   B. intelligent
   C. bald
   D. wise with money

6. What person did Saul approach when he wanted to know whether or not he would remain king?
   A. the fortune-teller from Jericho
   B. the palm-reader from Shechem
   C. the prophet from Bethel
   D. the medium of En Dor

7. How did God come to the aid of Deborah, the judge?
    A. He sent a flood to destroy the enemy.
    B. He struck the people down with a blizzard
    C. He sent a violent thunderstorm.
    D. He sent an earthquake.

8. Abimelech's killer was:
    A. a demon
    B. a woman
    C. a child
    D. his mother

TRUE OR FALSE 2

1. Bathsheba mourned the death of her husband, Uriah.

_____

2. Tamar was the daughter of King David and Princess Maacah.

_____

3. The wise woman of Tekoa lied to King David, influencing him to forgive Amnon for raping his daughter, Tamar.

_____

4. Jesus used the Queen of Sheba as an example when he rebuked the Pharisees.

_____

5. All of Solomon's wives worshiped Yahweh.

_____

6. Queen Jezebel provided a place of refuge for the prophet Elijah.

_____

7. King Ahaz killed a man in order to usurp his vineyard.

_____

8. The Shunammite woman and her husband built a lodging for Elisha in their home.

_____

9. Naaman's maidservant helped her master, despite the fact that he had her stolen from her family in Israel.

_____

10. Huldah was the prophetess to King Josiah and lived at the same time as Jeremiah and Zephaniah.

_____

SHORT ANSWER 1

1. Elijah provided constant bread and oil for whom?

_____

2. Jezebel worshipped which god?

_____

3. What prophecy was fulfilled when Queen Jezebel died?

_____

4. The widow came to Elisha for advice when what threat appeared?

_____

5. Elisha blessed the Shunammite woman with what?

_____

MATCHING 2

1. Queen Abijah

2. Queen Athaliah

3. Queen Azubah

4. Queen Bathsheba

5. Queen Esther

6. Queen Hamutal

7. Queen Hephzibah

8. Queen Jecholiah

9. Queen Jedidah

10. Queen Jehoaddan

A. Mother of King Manasseh of Judah

B. Mother of King Amaziah of Judah

C. Daughter of Zechariah; Mother of King Hezekiah of Judah

D. Wife of King Ahasuerus of Persia

E. Mother of King Azariah of Judah

F. Daughter of Jezebel and Ahab

G. Mother of King Josiah of Judah

H. Mother of King Jehoshaphat of Judah

I. Daughter of Jeremiah of Libnah

J. Mother of King Solomon

MULTIPLE CHOICE 3

1. Hosea's wife Gomer was a:
   A. prophetess
   B. prostitute
   C. leather worker
   D. soldier

2. The greedy women of Samaria were referred to by Amos as:
   A. harlots of Samaria
   B. pigs of Ashur
   C. cows of Bashan
   D. curs of Bashan

3. Zechariah had a vision of what as a representation of evil:
   A. a woman in a basket
   B. a female dog eating raw meat
   C. pigs
   D. a woman speaking in tongues

4. Ninevah was called what for enticing other nations?
   A. lamb
   B. deceptive
   C. a magician
   D. a harlot

MATCHING *(Jesus in His last days) 3*

Woman	Event	Action
1. Unnamed	A. the testing of	i. pleaded her husband to release Jesus
2. Servant Girl #1	B. the Resurrection	ii. stood by the cross, suffering with Jesus
3. Servant Girl #2	C. the Crucifixion	iii. prepared Jesus' body for burial
4. Pilate's wife	D. the journey to the Crucifixion	iv. asked Peter about his association with Jesus
5. Unnamed Women	E. the testing of Peter	v. used oil to anoint Jesus
6. Three Marys	F. the anointing of Jesus at Bethany	vi. asked Peter about his association with Jesus
7. Women from Galilee	G. the trial of Jesus	vii. mourned for Jesus
8. Mary Magdalene, Mary the mother of James, Joanna	H. the crucifixion and burial	viii. the first to announce his resurrection

ANSWERS

MULTIPLE CHOICE 1

1. A
2. B
3. A
4. D

TRUE OR FALSE 1

1. True
2. False
3. True
4. True
5. True
6. False
7. False
8. True
9. True
10. True

UNSCRAMBLE 1

1. Zipporah
2. Rachel
3. Ruth and Naomi
4. Mary Magdalene
5. Rahab
6. Bathsheba
7. Sarah
8. Mary and Martha
9. Jezebel
10. Rebekah